UNDERSTANDING AND SERVICING ALARM SYSTEMS

UNDERSTANDING AND SERVICING ALARM SYSTEMS

Second Edition

H. WILLIAM TRIMMER

Butterworth–Heinemann
Boston London Singapore Sydney Toronto Wellington

Library of Congress Cataloging-in-Publication Data
Trimmer, H. William, 1939–
    Understanding and servicing alarm systems / H. William Trimmer.—
2nd ed.
        p.   cm.
    ISBN 0-409-90204-7
    1. Burglar-alarms.   2. Fire-alarms.   I. Title.
TH9739.T74   1990
621.389′28—dc20   89-78308

British Library Cataloguing in Publication Data
Trimmer, H. William, *1939–*
    Understanding and servicing alarm systems.
    1. Buildings. Alarms. Maintenance & repairs
    I. Title
    621.38928
    ISBN 0-409-90204-7

Butterworth–Heinemann
80 Montvale Avenue
Stoneham, MA 02180

10 9 8 7 6 5 4 3 2 1

Printed in the United States of America

To Brandon, my son

Contents

Preface

Much has changed in the alarm industry since the release of the first edition of this book in 1981. This speaks well of the industry. We are fortunate to be part of these dynamics, for a static industry foretells a dying one. At the same time these dynamics place upon us the responsibility to constantly keep abreast of these changes. On me, too, it places the responsibility to update, hence this second edition.

What was commonplace during the first edition is no longer so. For example, the passive infrared (PIR) detector, then a relative newcomer, has virtually eliminated the old standby ultrasonic and microwave detectors. Another example is the virtual disappearance of copper telephone pairs, previously used for polarity reversal, McCulloh and direct wire circuits for silent alarm reporting. These have been replaced by digital communicators, carrier type multiplexing (MUX), derived channels, and long-range radio. Single zone or day-night zones and relay-operated panels have gone the way of the covered wagon. Today we see microprocessor-based panels with eight, sixteen, thirty, forty, or more zones, each of which is programmable with more features than I ever dreamed of when I wrote my article, "A Look at Some Advanced Alarm Concepts," for the July 1976 issue of *Security Distributing and Marketing (SDM)* magazine. Along with new equipment, new terms have entered the vocabulary, and others have become obsolete.

New opportunities are available to us and, yes, high false alarm rates are still with us. While reputable manufacturers of alarm equipment have greatly improved designs with new features to help overcome such problems, we are faced with ever-more alarm systems in service. The best way to deal with this problem is to gain a thorough understanding of alarm systems, detection devices, and their applications, as well as their limitations. Another method is the proper troubleshooting and maintenance of these systems. These are the main aims of this book.

As an incentive to improved installation and maintenance, many cities have adopted ordinances imposing financial penalties for false alarms and have reduced or dropped law enforcement response to locations experiencing excessive false alarms. A few states have already imposed licensing requirements on alarm companies. These require a demonstrated knowledge of alarm equipment operation and maintenance and are in addition to contractor licensing requirements. Expect to see more states adopt such requirements. Again, this book will assist you.

Preface to the First Edition

Some years ago, while attending the International Security Conference (ISC), I asked the editor of *Security Distributing and Marketing (SDM)* magazine if he would be interested in a technical article about magnetic contacts (switches). Open mouth, insert foot! I didn't realize until later the amount of work to which I had committed myself. This resulted in the four-part article "Magnetic Contacts from A to Z," appearing in the February, March, May, and July 1975 issues of *SDM*. This was the beginning of my writing career and has been followed by several other editorial articles and by several dozen contributions to the monthly "Kinks and Hints" column in *SDM*.

Somewhere along the line I was approached by Art Lilienthal, then Executive Director of the ISC, which was then a part of Security World Publishing Company, as was *SDM*. He requested that I do a seminar for the ISC on alarm installation. I had just observed a serviceman from a major Los Angeles alarm company spend four full days trying to repair an alarm system. This system had only fourteen openings consisting of foil and contacts. Further, the system was already divided into four zones. I could have completely rewired and refoiled the job in less than four days. Based on this, I suggested to Art that I do a session on alarm troubleshooting instead of on installation. He agreed and, again, I had committed myself to a gigantic task, as I was later to learn.

This book is the direct result of those seminars. However, the material in the book has been expanded beyond that in the seminar. The seminar was aimed exclusively at troubleshooting; this book presents additional information designed to help people understand how alarm systems and equipment work and the advantages and limitations of each type. Although step-by-step installation procedures are generally not covered, I feel this book is still far more valuable to the installer. Step-by-step instructions often tell "how" but not "why." In this book I place emphasis on the "why." The "how" can be picked up fairly easily. The book should also be of great value to salespeople, since it is usually they who decide what type of system to use and then sell that system. It is of the utmost importance that the system selected fits the need. This includes adequate type and extent of coverage and freedom from false alarms. Information in this book will help the salesperson understand the alternatives available so that he or she can choose wisely.

The incentive for every alarm company is to provide a high degree of protection commensurate with the cost and the degree of risk involved. Systems that are correctly selected, installed, and maintained will achieve the objective and will ensure the alarm company's profit picture by providing reliable systems that do the job and are free of false alarms and expensive service calls. It is my aim in this book to provide the knowledge and understanding of alarm systems and equipment necessary to enable alarm people to provide this kind of service.

PART ONE

For the benefit of the newcomer, Part One introduces the basic electrical theory for most alarm circuits. I do not go into electronics as I believe only the most advanced alarm people will need or even want to know what goes on inside a solid-state alarm control unit or motion detection device. Mainly, what the newcomer needs to know is how a device works in general, how it gets hooked up, and how to service it. These are the things I attempt to cover.

Even the more experienced person will be well advised to review Chapter 1, "Basic Electricity," and will benefit by reviewing Chapter 2, "Test Equipment." Many people know of only one or two test devices. Chapter 2 introduces newer, better devices.

1 Basic Electricity

Before we get into details of actual troubleshooting, we must understand a few very basic things about electricity. Without this understanding, troubleshooting is simply a matter of following a memorized or written procedure without knowing what is happening or why. When you run out of standard procedures without finding the problem, you have no idea of what to do next. Going through a list also wastes time. With a little understanding you can often go directly to the problem, which might be the last thing on a list. Another important reason for familiarity with the basics of electricity is to understand how various test and measuring devices work and how they affect the alarm system being tested. Without this knowledge, the test instrument can be incorrectly interpreted, wasting a lot more of your time.

When studying electricity it is not necessary to go into electron theory, although some books begin with this topic. Let's omit as much theory as possible and get down to the practical matters that will be of help in understanding alarm work.

1.1 ELEMENTS OF A SIMPLE ELECTRIC CIRCUIT

Let's start with batteries since most people are familiar with them. We have batteries in flashlights, portable power tools, cars, trucks, and most alarm systems. There are various kinds of batteries, which will be covered later. First, think of a battery as a source of electric energy. It is one place from which we can get electricity.

Another source of electricity often used in alarm work is the wall outlet. Here, the electricity is generated at a large power plant and comes over wires to the house or building where the alarm system is located.

Now, with electricity available to us, either from a battery or a wall outlet, we want it to do something useful for us. We use it to light a bulb to enable us to see in dark places, to run a drill motor so we can make holes to run alarm wiring, to ring bells to scare away intruders, to operate a radio for entertainment, and many more things. Each of these devices can be thought of as a user of electricity. We call each of these an "electrical load" or simply a "load."

The third element in simple electricity are the conductors, called wires, which are needed to get the electricity from one place to another.

The fourth and final element is control. An electric drill, for instance, would be

3

useless, or inconvenient at best, without a way to turn it on and off. A simple switch serves the purpose, although many newer drills also include variable speed control. Relay contacts also serve as a means of controlling electricity. Examples are turning a bell on and off or arming and disarming an alarm system. More modern alarm systems often use solid-state or transistorized devices for controlling electricity.

Now we have a practical and useful electrical system. Thinking in terms of source, load, conductors, and control may seem oversimplified, but it often helps to understand problems if we reduce alarm systems to these basic ideas.

1.2   DIAGRAMS AND SYMBOLS

Now, let's look at a simple electrical circuit. Since we cannot put an actual electrical circuit on paper, we will be looking at a diagram of one. Symbols that represent various electrical components are used in making such a diagram.

Sometimes, instead of using a complete diagram, only a box is shown on a drawing. The external terminals are all that are identified. This method is often used, for example, in a burglar alarm control unit. Usually an alarm installer or troubleshooter does not need to know all of the internal details. Unnecessary details just add to the confusion. A box diagram showing terminal connections and a brief description of how the unit works will give the troubleshooter all the necessary information. See Figures 1–1 and 1–2. Figure 1–3 shows other common symbols.

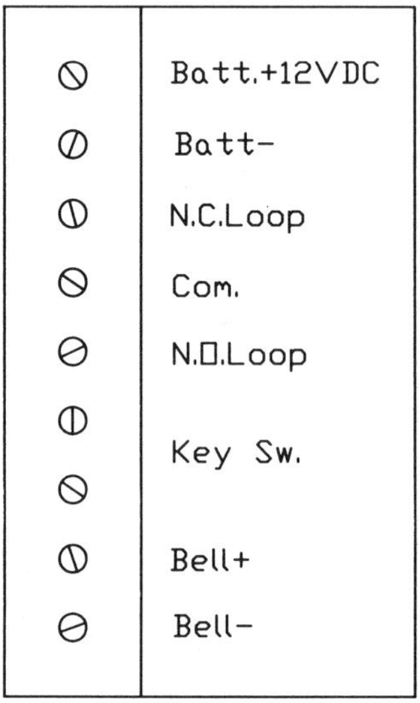

⊘	Batt.+12VDC
⊘	Batt–
⊘	N.C.Loop
⊘	Com.
⊖	N.O.Loop
⊕	
	Key Sw.
⊘	
⊘	Bell+
⊖	Bell–

Figure 1–1   Typical box diagram of simple alarm control. Only external connections are shown.

```
Battery:        12 V.DC, observe polarity

N.C. Loop:      1200 Ohms maximum loop resistance

N.O. Loop:      30,000 Ohms minimum loop resistance

Bell:           2 Amps maximum load

Key switch      50 Ohms maximum, system armed when switch open

Current drain:  Armed        3 mA. maximum

                Disarmed     0.5 mA. maximum

                Bell ringing 2 A. maximum


Bell output times out after approximately 10 minutes, at which

time control automatically resets if protective loop has been

restored, else system remains inactive until loop is restored.

Bell can be silenced at any time with key switch.
```

Figure 1–2 Typical instructions for alarm control unit.

1.3 ELECTRICAL UNITS

Now that we understand the "how" of simple electrical systems, we have to learn "how much." Knowing the amount is essential to finding and fixing alarm troubles. Before getting down to actual quantities, we'll have to identify the three kinds of electrical units because each has its own kind of "how much."

Most alarm systems work on DC, or direct current; therefore, just three units of measurement will tell us most of what we need to know about alarm systems. These units are voltage, current, and resistance.

1.3.1 Voltage (E)

Voltage is a measurement of electrical pressure. It is what forces electricity to flow through a circuit. All electrical sources have a voltage. A flashlight cell has 1½ volts. Batteries used in alarm systems are made up of many cells and usually have 6 or 12 volts. House power at a wall outlet usually is 120 volts. Note that batteries produce DC, or direct current, while house power is 60 Hertz AC, or alternating current. The

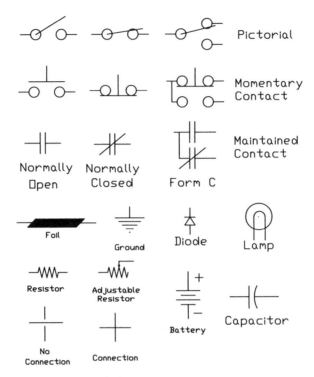

Figure 1–3 Some common symbols.

E, by the way, comes from "electromotive force." We will use the more common term "volts" as the unit of measure. The E, however, is used in Ohm's law by tradition. See Section 1.4.

1.3.2 Current (I)

Current is the amount or rate of flow of electricity and is given in amperes, or amps for short. The abbreviation I comes from the word "intensity." It, too, is used by tradition in Ohm's law.

1.3.3 Resistance (R)

Resistance is the opposition to or restriction of the flow of electricity. Think of it as electrical friction. Everything in an electrical circuit has resistance. Light bulbs have resistance. Relay coils and bell windings have resistance. Test meters have resistance. Wire has resistance, as does foil. Even batteries have resistance, which is called internal resistance.

From a practical standpoint, the internal resistance of a good battery is low, so we can usually forget about it. The resistance of wire can be a problem sometimes, and we will see why later. Most of our resistance is usually found in our load, or user of electricity.

1.3.4 Large and Small Units

In dealing with electrical units, volts, amps, and ohms, we often find the basic unit too large or too small. To simplify things, we use multipliers preceding the basic unit. For alarm work the volt is just right, but the amp is often too big, so we use milliamps (mA) (one-thousandths of an amp) or sometimes microamps (μA) (one-millionths of an amp). Sometimes the ohm is too small, so we use kilohm (KΩ) (one thousand ohms) or occasionally the megohm (MΩ) (one million ohms). Table 1–4 shows a more extensive range of multipliers. By tradition, the Greek letter omega (Ω) is used as the abbreviation for ohms.

1.4 OHM'S LAW

Ohm's law, "E = IR," tells how voltage, current, and resistance work together. As you can see, this formula is very simple. The voltage equals the current in amps times the resistance in ohms. The best way to get a feel for how this formula works is to hold one of these values constant, vary the second value, and see what happens to the third. In a simple alarm system, a battery or power supply is used that puts out an essentially constant voltage, so let's hold voltage constant in the formula. Again, in alarm circuits, some systems will have short protective loops and a low resistance. Other loops will be longer with a higher resistance. Still others may have a large amount of window foil and an even higher resistance, because foil has much more resistance per foot than copper wire. Let's use some different, typical values of loop resistance as our variable and see what happens to our third value, the current.

The first example is 5 ohms (about 150 loop feet of 22 gauge wire). The second example is 75 ohms (2000 loop feet of 22 gauge). The third example is 450 ohms (the same length of loop plus a large quantity of foiled windows). We can see what the loop current will be using a fresh 1.5 volt battery. In addition to the loop resistance, we must add the resistance of the coil of the sensitive relay, which would typically be about 300 ohms for a 1.5 volt system. For the present, we will ignore the internal resistance of the battery and resistance of switch contacts. While the battery's resistance will be very low, that of switches and other contacts will vary widely depending on their condition and can be significant. Table 1–1 lists the values.

As you can see, as the total resistance increases, the current decreases. A sensitive relay such as this needs 2.2 mA to operate, which is a typical value. In this case, the first two loops would function, but the third loop, with a total of 750 ohms, passes only 2.0 mA, which is not enough to operate the sensitive relay. If we did have a loop with this much resistance, we would have to increase the end-of-line supply voltage. This could be done by adding more dry cells or by using a power supply that puts out a higher voltage.

Another point must be considered. We need at least 2.2 mA to operate the relay,

Table 1–1 Holding voltage (E) constant

Example	$\dfrac{E}{Volts}$	Loop Ohms	Relay Ohms	$\dfrac{R}{Total}$ Ohms	$\dfrac{I}{Amps}$
1	1.5	5	300	305	.005~
2	1.5	75	300	375	.004
3	1.5	450	300	750	.002

Rearranging Ohm's law we have:

(1) $I = \dfrac{E}{R} = \dfrac{1.5}{305} = .005$ amps or approximately 5 mA

(2) $I = \dfrac{E}{R} = \dfrac{1.5}{375} = .004$ amps or 4 mA

(3) $I = \dfrac{E}{R} = \dfrac{1.5}{750} = .002$ amps or 2 mA

but we should add 50 percent more to allow for the eventual rundown of dry cells or for brownout low voltages from a line-operated power supply. So with our safety margin, we would want a current of about 3.3 mA (0.0033 amps). Let's use Ohm's law again, this time to find the voltage, $E = IR = 0.0033$ amps $\times$ 750 ohms = 2.48 volts.

Thus, we would need a three-volt battery or power supply, which is the next higher standard value. If we look back at Table 1–1, we see that a 375-ohm loop (total resistance) gives us 4 mA on 1.5 volts and that doubling the resistance to 750 ohms cuts the current in half to 2 mA. As the formula has just shown, we have to double the voltage when doubling the resistance in order to maintain the same current flow.

Now let's look at loop number two and see what happens as the end-of-line battery starts to run down. Table 1–2 compares decreasing voltages against a constant resistance. The loop current goes down as the battery runs down, while the resistance remains constant. At 0.9 volts, we have barely enough current to operate the sensitive relay. As the battery voltage drops even lower, the relay will fail to operate and the system can no longer be set or armed.

A note of interest is that the further a battery has run down, the faster it will continue to run down. For instance, a 1½ volt battery that is down to around 1 volt has spent most of its useful service life. Even though the loop resistance may be very low, as in example number one of Table 1–1, the battery would quickly run down from 1 volt to 0.67 volts. At this point the relay in the example would not operate. Shown graphically, the battery's output voltage looks like Figure 1–4.

Let's take another example where the loop resistance is marginally high, say 300 ohms. This plus the 300-ohm relay coil resistance gives a total resistance of 600 ohms. In Table 1–3, we again see what happens as the battery voltage begins to drop.

Table 1–2 Holding resistance constant

Example	Battery Volts	Total Resistance	Loop Current
1	1.5	375	.004 amps (4.0 mA)
2	1.3	375	.0035 amps (3.5 mA)
3	1.1	375	.0029 amps (2.9 mA)
4	.9	375	.0024 amps (2.4 mA)
5	.7	375	.0019 amps (1.9 mA)

(1) $I = \dfrac{E}{R} = \dfrac{1.5}{375} = .004$ amps or 4.0 mA

(2) $I = \dfrac{E}{R} = \dfrac{1.3}{375} = .0035$ amps or 3.5 mA

(3) $I = \dfrac{E}{R} = \dfrac{1.1}{375} = .0029$ amps or 2.9 mA

(4) $I = \dfrac{E}{R} = \dfrac{.9}{375} = .0024$ amps or 2.4 mA

(5) $I = \dfrac{E}{R} = \dfrac{.7}{375} = .0019$ amps or 1.9 mA

As we can see from this chart, the system would fail to set (arm) after probably only a few weeks. Now you can see why it is necessary to have a safety margin. Such a safety margin is usually provided by the manufacturer of the alarm control unit who will show, in the instructions, a loop limit of perhaps 100 ohms. In reality it might work with twice that amount but only if the batteries were brand-new.

The examples given are taken from earlier, relay-operated control panels. Virtually all modern panels are solid-state and most use integrated circuit digital logic. These newer panels have loop resistance limits in the thousands or tens of thousands of ohms

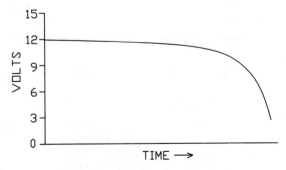

Figure 1–4 Typical battery discharge curve. Actual discharge time depends on battery capacity, battery condition, and the load.

Table 1–3   Voltage drop with marginal loop

Example	Battery Volts	Total Resistance	Loop Current
1	1.5	600	.0025 amps
2	1.4	600	(2.5 mA)
3	1.3	600	.0023 amps
			(2.3 mA)
			.00216 amps
			(2.16 mA)

$$(1)\ I = \frac{E}{R} = \frac{1.5}{600} = .0025 \text{ amps or } 2.5 \text{ mA}$$

$$(2)\ I = \frac{E}{R} = \frac{1.4}{600} = .0023 \text{ amps or } 2.3 \text{ mA}$$

$$(3)\ I = \frac{E}{R} = \frac{1.3}{600} = .00216 \text{ amps or } 2.16 \text{ mA}$$

and have loop currents in the microamp range. Also, window foil (made of lead and having a much higher resistance than copper wire) is seldom used any more. Photo beams or motion sensors are used instead of foil as they are usually easier to install and are less of a maintenance headache. Nonetheless, many foil installations and relay-operated control panels still exist and the examples above still illustrate Ohm's law. Also bear in mind that, while a solid-state closed loop control may have a loop resistance of tens of thousands of ohms, a typical end-of-line (E-O-L) resistor loop will have a

Table 1–4   Multipliers

femto	10^{-15}	.000,000,000,000,001
pico	10^{-12}	.000,000,000,001
nano	10^{-9}	.000,000,001
micro	10^{-6}	.000,001
milli	10^{-3}	.001
centi	10^{-2}	.01
deci	10^{-1}	.1
(unit)	10^{0}	1.
Deka	10^{1}	10.
Hecto	10^{2}	100.
Kilo	10^{3}	1,000.
Mega	10^{6}	1,000,000.
Giga	10^{9}	1,000,000,000.
Tera	10^{12}	1,000,000,000,000.

much lower limit because it operates a little differently. E-O-L loops are covered later in the book.

One very important point to remember is that in using Ohm's law all units must first be converted to basic units: volts, amps, and ohms. For example, 6 milliamps times 1000 ohms does not equal 6000 volts. But 0.006 amps times 1000 ohms does equal 6 volts. See Table 1–4 for a list of unit prefixes and their corresponding multipliers.

1.5 ELECTRICAL MEASUREMENTS

We have been talking about volts, amps, and ohms but have not said anything about how to measure them. Let's look at how this is done. You may already be familiar with a V-O-M or volt-ohm-milliamp meter and how to set the function and range switches. If not, study the instruction manual for your meter or have someone who is already familiar with it explain it to you.

1.5.1 Measuring Voltage

The voltmeter can be used to measure voltage outputs, as from a battery, and it can also be used to measure voltage drops. It is connected across (in parallel with) the source, load, or component being tested. For instance, assume we have a 6-volt battery powering a light bulb and that we have two long connecting wires. A meter at the battery would show 6 volts. A meter at the light would show, say, 5 volts, which is the drop across the light (our load). If we were to use a voltmeter with very long leads, we might read a half-volt drop along one wire and a half-volt drop along the other wire. Adding 5 volts for the light and ½ volt for each of the two wires, we get 6 volts, which equals the voltage output of our battery.

This is Kirchoff's first law, which says that the sum of the voltage rises around a circuit is equal to the sum of the voltage drops around the same circuit. A battery or power supply or any source of electricity is considered a voltage rise, and a voltage drop occurs along wires and across loads. The 6-volt rise from the battery is equal to the sum of the voltage drops or 5 + ½ + ½. This is illustrated in Figure 1–5.

When an open switch is added to the circuit, as shown in Figure 1–6, the current stops flowing and the bulb goes out. The voltmeter across the load reads 0 volts, as does the − W voltmeter. A voltmeter across the open switch indicates the battery voltage. This is because it has one test probe connected to the battery via the upper wire and the other test probe connected to the other side of the battery via part of the upper wire (right portion), the bulb, and the lower wire. Since the circuit is open, there is no voltage drop in the circuit so the meter reads full battery voltage. Technically, there is a tiny current flowing in the circuit, enough to make the meter work. But this current is so small it does not produce any measurable voltage drop, so the meter reads the actual battery voltage for all practical purposes.

With the switch closed, as shown in Figure 1–7, the bulb lights again. This diagram is the same as Figure 1–5 except it now shows a voltmeter across the switch.

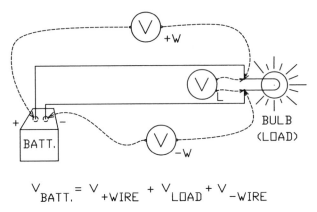

$$V_{BATT.} = V_{+WIRE} + V_{LOAD} + V_{-WIRE}$$

Figure 1–5 Three voltmeters (a circle with a V inside) are used to indicate the voltages at three points in the circuit. The formula illustrates Kirchoff's first law.

This voltmeter reads 0 volts. This is because the switch, when closed, has essentially zero resistance. Therefore, it will have zero voltage drop even though a current is flowing through it. If the voltmeter had read some voltage, it would have been an indication that the switch had a high internal resistance or was open. A good switch, when closed, should have zero voltage across it. This is an important point to keep in mind when troubleshooting.

Let's now place a second, similar bulb in series with the first one as shown in Figure 1–8. The voltage drop across each bulb is about half of what it was with only one bulb. The bulbs would glow dimly as each is receiving only half the voltage for which it was designed.

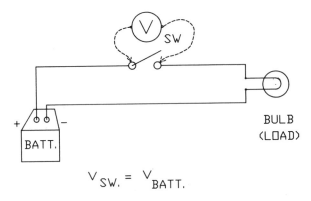

$$V_{SW.} = V_{BATT.}$$

Figure 1–6 The same circuit, now with an open switch. The entire battery voltage appears across the switch.

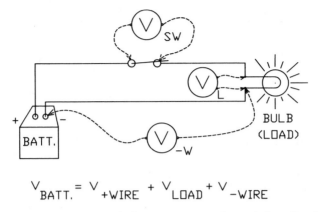

$$V_{BATT.} = V_{+WIRE} + V_{LOAD} + V_{-WIRE}$$

Figure 1–7 With the switch closed, the meter across the switch will indicate 0 volts, provided the switch is good, i.e., it does not have a high internal resistance.

1.5.2 Measuring Current

To measure current, we must break the circuit to be tested and put the meter in series with it. That is, the circuit is completed through the meter. If a bell draws 0.75 amps, the meter will read the same regardless of where it is placed in the circuit. It can equally well be inserted in the positive or the negative lead and can be located at the battery end, the bell end, or somewhere in the middle. See Figure 1–9.

Let's look at a similar circuit, Figure 1–10, this time with two bells in parallel. The ammeter in each bell wire measures the current going to its respective bell. The

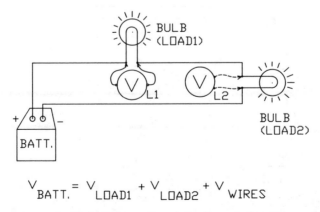

$$V_{BATT.} = V_{LOAD1} + V_{LOAD2} + V_{WIRES}$$

Figure 1–8 With two loads (bulbs) in series, the voltage drop across each will be about one-half that across a single load.

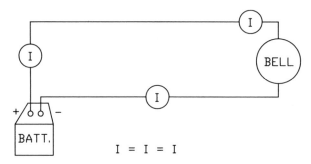

Figure 1–9 Three ammeters (circle with an I) will all show the same reading, regardless of where they are located in the circuit.

ammeter in the battery wire measures the total current provided by the battery. This will be the sum of all the loads.

Kirchoff's second law says the sum of all currents entering a point is equal to the sum of all currents leaving that point. In Figure 1–10, there are, say, 1½ amps entering the point with the asterisk from the left, coming from the battery. There are ¾ amps leaving that point and going downward to supply bell 1 and ¾ amps leaving to the right, to supply bell 2. Thus 1½ amps enter this point and ¾ + ¾ or 1½ amps leave the point, which is the same as the amount entering.

1.5.3 Measuring Resistance

An ohmmeter is an ammeter with a built-in battery and a built-in current-limiting resistor. The resistor, or part of it, is made adjustable to set the zero ohms reading.

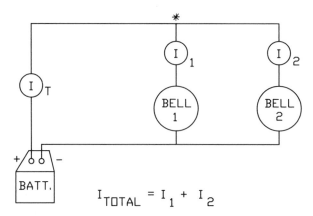

Figure 1–10 With two loads in parallel, the total current will equal the sum of the individual currents, illustrating Kirchoff's second law.

To set zero ohms, the ohmmeter probes are shorted together. The zero ohms knob is turned until the meter reads exactly zero on the ohms scale. This is on the right end of most analog type V-O-M meter scales. When this is done, the circuit resistance is set so that exactly the full scale meter current passes through the meter, which is why the meter moves to the right end of the scale. Since the test leads are shorted together, there is zero external resistance in the circuit, so the right end of the ohms scale is marked O ohms. As external resistance is added between the ohmmeter probes, it increases the total resistance of the meter circuit. From Ohm's law, we find that less current flows through the meter, and it doesn't deflect as far to the right. For example, when the external resistance being measured is equal to the meter's internal resistance, then the total (that is the external plus the internal) is equal to twice the internal resistance. Since the total resistance is doubled, the meter current is now halved and the meter deflects halfway.

The same method can be used to find the meter deflection for any amount of resistance being measured. Rather than do this every time, the meter manufacturer has simplified things for us by simply marking the ohms scale to read directly in ohms.

Figure 1–11 shows typical uses of an ohmmeter. The ohmmeter is shown as a circle with an "Ω" (the Greek letter Omega) inside. It can be used to check a bell. A good bell should read no higher than a few ohms unless it is designed for 120 volts. A reading of infinity (∞) indicates an open, such as the motor coil being burned out or the contacts stuck open on a vibrating (continuously ringing) type bell. (Single stroke bells do not have vibrating contacts.) Some fire alarm bells are polarized, that is, they have an internal diode in series. When testing a polarized bell with an ohmmeter first test one way, then reverse the test leads and test again. If one test shows infinity

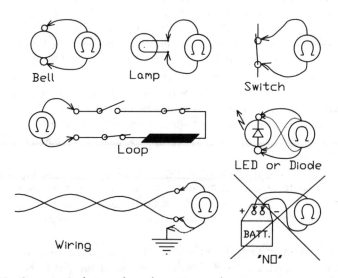

Figure 1–11 Some typical uses of an ohmmeter, and one way not to use it.

and the other test shows some reading higher than zero, the bell has an internal diode and is functioning. If the meter reads infinity (∞) on both tests, the bell or its internal diode is defective (open). Two words of caution when testing a bell with an internal diode (or any diode for that matter): (1) the resistance reading in Ohms is incorrect due to the forward voltage drop of the diode in the circuit, and (2) the ohmmeter must use an internal voltage source that is greater than the forward voltage drop of the diode in order for the above test to work. Most diodes have a forward drop of about 0.75 volts, so a single cell inside the ohmmeter is sufficient. However, a light-emitting diode (LED) typically has a drop of 2 volts. This would appear as an open circuit if your ohmmeter had only 1.5 volts. This is just one example of why it is so important to correctly understand your test equipment, how it works, and its limitations.

An ohmmeter can quickly test an incandescent light bulb. A reading of "∞" (infinity) indicates a burned-out bulb. Switch contacts can be checked to see if they are open or closed. The symbol "∞" (infinity) indicates open and "O" indicates closed. When closed, the resistance should be less than $\frac{1}{10}$ ohm. Readings higher than this usually indicate a defective or poor quality switch.

The coils of relays can be tested to see if they are burned out (open). If not open, the actual coil resistance is measured in ohms. Typical values are from a few ohms to 10,000 ohms, depending on the type of relay. The actual reading can sometimes help you sort out or identify types of relays if the part numbers are no longer readable on the relays themselves. Relay contacts can also be tested just like switch contacts, as explained previously.

A common use of an ohmmeter is to check continuity of an alarm system protective loop as shown in the middle of Figure 1–11. The meter would read "∞" (an open or no continuity) because one switch is open.

An ohmmeter can be used to test a pair of wires to see if they are shorted together. A reading of "∞" indicates no short. A reading other than "∞" indicates a short. The resistance reading will probably be greater than zero and will indicate the resistance of the wire between the short and the point of measurement. Of course, the wires could be intentionally shorted at the opposite end or they could be connected through the coil of a sensitive relay. To test for an accidental short, first disconnect the far end of the wire before testing. In this way any accidental shorts on the wire can be tested without anything at the far end confusing the test results. If one test probe is connected to an earth ground, the test would detect the presence of a ground on one loop wire or the other. Remember, sometimes one side of a protective loop is intentionally grounded.

The symbol in the bottom center of Figure 1–11 is a light-emitting diode (LED). These are commonly used as status indicators in place of incandescent pilot bulbs because they use very little power and practically never burn out if properly used. Since an LED is a type of diode, the same cautions apply as for testing polarized fire alarm bells.

The most important thing to remember when measuring ohms is to remove all voltage sources (batteries, power supplies, etc.) from the circuit being measured.

Failure to do so will give a false reading or could damage the meter because the extra voltage will cause too much current to flow through the meter.

Resistors are occasionally used in alarm work, particularly as end-of-line (E-O-L) resistors (sometimes called terminators) and for limiting current in LED circuits. Table 1–5 shows the color coding used to mark the value on the resistors.

1.6   POWER

Before leaving the subject of basic electricity, there is one other electrical unit that is occasionally needed: power, which is expressed in watts. This tells us the amount of electricity being used and is simply equal to the volts times the amps: $P = E \times I$. Most of us are already familiar with wattage ratings such as a 100-watt light bulb or

Table 1–5   Resistor color code

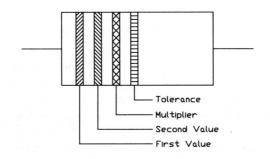

Color	1st/2nd Value	Multiply	Tolerance
Black	0	1	–
Brown	1	10	–
Red	2	100	–
Orange	3	1,000	–
Yellow	4	10,000	–
Green	5	100,000	–
Blue	6	1,000,000	–
Violet	7	10,000,000	–
Gray	8	–	–
White	9	–	–
Silver	–	.01	10%
Gold	–	.1	5%

a 1200-watt hair dryer. Alarm systems usually take only a few watts. Occasionally, you will see the term "VA," which is volt-amps, or simply the volts times the amps. This symbol is sometimes used in AC circuits. Technically, the wattage in an AC circuit is equal to volts times amps times the power factor. The power factor is equal to or less than one. For most practical purposes in alarm work, you can think of VAs in the same way as watts.

1.7   ALTERNATING CURRENT

Most alarm systems you will encounter will operate on direct current, or DC. There are a few uses for alternating current, or AC, in alarm systems, such as the AC line cord or the plug-in transformer. Usually, the only thing you are concerned with is determining that you have the correct AC voltage needed to power the alarm equipment. This is done by setting the V-O-M meter to AC and to the proper voltage range. Beyond this, I will not go into AC theory because it is much more complex than DC. Proper coverage of the subject would take up many chapters in this book and you would not have much use for it in most alarm work.

1.8   FURTHER STUDY

For further information about DC electricity, there are many books available in public libraries, bookstores, and the book shelves in better electronic parts stores. High school and college physics books also include chapters covering basic DC. In this book the material on DC electricity is intended mainly as a brief review. It has been presented with a slant toward understanding alarm systems. For further study on the subject, consult the above sources. Different books present the same ideas in a variety of ways, some of which may be more understandable than others.

A number of readers of the first edition have inquired why I have not included a more complete coverage of the electronic components that make up alarm equipment. Let's leave the insides of alarm equipment to the design engineers. The alarm installer is interested in the external connections and how the alarm works, not how transistors or integrated circuits work. If you are interested in such detail, I encourage you to read additional books that cover such topics. Also consider signing up for classes through adult education, community colleges, or universities. My goal is to keep this book simple and practical.

2 Test Equipment

Humans cannot measure electricity with any of our senses. At least we cannot do so safely on high voltage and cannot do so at all on the low voltages used in most alarm systems. We must, therefore, depend on various test instruments to make the measurements and to give us useful indications. Test devices can range from a simple light bulb to a buzzer, to a complex digital voltmeter, which presents its readout in illuminated numbers.

Each kind of test device has its advantages and disadvantages. Some are extremely accurate, others very crude. Some are expensive, others are quite cheap. Some are flexible and can do many different tests. Others are readily available and can be pressed into service if the preferred test instrument has been broken or left behind in the shop.

Let's look at various kinds of test devices, their advantages, their limitations, and how to use them. I'll start with common, simple devices, progress to the better quality devices, and finally get into some specialized test equipment.

One additional clarification is in order before going on. This chapter describes kinds of test instruments but does not go into much detail about how to use them. This information is covered in later chapters. Right now I just want to point out available devices and their advantages and limitations so you can select what best suits the job.

2.1 THE EYE

The eye is free and always with us, but is seldom thought of as a test instrument because we cannot see electricity. Yet in the overall context of getting the trouble fixed, we can sometimes spot obvious troubles such as open doors or windows, broken foil or cut wire and thus save time. This is not to say that you won't end up wasting time looking. After a little experience, however, you will get the feel for the correct amount of time to spend looking and when to haul out the test instruments.

2.2 THE SYSTEM ITSELF

The alarm system itself can sometimes be used as a test device. For example, you can short various points along a single, closed loop system and observe its operation for each trial. This is a method that is always available. Such testing, though, requires constant running between each test point and the control or on-off station to observe the results. If available, a partner can communicate the results verbally or via walkie-talkies. This method is generally impractical and too time-consuming to use as a basic method of troubleshooting. Do keep it in the back of your mind as it can get you out of a pinch occasionally when you don't have the right test instruments with you.

Modern control panels have extensive indications that will help you in trouble-shooting. Some have an indicator light for each zone, some have numeric displays to indicate zone problems, and others have displays in English. Some systems duplicate or partially duplicate such indications at arming stations. Learning to use these indications can save you much time.

2.3 SIMPLE TEST DEVICES

2.3.1 Light Bulbs

A low-voltage light bulb can be used as a simple test device, but it draws far too much current for use in testing protective loops. Its use is limited to testing bell or prealert circuits or perhaps as a quick and dirty check of a battery.

2.3.2 Buzzers

Buzzers also draw too much current for testing, and they generate severe, high-voltage transients that may damage solid-state devices. Don't use one except as a temporary substitute for a bell.

2.3.3 Sonalert®

Sonalert is a trade name of R. P. Mallory & Co., Inc. It is an electronic substitute for a buzzer. Although it has a lower current draw than a buzzer, it is still not sensitive enough for use on modern alarm systems. This device is often used as a prealarm alerting device and is built into some test devices to provide an audible indication.

2.3.4 Light-Emitting Diode (LED)

LEDs are also not sensitive enough to test modern protective loops, as they need a minimum of 2 volts and about 5 milliamps to operate. These devices are often used as status indicators and as walk test lights. If you do use an LED for any application, remember that they are polarity sensitive and must also have a current-limiting resistor in series with them, or they will instantly burn out. If connected with incorrect polarity, they will not light. Their current draw depends on the applied voltage and on the value of the limiting resistor. They need at least 5 mA to light dimly and most of them must not exceed 50 mA to prevent overheating and destruction. They must have at least 2 volts to work at all.

2.4 SIMPLE CONTINUITY TESTERS

A simple continuity tester is just a battery in series with some sort of indicating device such as a bulb, LED, or Sonalert. Polarity must be observed when connecting a battery to an LED or Sonalert. Each indicating device has the same limitations as previously described. They are therefore not suitable for testing since most end-of-line resistor loops use a resistor value of several thousand ohms.

Since continuity testers have their own battery, you can use them to test dead circuits, that is, circuits that are not connected to any other source of voltage. Although it is sometimes done, it is best not to use them to test circuits with other voltages already present. For instance, if connected backwards, the external voltage would cancel the tester's internal battery voltage. It would then falsely indicate an open circuit when the circuit was not open. If hooked up with the correct polarity, the internal and external voltages would be added together. The total might be high enough to damage the tester or something else in the circuit. For these reasons, it is best to use continuity type testers only on dead circuits. The same is also true for ohmmeters.

2.5 RELAY-OPERATED CONTINUITY TESTERS

The addition of a relay or two can increase the sensitivity of a test device and provide greater flexibility of testing, as we will see in the following sections. A relay will also approximate an alarm control in speed of response and is a fairly rugged device. Unless carefully designed, a solid-state test device can be damaged easily when accidentally connected to the wrong voltage, can be far too sensitive to give useful results, and can respond too quickly to test conditions. The last two problems can be an advantage, as we will see in Section 2.9.1.

2.5.1 Increased Sensitivity, Normally Open (NO) Operation

You can build a continuity tester by using a sensitive relay as shown in Figure 2–1. The relay contacts are then used to operate a light or buzzer or both. If you use the correct relay, the tester will be sufficiently sensitive for almost all alarm work, including end-of-line resistor loops. Since the current to operate the horn or light does not go through the loop, you can use a loud horn or bell or a bright light. This is handy when in a noisy location or when a long distance from the tester. This simple device is an introduction to the following testers, which have additional features.

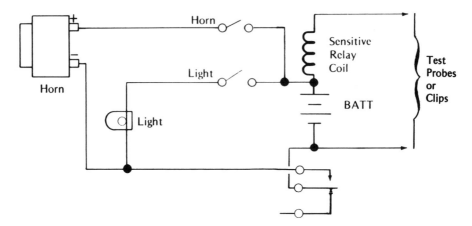

Figure 2–1 Simple NO continuity tester.

2.5.2 Normally Closed (NC) Operation

By moving the wire "X" to the opposite relay contact, that is, the break contact, you will get a reverse operation as shown in Figure 2–2. Now the light will be lit or the horn sounding when the circuit being tested is open rather than when it is closed, as was the case in Figure 2–1. This is handy for checking circuits that normally have continuity. This way the buzzer or bell will be silent or the light will be out most of the time, and will sound or light to indicate a break.

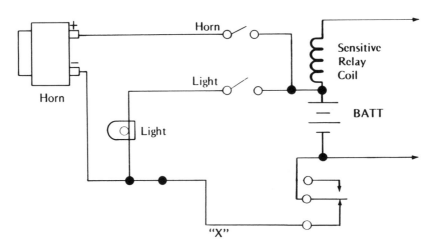

Figure 2–2 Simple NC continuity tester.

2.5.3 Normally Open/Normally Closed (NO/NC) Operation

By adding one, single-pole, single-throw, two-position toggle switch, as shown in Figure 2–3, you can now use the unit as either a normally open or as a normally closed continuity tester. In fact, you can use a three-position toggle switch with the center position as "off." When using this tester, remember the switch setting you have chosen, because it reverses the operation between NO and NC. If in doubt, short the test clips to see if the buzzer sounds or is silenced.

2.5.4 Latching Operation, Normally Open

By adding a second relay, sometimes called a drop relay, you can add a latching function as shown in Figure 2–4. The latching feature is very useful for checking intermittent or "swinger" type problems. Often this kind of problem occurs for such a brief time that you might not notice a light bulb that blinked only briefly or a buzzer that gave only a click. With the latching function, the light remains on or the buzzer sounds until manually reset by the reset push button on the tester.

2.5.5 Latching Operation, Normally Closed

By moving the wire marked "X" in Figure 2–5 to the break contact, the tester will now latch on a momentary open. This is very useful for testing normally closed loops.

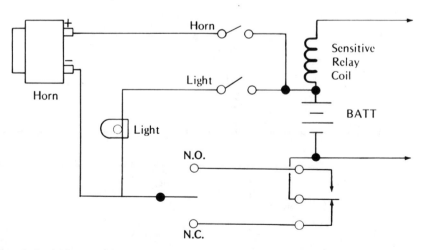

Figure 2–3 NO-NC continuity tester.

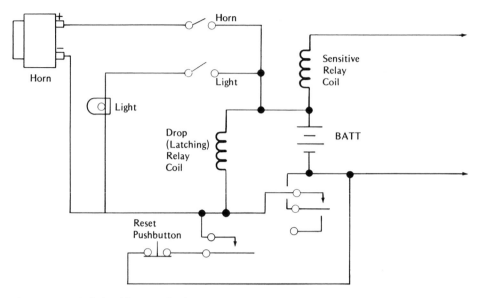

Figure 2–4 NO latching continuity tester.

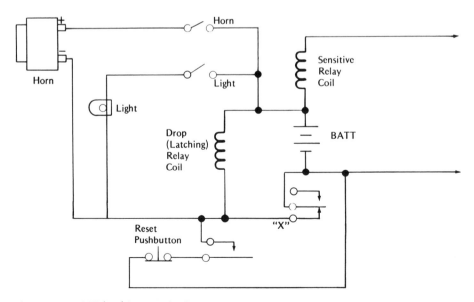

Figure 2–5 NC latching continuity tester.

TECHNOLOGY WORKSHOP
CORNWALL COLLEGE
POOL, REDRUTH,
CORNWALL TR15 3RD

2.5.6   Normally Open-Normally Closed Latching Operation

By adding a single-pole, double-throw, two-position switch, as shown in Figure 2–6, both normally open and normally closed latching operation is available at the flip of a switch.

2.5.7   Four-Function Continuity Tester

By adding a single-pole, single-throw switch, as shown in Figure 2–7, the following four test functions are available: normally open nonlatching, normally open latching, normally closed nonlatching, and normally closed latching.

2.5.8   Voltage Tester

Very often it is desirable to test for the presence of a voltage in an alarm system rather than for continuity. This is very easily done by adding a single-pole, double-throw, two-position switch as shown in Figure 2–8. In one position, the unit operates as a four-function continuity tester as previously described. In the "voltage" position, the following four additional functions are available using a voltage input (3 to 12 volts DC): voltage present at input = horn/light on, nonlatching; voltage present at input = horn/light off, nonlatching; voltage momentarily present at input = horn/light latches on; and voltage momentarily interrupted at input = horn/light latches on.

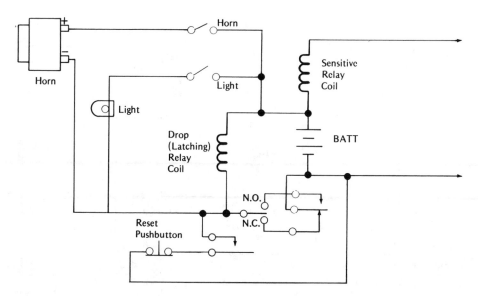

Figure 2–6   NO-NC latching continuity tester.

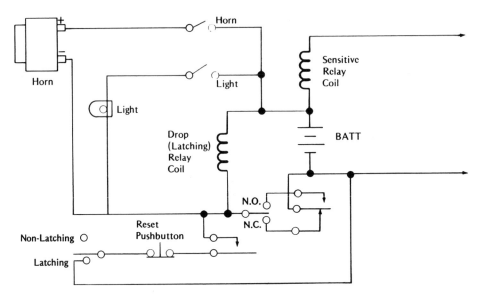

Figure 2–7 Four-function continuity tester.

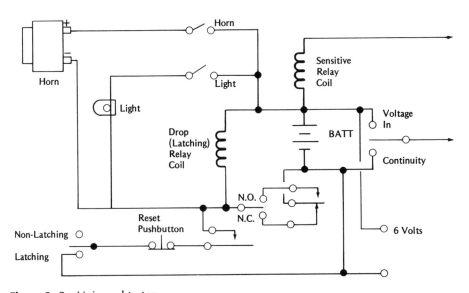

Figure 2–8 Universal tester.

2.5.9 Universal Tester

Adding an extra pair of test jacks, as shown on the lower right of Figure 2–8, makes 12 volts available from the battery for testing bells, bulbs, etc. You can use these same terminals for recharging if a rechargeable type battery is used to build the tester.

2.5.10 Build It Yourself

You can build any of the testers shown in the various diagrams, for your own use. Choose the one or ones that will meet your testing needs. For greatest flexibility, build the universal tester, shown in Figure 2–8, as it can handle most testing problems. It includes all the features of the various testers in Figures 2–1 through 2–7 in one unit.

Here is a parts list for universal and other testers:

- *Sensitive relay*. Sigma type 4 extra sensitive relay, cat. no. 5F-10,000 (Allied radio stock no. 917-0214) or use Ademco catalog 90695. (Insulate relay from chassis when mounting.)
- *Battery*. 12-volt rechargeable (preferred) or use dry cell type.
- *Drop (latching) relay*. Any 12-volt DC relay with SPST normally open contact can be used. To reduce current drain, the same type relay can be used here as for the sensitive relay.
- *Horn*. Mallory Sonalert preferred, but any small buzzer, bell, or horn can be used.
- *Light*. Pilot light assembly with matching 12-volt bulb. If you wish, you can use a large, red LED with a 180-ohm, ½-watt (or larger) current-limiting resistor instead of a bulb. (Install with correct polarity.)
- *Switches for horn, light, latch/nonlatch operation*. Each is a single-pole, single-throw toggle switch.
- *Switches for NO/NC, voltage-in/continuity*. Each is a single-pole, double-throw, two-position switch. The NO/NC switch can be a three-position switch with the center position for "off."
- *Reset push button*. Single-pole, single-throw, normally closed, momentary (or use the normally closed contact of a SPDT push button).
- *Jacks*. Four each banana jacks (or pin type jacks if you prefer), two for testing, two for 12-volt power out (and for recharging, if a rechargeable type battery is used).
- *Miscellaneous*. Minibox, handle, labels, screws, test leads to suit.

2.5.11 Solid-State

You can duplicate all of the test features just described, using solid-state circuits in place of the relays. Solid-state circuits can be more sensitive than relays. In fact, they can be made too sensitive. A practical tester should approximate the sensitivity and speed of response of typical alarm control instruments. For many purposes it is useless having a tester indicate that you have continuity through 100,000 ohms when the control panel only works with a loop of 2,000 ohms or less. Nor is it practical to have a tester respond so fast (which is typical of electronic circuits) that it latches onto transients or to radio interference that would be filtered out by good, solid-state alarm control panels. Such false test signals would be misleading and a waste of time.

2.6   METERS

Because of its versatility, sensitivity, and accuracy, the meter will be the test instrument most used by the alarm troubleshooter.

2.6.1   Sensitivity

Short of an electronic test device, a good meter is the most sensitive test tool you will use. Although I have just warned against excessive sensitivity, this is not of concern with a meter because it gives an actual reading, not just a yes-no indication as does the continuity tester. You are concerned with the operating limits of the alarm control panel you are testing. For instance, if you measured a loop resistance of 820 ohms and the maximum limit of the alarm control is shown by the manufacturer to be 500 ohms, then you must either reduce the resistance of the loop or replace the control with one having a higher loop resistance limit. By the way, most modern alarm control units have loop resistance limits that will handle any practical length of protective loop. This, however, is not true of some earlier, relay type controls. Also note that when you are measuring the resistance of an E-O-L resistor loop with the terminating resistor included in the measurement, there will be both a maximum and a minimum resistance limit specified by the manufacturer.

In this discussion on meters, I am referring to the V-O-M, that is, volt-ohm-milliamp meters. These do not need any power, either line cords or batteries, for operation (other than an internal battery for ohms measurement). A small amount of power is taken from the circuit being tested to directly operate the meter. This is usually no problem with better-quality meters as the amount of power taken is very small.

2.6.2   Functions

One of the big advantages of a meter is that it can measure volts, amps (and milliamps), and ohms, which are the three basic units of electricity. Special meters are also available to measure power directly in watts, but this measurement is seldom needed in alarm work. If necessary, you can obtain the watts by measuring volts and amps and multiplying the two. This is true for DC circuits, and is approximately true for AC, however not all V-O-Ms are able to measure AC current. Since most alarm circuits are DC, you should have no trouble.

2.6.3   Ranges

Multimeters, of course, have many ranges to add to their usefulness. By selecting the proper range, you can get more accurate measurements. For instance, if you tried to measure 1.5 volts on a 0–150 volt scale, the meter would only move ⅟₁₀₀th of its total possible travel. It would be impossible to tell if you were measuring 1.5 volts or 1.4 volts or even 1 volt. If you tried a 0–15 volt range the meter would move ⅟₁₀th of its total possible travel so you could distinguish between 1.5 volts and 1 volt. If you used a 0–1.5 volt range on the meter you could tell the difference between 1.5 volts and 1.45 volts. Generally, you will want to select the lowest range on the meter that will take the measurement without pegging the meter against the top. When you don't know what range is needed, start with a higher range and work downward. To start at too low a range can result in a damaged or burned-out meter. Digital multimeters (DMMs) usually have automatic range selection, which eliminates this worry.

2.6.4   Accuracy

The meter, because it gives a definite reading, is more accurate than the other test devices, which usually provide only a yes-no indication such as a light on or off or a horn buzzing or silent. Meters have different accuracy (error) ratings of from 5 percent (poor) to ½ percent of full scale (very good) on DC, depending on their quality and price.

Accuracy is the nearness of the indicated reading to the true reading. Although mistakenly called "accuracy" in published specifications, the figure usually given is the "error." This error is usually expressed as a percentage of full scale for V-O-Ms. Suppose you get a reading of 12 volts on a 0–15 volt scale on a meter having an error of 5 percent of full scale. Five percent of 15 volts is 0.75 volts. So the true reading could be anywhere from 11.25 to 12.75 volts. For most alarm work, it would be sufficient to know you have about 12 volts. Such a meter would handle most alarm field work. By comparison, a more expensive, higher-quality meter might have an accuracy (error) of only 1 percent of full scale. One percent of 15 volts full scale is only 0.15 volts. Now a meter reading of 12 volts would have a true reading of 11.85 to 12.15 volts. As you can see, this is more accurate than the previous 11.25 to 12.75 volts obtained with the cheaper, 5 percent meter. Accuracies of 0.1 percent or even better are obtainable with some digital-type meters.

2.6.5   Price

The price will probably determine what kind of meter you will be using. Balanced against price should be ease of use, accuracy, ranges and functions required, ease of reading, and sensitivity.

Cheap meters are available for less than $20. Their small size allows them to be carried in a shirt pocket, but they have relatively low accuracy (high error) and a limited number of ranges, particularly on milliamps and ohms functions. The sensitivity is low, usually 1000 ohms/volt, which is about the same as a relay-type control panel. Figure 2–9 shows a typical unit. Meters in the $30 to $60 range provide larger, easier to read scales, more ranges, better operating convenience and much better sensitivity, usually 20,000 or 30,000 ohms/volts. This higher sensitivity will affect the circuit being tested much less than will the 1000 ohms/volt meters. Meters in this price range are the most used because they offer a good balance of cost versus usefulness. See Figure 2–10.

If you want high accuracy and sensitivity, the digital multimeter (DMM) is unbeatable. Prices of these units have dropped over the years and suitable units are now available for about the price of a good V-O-M. They have very good accuracy, are quite rugged, and will meet most alarm testing needs. They all require batteries for operating the internal circuitry and periodic recharging or replacement is required. The operating time is typically 5 to 10 hours per charge for DMMs that use LED displays. These do have the advantage of being readable in the dark. Units having liquid crystal displays (LCD) typically have operating times of hundreds of hours per charge. Figure 2–11 shows a high-quality, 4½ digit DMM with LED display.

Some special comments are in order concerning DMMs. They use a sample and hold method of operation. That is, they briefly sample the voltage or current, convert it to the appropriate readout, then hold that reading while taking and analyzing the

Figure 2–9 Low-cost V-O-M meter.

Figure 2–10 Medium-cost V-O-M meter.

Figure 2–11 High-quality 4½ digit DMM with LED display.

next sample. Because of this, it is very likely that a DMM will miss "seeing" a momentary event such as a brief pulse or intermittent trouble condition. For the same reason the readings will jump widely when measuring bell current, which varies each time the bell's interrupter contacts open and close. By comparison, a V-O-M will give a steady, average reading because the indicating needle is inherently slow. DMMs will usually read only AC when set to an AC function and only DC when set to a DC function. If you have a DMM set to AC when you want to measure DC you may get a reading much lower than expected, which can be very misleading. What you may actually be reading is the AC ripple from a battery charger, for instance. I've had this happen when I first started using a DMM and didn't realize it immediately. By comparison, a V-O-M (an analog device) will usually read a DC voltage approximately correctly even when set to AC. The reading obtained may be approximately correct, may be about twice what it should be, or may be zero, depending on the design of the meter and the polarity of the test probes. When testing, make sure you have set your meter to the correct function to avoid confusion.

2.7 TEST CABLE REEL

The test cable reel is simply a 200-foot-long 8-conductor test lead arranged on a reel for ease of testing (See Figure 2–12.) It is intended as an aid in one-man trouble-shooting. To avoid running between two points, the troubleshooter can use the cable reel to extend test indications from the main control to the point in the loop being checked. For example, the test reel can be used to extend testing circuits such as meter leads as well as indicator light and control functions of the system itself. The unit is limited to about 200 feet as a matter of practicality, but this will cover many alarm jobs.

The cable reel is mounted in a box with a geared hand crank for easy, fast rewinding. Slip rings allow the cable to pay out or to be cranked in freely without the wires having to be disconnected, although this feature is not essential. Four 2-conductor, 8-foot-long wires with color-coded test clips extend from the top of the box. These are used to make connections to points in the system (usually the control panel) with the reel sitting on the floor. These wires are spring rewound. Again, this feature could be replaced with a straight piece of cable to simplify construction.

The free end of the 200-foot main cable is equipped with an 8-conductor jack that can be connected to a variety of test boxes having matching plugs. These can accommodate a wide variety of testing. The universal continuity tester, previously described, is also equipped with both an 8-pin plug and a jack to permit using it at either end of the cable. Figure 2–13 shows several of these test devices.

I have found this device to be useful in both alarm installation and troubleshooting work. It has been included to stimulate your thinking in building test devices to meet your special needs. You can build one of these if you wish, but I would suggest building or obtaining other more basic equipment first.

Figure 2–12   Test cable reel.

2.8   FOIL ZAPPER

I've had alarm troubleshooters tell me they connect 120-volt AC house power directly to alarm circuits and particularly to foil for troubleshooting. Needless to say, this is a very dangerous practice. The high current resulting from a short or ground could easily start a fire and a dangerous shock hazard exists. Alarm equipment can also be damaged by the high voltage and current.

Another practice is to charge a capacitor, then discharge it across the closed loop to "weld" shut any poor joints. The danger of starting a fire or of electric shock are reduced because the capacitor is quickly discharged, if the loop is not open. Although this procedure works, it is just as likely to weld switch and relay contacts closed, causing undetected break-ins at some later time. It could also damage the contacts enough to cause swingers (intermittent problems) later. This is particularly true of the smaller reed switches, but the problem is not limited to them. For a much better way of testing loops, see Section 2.9, "Exor-System®."

A capacitative discharge tester, which I call a "zapper," is best used across foil and will give excellent results. The current is high enough to burn open a hairline crack so that it can be located and repaired. In this way, the otherwise hard-to-find

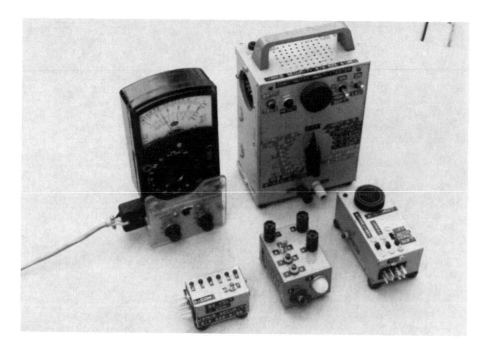

Figure 2–13   Various test devices designed to work with the 200-foot test cable reel.

swinger in foil can easily be located. Good foil and properly made patches and joints will not be damaged, but poorly made joints or patches will be burned open. In this case, the open can easily be located with a meter or by visual inspection and repaired. The zapper should be used across the foil on only one window or door at a time because best results are obtained when the foil resistance is less than 15 ohms. The foil must be completely disconnected from the loop to prevent unnecessary shock hazard and to prevent damage to the rest of the system.

Grounds can often be cleared with a zapper as well. To do this, connect both ends of the foil together on one terminal of the zapper, and connect the other terminal to a good ground, with the foil disconnected from the loop.

You can build this device by following the diagram in Figure 2–14. Read and follow all construction notes, as follows, to avoid shock hazards.

2.8.1   Construction

The switch must be a heavy-duty toggle switch because light-duty switch contacts will weld together. The switch isolates the output from the AC line for increased safety. A two-position, spring-return switch is mandatory. When released, the switch will return to the ''charge'' position to prevent accidental shocks to the user handling the

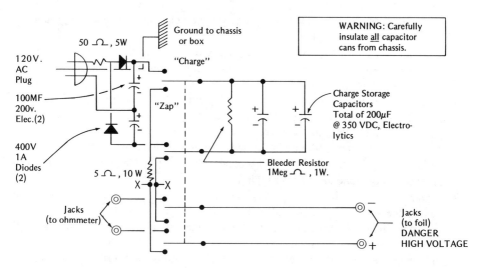

Figure 2–14   Foil zapper circuit. (Warning: high-voltage output.)

test clips. For added safety use rubber insulating boots over the test clips. A four-pole switch is preferred so that the test leads to the foil are automatically switched to a second set of test jacks to which an ohmmeter can be connected. Thus, you can check resistance easily while the zapper is in the "charge" position. Better yet, you can build your own ohmmeter or continuity tester right into the zapper. Use a Smith model 3925 switch. If you cannot find a four-pole switch or are not interested in the ohmmeter connection, use a two-pole, two-position, spring-return switch and connect the wires marked X-X to the foil jacks. This eliminates the lower half of the switch and the ohmmeter jacks shown on the diagram.

The capacitors are charged directly from the AC line with a voltage doubler rectifier, without any transformer to provide isolation. It is mandatory that all capacitor cans and all circuit components be adequately insulated from the chassis or metal box housing the unit. Without this precaution, a dangerous shock hazard *will* exist. Use a three-prong line cord and ground the green wire to the chassis or box, and use only three-wire extension cords and three-prong grounding outlets. Also use a spring-loaded zap switch and rubber boots over test clips.

The zapper requires high voltage to do its job. Although it is much safer than the direct application of 120-volt AC house current to an alarm protective loop, there are still dangers involved. For safe usage read and obey the following instructions carefully:

1. To charge the unit, plug it only into a three-prong, grounding type outlet. If necessary, use only a three-wire extension cord that is plugged into a three-prong outlet.
2. Connect only to a 110–120 volt AC outlet.
3. Do not use a three-wire to two-wire adaptor unless the third wire is properly

grounded at the adaptor. Do not use an extension cord that has had the grounding pin removed from the plug.

4. The unit can be unplugged after charging and carried to the point of testing, to avoid the need for extension cords. It will hold a sufficient charge for about one minute. Recharge after each test.

5. This device is intended for use on foil. Disconnect both ends of the foil from the protective loop before using it to reduce the danger of shock hazard at any other point along the loop and to prevent damage to the system.

6. The unit can also be used on wire having poor connections to weld the connections solid in many instances. Always disconnect the section of wire to be tested from all system components before zapping.

7. Never use this device on any switches, contacts, or relay contacts or on wire having these devices connected to them. To do so may weld the contacts inoperative and could later result in an undetected break-in. If in doubt, test all contacts for proper operation. Even if contacts are not welded shut, they are likely to be damaged, which can result in unreliable operation and possible false alarms in the future.

8. The high voltage and current will damage control units and electronic devices such as mat converters.

9. Always handle test clips by the protective rubber boots to prevent shock hazard.

10. When used on foil, the zapper often produces sparks. Stand back at least five feet. Wear eye protection. Also, remove curtains, decorations or other combustible items before using to prevent damage and possible fire.

11. Do not touch any part of the circuit while testing.

12. Never block or defeat the spring-return zap switch and never hold for more than one second. This is adequate to do the job.

13. Limit the circuit under test to 15 ohms or less, that is, test foil one window or door at a time.

14. Remember the danger: output is approximately 330 volts DC at up to 65 amps pulse, until capacitors discharge.

15. After repairing defective foil, test again to find any additional defects.

Post a copy of these instructions on the zapper under a plastic cover for protection. Instruct all personnel in its safe use before operating. Also post a clear sign at a conspicuous location on the unit: "DANGER, HIGH VOLTAGE—330 volts DC."

In use, I have found the zapper to be a highly effective tool to find intermittent problems in foil, such as those which result from bad patches (often applied by the customer) and hairline cracks. This test device may or may not work if the foil circuit is open, but you can easily find an open using a meter.

When a hairline crack or bad patch is zapped, the momentary high current from the capacitor will melt the foil at the defect and will emit a small shower of sparks. Stand clear and keep curtains and other flammables away. Once the foil is burned, clean the defective spot and repair the foil properly. Be sure to retest, as there could be other bad spots in the foil. If the window has many foil patches, better results will be obtained by entirely refoiling the window. A good foil job will not be damaged by the zapper. See Figure 2–15.

2.9   EXOR-SYSTEM®

The Exor-System (Wiloak Industries) is, in my opinion, one of the best test devices ever to hit the market for the benefit of the alarm troubleshooter. This device can be used to test any open or closed loop system, but its greatest advantage is its ability to accurately and easily detect swingers. It is also very useful in walk testing motion sensors, and it is easy to use.

Basically, this unit is so effective because it is highly sensitive to resistance change and is extremely fast in response, about a microsecond, or one one-millionth of a second. Because of these features this unit will detect potential swingers before they start causing false alarms and, since it automatically resets itself, it is very convenient to use.

When the Exor-System was first invented, its manufacturer contacted me because of my speaking engagements at the International Security Conferences on alarm trouble-

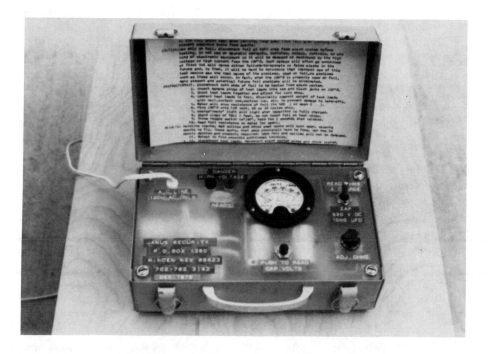

Figure 2–15   Foil zapper. Note "Danger" label above jacks and instructions in lid. Components can be seen through translucent cover.

shooting. During a phone conversation I was told, "It will locate swingers before they cause problems." I doubted this statement, although I very much wanted to believe it. After receiving a unit, actually a prototype, I went back to one of my own installations on which I could not locate the cause of a false alarm. I quickly found and replaced a mechanical switch/foil takeoff. My confidence in Exor-System started to grow.

Next, I approached one of the large alarm companies in the Los Angeles area and talked to the service manager. After a brief table demonstration, he remained skeptical. When I suggested we put it to the test, he broke out in a big grin and said, "I know just the place."

After meeting one of the company service people, we entered a small ladies' apparel shop in downtown Los Angeles. No sooner did the shop owner spot the company insignia on the serviceman's uniform than he became very upset. After four prior unsuccessful repair attempts, he was tired of getting called out of bed in the middle of the night for false alarms.

After assuring the owner that we were armed with better equipment this trip, we proceeded to the McCulloh transmitter and control in the back room. After an ohmmeter confirmed we had continuity, both ends of the loop were lifted, one end shorted together, and the other connected to the Exor-System. With a quick adjustment of the sensitivity knob, we were ready to begin.

The very first window that we rapped with our knuckles produced a half-second beep from the Exor-System, which then automatically reset itself. Repeated rapping quickly confirmed the results. The foil looked fine, but closer inspection from a ladder revealed a poor takeoff at the top of the plate glass. This was quickly fixed. Everybody was happy and were ready to go home. I quickly suggested, "While we are here . . ."

Leaving the Exor-System in place, we switched from "local beeper" to "transmit" mode. We turned on the portable walkie-talkie and proceeded to the front of the store. Rapping on windows produced no response, but the walkie-talkie gave its characteristic beep each time the door cord on the front door was wiggled. This time there was no hesitation. On went a new door cord. The smiles grew broader.

Tapping along the loop wire (about ten feet high) with a long stick (no ladder needed) produced more beeps. Once a problem was located, up came the ladder to the exact spot, off came the old tape to reveal two twisted but unsoldered splices that had corroded over many years. Two additional unsoldered splices were also quickly found and repaired. The smiles turned to grins of amazement. Magnetic contacts were checked by firmly rapping the doorjamb four to six inches away from the contact with a screwdriver handle. (Don't hit the switch directly or you will usually get a beep, even from a good contact.) The contacts checked out clean as did the rest of the loop. A recheck with an ohmmeter indicated the loop resistance had dropped from 138 ohms to 74 ohms, close to the reading of 68 ohms as recorded when the system was installed.

We suspected the defective foil takeoff on the first window checked as being the most probable cause of the current string of false alarms because it had a loose screw. Wind, traffic vibrations, pedestrians on the sidewalk, or small earthquakes could easily have triggered these false alarms. Yet we also found a bad door cord and four unsoldered wire splices, any of which could have been the cause. Even if these others didn't contribute to the present problems, they probably would have done so in the future. The Exor-System did find problems before they caused falses.

Here is a sum-up of the results:

- The alarm company got the system not only working but also completely cleaned up.
- They avoided the near-loss of a subscriber.
- The subscriber no longer had to get out of bed in the middle of the night.
- The police were happy to have one less false-alarming system to answer.
- The alarm company got a job done in less than an hour that four prior service calls had failed to fix.
- Several follow-ups up to one year later revealed a clean system.

After reporting this wonderful story, I am saddened to report that this device is no longer available. Do not despair; read on!

2.9.1   Loop-Sticks®

The Loop-Sticks is a device that performs a function similar to that of the Exor-System and is currently available (from Labor-Saving Devices, 815 Benton Street, Lakewood, Colorado 80214). See Figure 2–16. If the Loop-Sticks had been available when I tested the Exor-System, I believe it would have given similar results.

The design is different and consists of a transmitter and a receiver, each of which is built into a 12-inch-long piece of 1-inch PVC plastic pipe. Each is powered by a 9-volt battery. The transmitter is clipped to the protective loop, which can be NO (normally open), NC (normally closed), or E-O-L (end-of-line resistor) type. Whatever the type, the loop wires must be disconnected from the control panel or other source of voltage while being tested. The device responds to very small changes in loop resistance. The resulting test signal is transmitted over the loop at a low radio frequency, with the loop wires acting as the antenna. (The Exor-System transmitted over a CB walkie-talkie at 27 MHz.) This signal is detectable by the receiver anywhere along the loop wiring but only at a distance of a few feet from the wiring. This allows the receiver, which is carried by the troubleshooter, to locate hidden wiring and switches as well as to locate troubles in a manner similar to that described above for the Exor-System.

2.10   BATTERY FLOAT CHARGE VOLTMETER

Much of today's alarm equipment uses rechargeable standby batteries. It is important that gel-type batteries be float-charged at the correct, constant voltage. See Figure

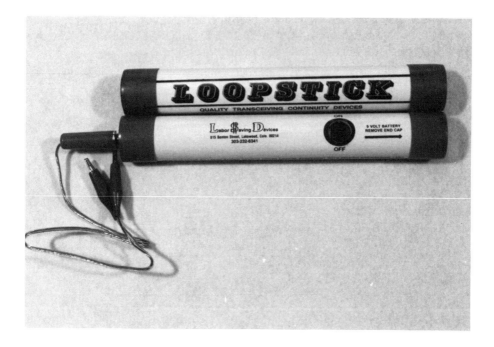

Figure 2–16 Loop-Sticks® wireless test device. (Courtesy of Labor-Saving Devices, Inc., Lakewood, Colorado.)

2–17. If the float voltage is too low, the battery will not deliver its maximum energy when needed. If the float voltage is too high, battery life will be shortened.

Most of the analog meters (V-O-M type) used in alarm work are not accurate enough to give a meaningful test of the float charge voltage. You should have a meter with an accuracy (actually an error) of 1 percent, and preferably 0.5 percent or better. Many digital multimeters will meet this requirement. If you do not have a DMM, an alternative is to make your own meter that reads from about 13 to 14 volts (for 12-volt batteries).

To build such a meter, I would suggest a 0–1 mA meter that can be mounted in a suitable box with test jacks. See Figure 2–18. Before mounting in the box, the meter must be disassembled and the scale removed, painted white, and reinstalled when dry.

The circuit is temporarily connected as shown in Figure 2–17. Using an accurate digital multimeter, set the power supply to 13.0 volts. Now select and try a variety of diodes and zener diodes until the meter reads near but not at the left side. Increase the supply to 14.0 volts on the digital meter and see that the meter reads near the right side without pegging. Increase the value of ''R'' if the meter pegs or decrease it if the meter is near the center.

Note that the meter does not have to read exactly from 13.0 to 14.0 volts. It could read from 12.8 to 14.1 volts. This makes it easier to select components, as you don't have to try many different ones to be exact.

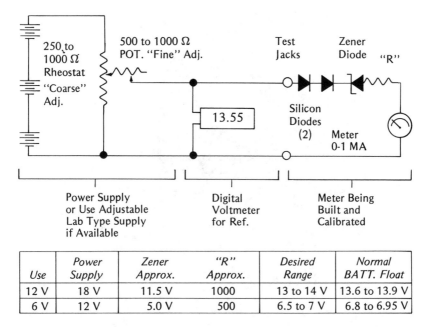

Figure 2–17 Meter (and calibrating circuit) for measuring float charge voltage of gel-type (lead-acid) batteries.

Use	Power Supply	Zener Approx.	"R" Approx.	Desired Range	Normal BATT. Float
12 V	18 V	11.5 V	1000	13 to 14 V	13.6 to 13.9 V
6 V	12 V	5.0 V	500	6.5 to 7 V	6.8 to 6.95 V

To calibrate the meter, adjust the power supply in 0.1-volt increments (as read on the digital meter) and mark the meter scale lightly with a pencil. When the entire scale has been marked, remove it and draw in the entire scale and numbers (see Figure 2–17) with a black pen or pencil or permanent marker. You can also mark "LO," "OK," and "HI" as shown in Figure 2–18.

The reason for using two silicon diodes plus a zener is that you now have three components to vary rather than just one, which makes it easier to get the meter to read from near 13 to near 14 volts. Also, this arrangement provides some temperature compensation.

For testing 6-volt systems, the same arrangement can be used except the meter will be calibrated approximately 6.5 to 7 volts.

Do not attempt to use voltage measurements as a means of testing Ni-Cad batteries, as they use constant current charging rather than constant voltage charging.

2.11 FUTURE TEST EQUIPMENT

After many years of neglect, it is indeed heartening to see new test equipment for the alarm industry, and this trend will continue. As more sophisticated alarm equipment is introduced, more and better test equipment will be needed to keep pace.

I urge each alarm company to seek out and evaluate new test equipment. Those

Figure 2–18 Special meter to accurately read float charge voltage on 12-volt gel-type (lead-acid) batteries.

items that prove their worth should be used to their best advantage and the appropriate people trained in their correct use. Only by so doing can we in the alarm industry provide the best in protective service and reduce the number of false alarms. This becomes all the more important as we start using ever-more sophisticated equipment.

PART TWO

Part Two explains the various problems that arise in alarm systems, the types of protective loops found in the systems, and the effect each kind of trouble has in the various types of loops. Rather than trying to absorb all of this material, newcomers may be tempted to study only the types of protective loops on which they will be working. Although this may be expedient at times, they will miss out on starting simple and going a step at a time. This is usually the best, although not the shortest, way.

To pull everything together, the "seven basic steps" will guide you through troubleshooting any kind of system. These steps will put things in perspective and direct you even when servicing unfamiliar equipment.

3 Kinds of Trouble

To continue to establish the big picture, let's look at different types of possible problems we might encounter. We can have shorts, opens, grounds (the unintentional kinds), foreign voltages, swingers (intermittents), dead batteries, equipment faults of all kinds, phone line problems, and subscriber errors. We can also have problems of equipment misapplication on installation. Later chapters will help you understand how detection devices work, which will help you spot and correct such misapplications. This chapter will cover only the types of commonly encountered problems.

One of the more difficult problems to deal with is that of subscriber error. Subscribers aren't always willing to admit they made an error, or they may not be aware that they had done so. Careful but courteous questioning may uncover what actually happened. Otherwise it may be difficult to determine whether the trouble was really caused by a subscriber error, by a swinger, or by some other problem that did not leave any physical evidence behind.

3.1 EQUIPMENT TROUBLES

There are a number of general troubleshooting steps that apply to any piece of equipment such as a control panel, photoelectric beam, passive infrared detector, or the like. On the other hand, alarm detection devices each have their own kinds of problems that are related to the way they work. These are so varied that they will be covered in more detail in a later chapter. Right now, let's look at the common things.

3.1.1 Power

Make sure the correct power is being supplied to the unit. Batteries may have run down; power supplies may have failed or been turned off or unplugged; wires may have become loose, broken or shorted; or the wrong voltage may have been used. Also make sure that AC is not being supplied if DC is required by the specific unit, and vice versa. Don't overlook the fact that 120-volt house power is sometimes controlled by wall switches or timers. This could be the reason behind unexplained dead batteries. Also look for unplugged transformers and for wire that is too small and thus causes excessive voltage drop. This is particularly true of long wire runs. When checking for proper voltages or for excessive voltage drops, do so under maximum load, such as with bells ringing. Also check battery condition under maximum load. Many systems have power supplies adequate only for normal operation and for slow recharging of batteries. Such systems depend on healthy batteries to deliver the higher current draw needed to ring bells and so forth. A unit may operate normally with a nearly dead battery, so long as the power supply is on, but will fail under maximum load, such as with bells ringing.

3.1.2   External Connections

Inspect all external connections to see that wires are connected to the right terminals and that they are clean, tight, and not broken inside the insulation close to the terminal. Also look for evidence of corrosion. White, gray, or greenish blue powdery coatings on exposed metal wires or terminals are telltale signs of this problem. Crimped connections, such as crimped lugs, must also be checked for proper crimping. Any signs of looseness requires replacement. Recrimping previously crimped connections should be avoided. It is better to replace the lugs if old crimp connections are loose. Sufficient slack should be allowed in all leads to prevent tension, particularly when covers are closed or replaced.

3.1.3   Switches

Make sure switches have not been turned off or set to a test position if the unit has such switches.

3.1.4   Tamper Switches

Be sure temporarily to bypass or defeat any tamper switches that have been operated, such as when opening covers for testing. Don't forget to remove such bypasses when done testing.

3.1.5   Adjustments

Make sure sensitivity, pulse count, and other adjustments are correctly set. Follow the manufacturer's instructions or guidelines unless your previous experience dictates otherwise. As previously mentioned, additional information is presented in a later chapter.

3.1.6   Test Jumpers

Sometimes test jumpers are temporarily attached to a unit during certain tests. Be sure these jumpers have been removed when testing is completed. Other units may have a jumper with one end permanently attached. The free end is placed in one position for testing and a different position for normal operation. Be sure jumpers are correctly positioned.

3.1.7 Mechanical Adjustments

Relays, McCulloh code wheels, bells, and other mechanical type devices can sometimes be repaired, cleaned, or lubricated to restore them to proper service. (Do not lubricate bells or relays.) Electromechanical contacts (relays, bells, etc.) are best cleaned with a contact burnisher, made specially for that purpose. These are available from alarm equipment suppliers, electronic parts distributors and small tool specialty houses. Files are too rough and, when used to clean contacts, will often remove the precious-metal plating from the contact surface. This exposes the base metal, which is more likely to corrode and give further problems.

Any lubrication of moving parts should be done per the manufacturer's recommendations or should be based on your own experience if you have reason to deviate from the instructions. Nongumming lubricants, such as clock oil, should be used for long, trouble-free operation. Lubricant should be applied very sparingly. When lubricating, it may first be necessary to disassemble and thoroughly clean the parts for long-lasting results.

Some items, such as bell plungers, are designed to operate dry. Oil could trap enough dust and dirt over a period of time to cause sticking, so do not lubricate them. The same is true for relay armatures. Fortunately, solid-state electronics have replaced most electromechanical devices.

3.1.8 Fuses

Some alarm equipment has one or more fuses or circuit breakers. Inspect them and replace or reset them if they are blown or tripped. Before doing so, look for the cause of the blown fuse or tripped breaker, or the same thing may happen again. Examples are an overloaded power supply, shorted wires, or a foreign voltage.

3.1.9 Indicators

Many alarm systems are equipped with a built-in meter, indicator lights, LEDs, or digital or alpha display. A glance often gives clues to problems. Also observe the positions of switches, knobs, and other controls for clues.

3.1.10 Replacement

If you do not have the necessary replacement parts or if experience has shown that certain kinds of repairs are unreliable, then the only course of action is to replace the entire unit. This will particularly be true of the solid-state electronic equipment now in widespread use. Unless you have schematics (and know how to read them), correct replacement parts, a thorough knowledge of electronics and of electronics trouble-shooting, the correct tools, the correct test instruments, and a very steady hand to work on the tiny components, you will do more damage than repairs. Most of us will end up substituting a known good item for one that is bad or is suspected of being bad. Chapter 6, Section 6.2 provides more detailed procedures you can use before determining the need to replace an item. If you do determine that a piece of equipment is defective, it is generally more economical to replace it rather than to attempt repairs.

3.2   LOOP AND WIRING TROUBLES

Most alarm components are connected into a system with wires. Even radio-operated systems often have wire for bells or other warning devices and for on-off switches or control stations. This wire is subject to deterioration, abrasion, flexing, corrosion, cutting, pulling, tearing, vibration, and other kinds of damage, both accidental and malicious. Magnetic and mechanical contacts, traps, mats, and other intrusion sensors are subject to much the same problems as wire, with more troubles of their own. All of these troubles require troubleshooting. Let's look at what kinds of trouble we can encounter. By grouping them appropriately, we can better direct our efforts to locate and repair them.

3.2.1   Foreign Voltage (Potential)

The most dangerous fault is a foreign voltage on an alarm circuit. This would result if a bare alarm wire came in contact with a bare, hot wire from another circuit such as a 120-volt house wire, a doorbell, a thermostat or control circuit, a telephone line (other than an alarm-reporting drop), or any other circuit or equipment. Anything over about 60 volts can pose a shock hazard, and any foreign voltage can seriously damage alarm equipment. Even if there has been no damage, erratic or unexplainable system operation may be traced to a foreign voltage. Remember, though, that these foreign voltages may be intermittent due to the nature of their operation. For example, ther-mostats turn on and off, telephone bells ring only occasionally, and lights are turned on and off. This can make troubleshooting difficult.

Foreign voltages (potentials) on an alarm circuit are dangerous and can cause damage to the equipment. Fortunately, they are relatively rare, so let's move on to more common troubleshooting matters.

3.2.2   Opens

Opens account for the largest percentage of wire troubles. They can result from torn or cut wires, bad splices, loose connections at equipment or detection devices, cold solder joints, fatigue from overflexing, and defective wiring inside equipment. Opens are detected in closed circuit loops as immediate alarms when arming or as an inability to arm a system, depending on the kind of system used. Opens in open circuit loops can go undetected until tested or possibly until after a successful attack.

3.2.3 Shorts

Shorts are also common and are likely to result from staples cutting through wire insulation, improperly insulated splices, sharp edges of objects cutting through the insulation, moisture or corrosion of terminals or splices, or from wet or damp wires.

Another source of shorts is physical pressure on the wires. Such pressure can result from insulated or uninsulated staples driven too tightly against the wires or from the weight of objects resting on or leaning against the wires. Such objects can be insulating or conducting. When the pressure is applied at a point where the wires cross, which happens every few inches in twisted pair wire, the pressure causes plastic insulation to "cold flow" away from the pressure point. Eventually, the two wires can press through the insulation and cause a short. Twisted pair wire is more susceptible because of its regular twist, but parallel type wire also gets twisted and so is not immune to the problem. Metal objects, which are conductors, can press through insulation in a similar manner even where wires are not crossed. Thus the short is completed through the metal object such as an uninsulated staple. Jacketed wire and cable is less susceptible to such problems because of the extra protection afforded by the jacket, but it is not completely immune.

Short circuits due to cold flow can occur within seconds after the pressure is applied, or it may take days, weeks, or months for the short to occur. The time interval depends on the amount of physical pressure, whether the pressure is continuous or intermittent, whether there is any motion or vibration involved, and on the temperature, which can soften or harden the plastic insulation.

As an example, an open loop panic circuit wire came loose from the wall and found its way under one of the feet of my bed just where a twist happened to occur in the parallel wire. The bed itself caused no problem but a few minutes after I went to bed, the added weight caused the plastic to cold flow. Off went the alarm when the wires shorted. I got up, reset the alarm, and investigated for a break-in, not realizing at that point what had caused the alarm. Finding nothing, I returned to bed. This time, it took only thirty seconds before it went off again. Again the routine. Back to bed. After the third ring, I disabled the system for the night. Examination the next morning revealed the problem.

Shorts in open loop, double loop, and end-of-line systems will be detected because they will cause an alarm condition. The big danger of shorts in a single, closed loop system is that they may not cause an alarm condition. They will therefore not be detected until all openings are tested, or worse yet, until a successful break-in occurs.

3.2.4 Grounds

When speaking of grounds, we must first distinguish between accidental and intentional ground connections. In an ungrounded system, if an accidental ground occurs in the loop, there will probably not be any alarm occurring to call attention to this event. Later, perhaps years later, another accidental ground can occur that bypasses all or part of the protection. Again, there will probably be no alarm to alert anybody to the loss of protection or to the need for corrective action. The loss may be discovered only after a successful (undetected) break-in occurs. For this reason, one side of some protective loops is intentionally grounded to an earth ground. It is then necessary to connect all detection devices in the ungrounded side of the loop. More detail will be presented on this topic in Chapter 4.

Sometimes we end up with a grounded loop even though no intentional connection is made from the loop to earth ground. This can happen through some other portion of the alarm circuit. An example would be where the bell or other wire is run through a conduit for physical protection. The conduit is connected to the metal control box and is very likely to be fastened to some grounded metal part of the building. If the manufacturer has connected a common point of the circuitry to the box, you will most likely have a ground on one side of the loop, even though you are not aware of its presence. This usually causes no problem. The system will behave just as if you had made an intentional ground connection.

There is some controversy in the alarm industry as to the relative safety of a grounded versus an ungrounded system. I've heard statements that favor both methods. Lightning can cause serious damage to, or total destruction of, alarm equipment. I have seen equipment that was "fried" by lightning. Components were literally blown up and traces were burned off the circuit board. This occurred in spite of the presence of surge protectors. Lightning does not have to score a direct hit on a system or even on a building to cause such damage. Very high voltages can be induced into alarm systems by nearby strikes.

Unfortunately, I do not have sufficient evidence to advise grounded or ungrounded systems. Since lightning can jump a mile or more through the sky, I doubt it will stop at a few inches or feet between an alarm system and a metal object, grounded or not. I recall the following excerpt from a book about lightning that I read some years ago. A particular strike hit a tree, came down the tree, jumped to a wash line, followed it to a house, jumped through the wall and hit a bed spring, killing the person in the bed. Lightning behaves strangely. It is a very rapid transient and the electrical laws it obeys are very different from the laws of steady-state electricity we encounter in normal alarm system operation.

For troubleshooting purposes, a ground is nothing more than a short between one wire and a grounded object. Grounds result from the same causes as shorts. The results are a bit different, though.

A double, closed loop; an E-O-L resistor loop; or a break and cross loop, any of which has one side intentionally grounded and no detection devices in the grounded side, are generally safer than single-loop systems or ungrounded-loop systems. An accidental ground on the ungrounded wire of such a system causes an alarm condition. An accidental ground on the already grounded wire causes no problems. More will be said on results in the next chapter.

The best advice on intentional grounding of an alarm system is to follow the recommendations of the alarm equipment manufacturer. Most, if not all, manufacturers of the microprocessor-based systems demand that a system be properly connected to an earth ground.

3.3 RESISTANCE FAULTS

Resistance faults are not a kind of trouble in themselves, as are opens, shorts, grounds, and foreign voltages. Rather, they are a variation of these four. In the preceding discussion it was assumed that we had "dead" or "solid" shorts, grounds, and foreign voltages. That is, it was assumed that such faults were of very low resistance (usually less than an ohm, or a few ohms at most), such as would be caused by bare metal touching bare metal. Opens were assumed to be clean breaks with resistances approaching infinity. Quite often we do find such faults.

Sometimes we find that a short or ground has a high resistance. The short resistance might be high enough not to adversely affect alarm operation, or it may be low enough to cause an alarm condition or to effectively bypass part of the protection. Similarly, an open may have leakage resistances. Again, it may or may not affect alarm system operation, depending on the actual resistance. Whether or not any given resistance value will adversely affect an alarm system depends on the type, make, and model of alarm control unit; the type of protective loop; the resistance of the loop (without the fault); and where the fault occurs in the loop. It also depends on the voltage the system is operating on. Most units will operate over a range of voltages, such as from 9 to 14 volts for a nominal 12-volt system. Unfortunately, it is not possible to make any generalizations. For example, a relay-type alarm control unit using a 1½-volt battery has a loop resistance limit of 100 ohms. A solid-state control may work through 100,000 ohms. For this reason, it is necessary to find the loop resistance limits from the manufacturer of the make and model of control you are testing. This information is often, but not always, included in the sales literature, catalog or instruction sheet. You can determine these values yourself by substituting a decade resistance box or resistance substitution box for the protective loop.

A metal-to-metal solid short or ground is easy to understand, but what might cause a resistance short or ground? What would cause a resistance open? Consider wires running through water or through a damp location. The insulation is seldom perfect. It often has pinholes. Water can leak in. The same goes for splices, which often are not taped watertight or may not be taped at all. Water, which almost always has some impurities in it, conducts electricity well enough to cause shorts and grounds.

Sometimes a wire is spliced but poorly insulated or not insulated at all and is thus exposed to air, moisture, and corrosion. The same is true of screw terminals. Over the months or years, corrosion can eat away at the copper wire. When the wire has been entirely eaten through, an open results. The corrosion products (chemicals) remain and can conduct electricity, but they usually have a high resistance. Thus, you have a resistance open. Moisture and corrosion are the cause of most resistance fault.

Fortunately, resistance faults are not often encountered, but when they do occur they can be very elusive. Continuity testers often prove unreliable for this kind of problem because the resistance limit of the tester is different from that of the alarm control unit. Most accurate results are obtained by measuring the loop with an ohmmeter and comparing this number with the manufacturer's limits for the alarm control unit. More meaningful results can be obtained by comparing present loop resistance with similar measurements made during installation or during previous troubleshooting. It is helpful to keep such written records. Post values and dates for each zone inside the control box.

Bear in mind that weather conditions can change by the time you arrive to troubleshoot and that such changes can affect alarm system conditions. A good example is that moisture from rain or fog can cause corrosion of poorly made electrical connections. Wet and dry cycles of weather can be particularly difficult times to troubleshoot.

3.4   THE SWINGER

The swinger is the worst problem of all to troubleshoot. Once again, this is not the same kind of fault as opens, shorts, and grounds, but is a variation of any of these. It can be, and often is, a variation of a resistance fault. The name ''swinger'' is a general term in the alarm industry used to indicate an intermittent problem. Like the back-and-forth motion of a swing, the problem comes and goes. It seems as though it always comes in the middle of the night or at a time when you're swamped with work and always goes as soon as you arrive to look for it. Remember this about swingers: they are time-related problems.

4 Types of Protective Loops

Before doing any troubleshooting, we must know the types of protective loops that we might be working on. Each reacts somewhat differently to the various kinds of wire faults, and each requires the correct troubleshooting approach. The following types of loops are listed in an approximately increasing level of security afforded. A few comments are in order concerning the diagrams in this chapter. First, the various types of protective loops are shown in the nonalarm and then in one or more of the alarm conditions to illustrate how that particular type of loop works. Additional diagrams show how different kinds of troubles affect the different types of loops. Second, the diagrams are typical and do not represent any given job. Third, refer to Figure 4–1 for an explanation of the symbols used in the diagrams. If the symbols you use are different from the illustration, you may wish to redraw the diagrams using your own symbols. Unfortunately, I do not know of any standard on symbols for the alarm industry.* Fourth, the box shown at the left of the diagram represents the control function. You may call it a panel, a control module, or by some other name. The control function may also be part of a transmitter, dialer, or other combination device.

4.1 OPEN LOOP

An open loop is the simplest type of protective loop but is not often used because there is no supervision of the wiring. The loop is open during nonalarm conditions (Figure 4–2) and is closed by a switch in some sort of intrusion-sensing device, such as a door contact, when an intrusion occurs (Figure 4–3). All switches are wired in parallel. If a wire is broken, then any switch closure beyond (to the right of) the break (Figure 4–4) will not be "seen" by the alarm control, so it will not cause an alarm. This is what we mean by "no supervision." This leaves a possibility of a successful, undetected break-in. A short across the loop (Figure 4–5) will result in an alarm condition and will thus be detected. On the other hand, a single, accidental ground on either side of the loop (Figures 4–6A and B) will not affect normal operation. This assumes the system has no intentional ground. But if two accidental grounds occur

---

*N.B.F.A.A. does have standard symbols, but they are used to locate alarm detection devices and other equipment on architectural drawings rather than to make electrical diagrams.

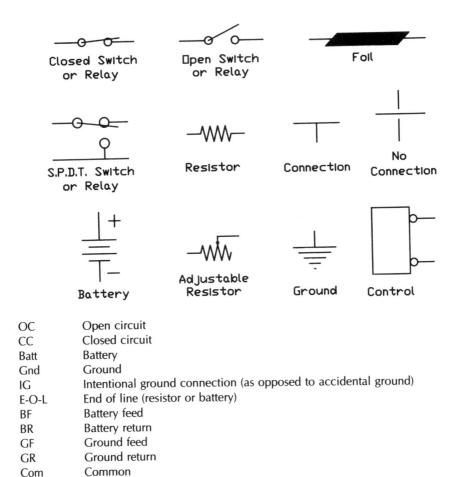

OC	Open circuit
CC	Closed circuit
Batt	Battery
Gnd	Ground
IG	Intentional ground connection (as opposed to accidental ground)
E-O-L	End of line (resistor or battery)
BF	Battery feed
BR	Battery return
GF	Ground feed
GR	Ground return
Com	Common

Figure 4–1 Symbols and abbreviations used in this book. An asterisk on the diagrams indicates an alarm or fault condition.

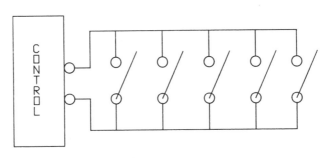

Figure 4–2 Open loop, secure condition.

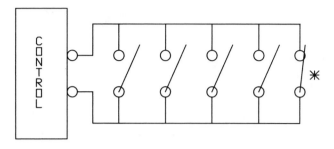

Figure 4–3   Open loop, alarm condition.

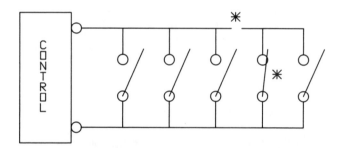

Figure 4–4   Open Loop. Broken wire does not signal an alarm, yet prevents detection of alarm condition beyond the break, so there is no supervision against breaks.

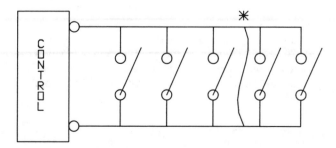

Figure 4–5   Open loop. A short causes an alarm condition.

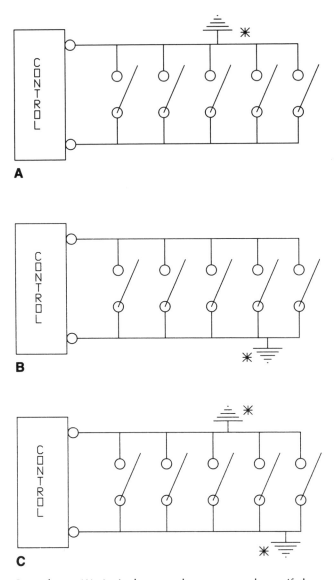

Figure 4–6 Open loop. (A) A single ground causes no alarm, if the system has no intentional ground. (B) A single ground on the opposite side of the loop causes no alarm, again only if the system is not intentionally grounded. (C) Two ground faults on opposite sides of the loop cause an alarm condition, if the leakage resistance of the ground path is low enough.

(Figure 4–6C), an alarm will occur because the loop will be completed via the two grounds.

Sometimes an open loop system has one side intentionally grounded, perhaps through the control. In such a system, an accidental ground on the other side, would, of course, cause an alarm.

4.2   SINGLE CLOSED LOOP

The single closed loop is better because it does provide supervision. The loop must be closed (Figure 4–7) during nonalarm conditions and is opened (Figure 4–8) to give an alarm. Thus a broken wire (Figure 4–9) or broken foil (Figure 4–10) will be detected because it will provide an open, or alarm, condition. The loop is supervised at least against opens. A short across part of the loop will bypass the portion of the loop beyond the short. An intrusion (Figure 4–11) will go undetected, and there is no warning of this loss of protection. A single, accidental ground (Figure 4–12A) will not affect operation. No indication will be given of this ground fault. A second ground, possibly occurring later (Figure 4–12B), will bypass part of the loop. A subsequent intrusion will go undetected. Again, there is no indication of this loss of protection. Switches are wired in series. A single closed loop can be run with a single conductor looped around the premises but this can make troubleshooting very difficult. Two-conductor wire makes troubleshooting much easier, as I will point out in Chapter 6, "Specific Troubleshooting Procedures."

4.3   OPEN AND CLOSED LOOP

Some alarm control units can accept both open and closed loops so that a trip on either the closed loop (Figure 4–13A) or on the open loop (Figure 4–13B) will cause an alarm condition. These controls are often wired with two physically separate loops

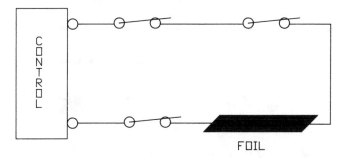

FOIL

Figure 4–7   Single closed loop, secure condition.

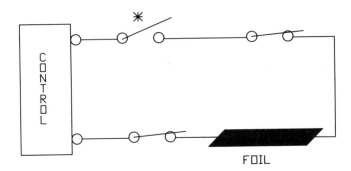

Figure 4–8   Single closed loop, alarm condition.

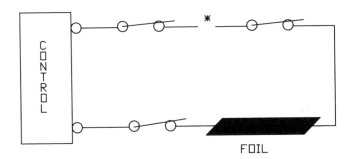

Figure 4–9   Single closed loop. Broken wire causes alarm condition.

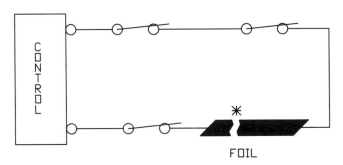

Figure 4–10   Single closed loop. Broken window foil causes alarm.

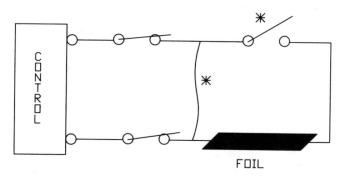

Figure 4–11 Single closed loop. A short does not signal an alarm, yet prevents detection of an alarm condition beyond the short.

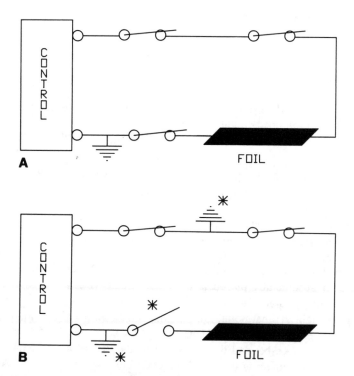

Figure 4–12 Single closed loop. (A) A single ground fault does not cause an alarm. (B) Two ground faults do not cause an alarm, yet prevent detection of an alarm condition beyond the ground faults.

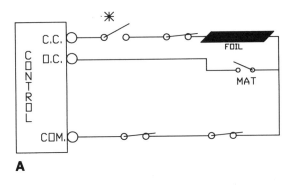

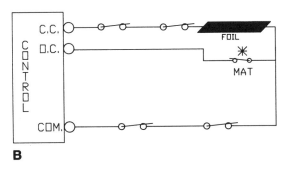

Figure 4–13 Open and closed loop. (A) Alarm condition on closed circuit (loop) side. (B) Alarm condition on open circuit (loop) side.

(Figure 4–14A). That is, one pair of wires is used for closed circuit devices such as magnetic contacts, foils, lacing, etc., and another pair of wires is used for open circuit devices such as mat switches.

This type of alarm control often has one terminal common to both the closed circuit and the open circuit. In this case a combination loop could be run, similar to a double loop, and both open and closed circuit devices could be used (Figure 4–14B). When doing this, all closed circuit devices must be connected in the closed circuit wire. If accidentally placed in the open circuit wire, a closed circuit device will not only fail to signal an alarm, it will also disable any open circuit devices beyond (to the right of) that point. Also, unlike a true double closed loop, there is no supervision of the open circuit wire. Thus, a wire break (Figure 4–15A) would disable the open circuit device beyond the break. Also, the loss of coverage would go undetected. An improvement is to extend the open loop wire on around to the control (Figure 4–15B) where the wire is connected to the normally open circuit terminal, along with the original end. This still does not provide supervision of the NO (open circuit) wire, but no protection would be lost if a single break were to occur in this

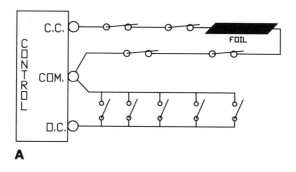

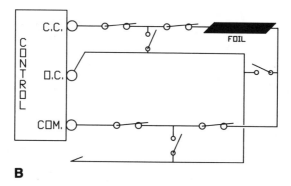

Figure 4–14 Open and closed loop. (A) Wired as separate loops, secure condition. (B) Wired in combination, secure condition.

wire (Figure 4–15C). A double break in this wire (Figure 4–15D) could cause loss of protection.

A break in the closed circuit part of the loop (Figure 4–16) will cause an alarm. A short between the closed and open circuits (Figure 4–17) will also cause an alarm. A single, accidental ground on the closed circuit (Figure 4–18A) or on the open circuit (Figure 4–18B) will not cause an alarm nor will it affect operation, assuming the circuit is not intentionally grounded anywhere. If a ground occurs on both sides of the circuit (Figure 4–18C), an alarm will result. If, on the other hand, two grounds occur on the closed circuit (Figure 4–18D), part of the protection will be bypassed. All of the points in this paragraph are the same as for a separate open loop or for a single closed loop.

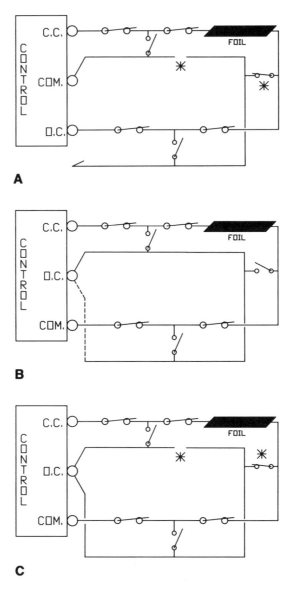

Figure 4–15 Open and closed loop. (A) A break in the open loop wire does not signal an alarm, yet prevents detection on an open circuit device beyond the break. (B) Connecting the return end of the open loop wire to the OC terminal (dashed line). (C) Now a single break in the open loop does not prevent detection of an alarm condition. (D) There is still no supervision of the open loop wire, so a second break will cause loss of detection of an alarm condition beyond the breaks.

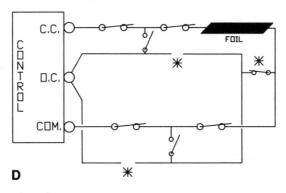

D

Figure 4–15   (*continued*)

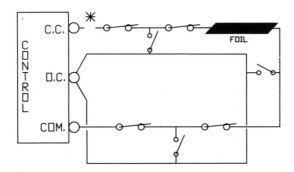

Figure 4–16   Open and closed loop. A break in the closed loop wire will signal an alarm.

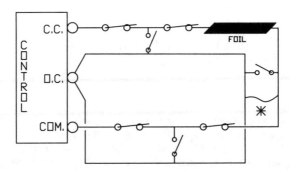

Figure 4–17   Open and closed loop. A short between the open and closed loops will cause an alarm.

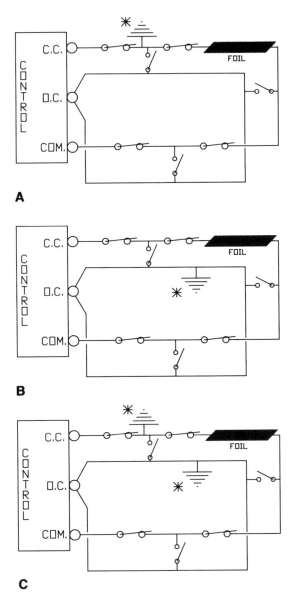

Figure 4–18 Open and closed loop. (A) A single ground on the closed loop will not cause an alarm, as long as the system has no intentional ground on the open loop side. (B) A ground on the open loop side causes no alarm, as long as there is no intentional ground on the closed loop side. Note: a closed loop should never be grounded, as an accidental ground fault will bypass part of the protection and will not cause an alarm. See Figure 4–18D. (C) Ground faults on both open and closed loops will cause an alarm, if the leakage resistance is low enough. (D) Two ground faults on the closed loop will bypass part of the protection and will not cause an alarm, if there is no intentional ground on the open loop.

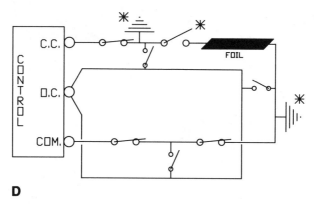

D

Figure 4–18 (continued)

4.4 DOUBLE CLOSED LOOP

A more common and more secure wiring method is the double closed loop, which is often referred to simply as a double loop. There are a number of variations. They all share the characteristics that they use two circuit conductors (one positive and one negative), they have both conductors supervised, and they can employ both closed circuit and open circuit intrusion detection devices. Usually, closed circuit devices are preferred because their contacts are supervised. Mat switches, which are open circuit devices, can also be used. I will begin with a simple, double closed loop. Next I will add intentional grounds. Finally, I will advance to end-of-line resistor (terminator), direct wire (break-and-cross), and distributed resistance loops, which are variations of the simple, double closed loop.

A double closed loop is shown in the secure condition in Figure 4–19. It can be tripped by the opening of a closed circuit device (Figure 4–20A) or by the closing of an open circuit device (Figure 4–20B). These diagrams show the double loop with

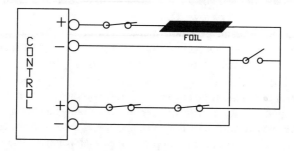

Figure 4–19 Double closed loop, secure condition.

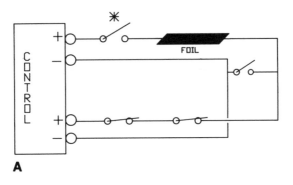

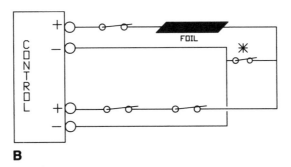

Figure 4–20 Double closed loop. (A) Alarm on closed circuit device on + side of loop. (B) Alarm on open circuit device between + and − sides of loop.

both ends connected to the control. With this arrangement, only one power supply, located in the control, is required.

Many earlier systems used an end-of-line battery or power supply with standby battery (Figure 4–21). Another battery or power supply with standby battery was also required in the control to ring a bell or to transmit a silent alarm. Note that a short in the loop near the E-O-L battery creates a high current draw, which will quickly drain a battery (Figure 4–22). To prevent this, a resistor is added (Figure 4–23). A small light bulb is an excellent resistor for this service. In normal operation, the filament is cold and its resistance is very low. Thus it does not add much to the loop resistance. During a short, the filament gets hot; that is, the bulb lights up and its resistance greatly increases. This reduces battery drain and provides a short indicator. Some E-O-L power supplies have a bulb built in for this purpose. This short indicator can not always be relied upon, though. If the loop resistance between the power supply and the short is high enough, too little current will flow and the bulb will not light. Systems having the loop voltage supplied from the control will have a similar resistor or bulb.

In a double closed loop, the loop voltage holds a relay operated in the secure condition. Opening or shorting the loop removes this voltage. The relay drops out,

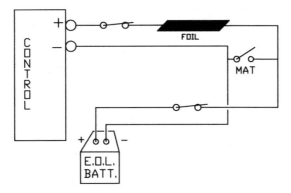

Figure 4–21 Double closed loop, using an end-of-line battery or power supply. May be located at control or at another location.

signaling an alarm. The same function is performed electronically in solid-state systems. Let's start by assuming that there are no intentional grounds on the loop.

Opening the positive side (Figure 4–24A) or the negative side (Figure 4–24B) of the loop will cause an alarm. Thus both sides of the loop are supervised. If you recall, the negative side of the open and closed loop was not supervised. A short (Figure 4–25) will also cause an alarm. An accidental ground on the negative side (Figure 4–26A) or on the positive side (Figure 4–26B) will not cause an alarm nor will it affect normal operation. A ground on both sides (Figure 4–26C) will cause an alarm. Two ground faults on the positive side (Figure 4–26D) will not cause an alarm but will cause loss of protection (Figure 4–26E). Since no indication is received on the

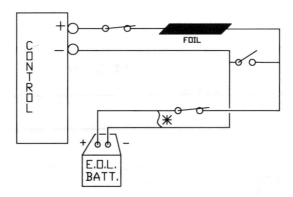

Figure 4–22 Double closed loop, with short across + and − sides. If short is physically close to battery power or power supply, a high current will flow, causing a blown fuse or rapidly discharged battery. The short will cause an alarm.

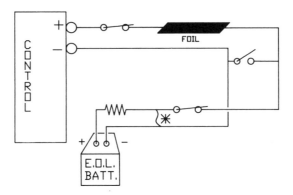

Figure 4–23 Double closed loop, same, with addition of current-limiting resistor. A small light bulb makes a good limiter for this service.

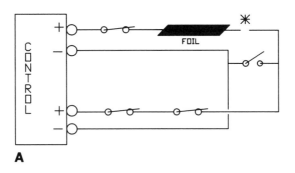

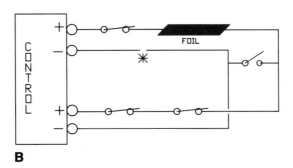

Figure 4–24 Double closed loop. (A) Break in + loop causes alarm, thus the + side is supervised against breaks. (B) Same for the − side.

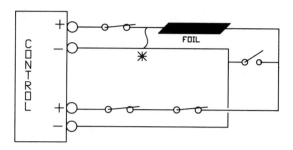

Figure 4–25 Double closed loop. A short also causes an alarm, thus this system is also supervised against shorts.

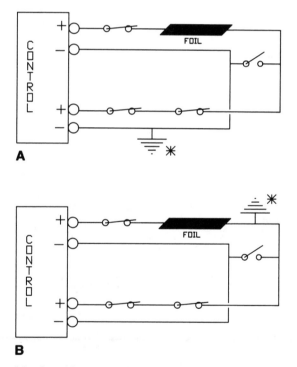

Figure 4–26 Double closed loop. (A) Ground on the − side causes no alarm nor other problem, whether or not there is an intentional ground as well. (B) Single ground on the + side will not cause an alarm or other problem, as long as the − side is not intentionally grounded. (C) With grounds on both + and − loops an alarm will result, if the leakage resistance is low enough. (D) Two grounds on the + side will not cause an alarm, if the − side does not have an intentional ground. (E) Two grounds on the plus side cause no alarm, yet an intrusion goes undetected because part of the circuit is effectively bypassed via the grounds. *Continues on next page.*

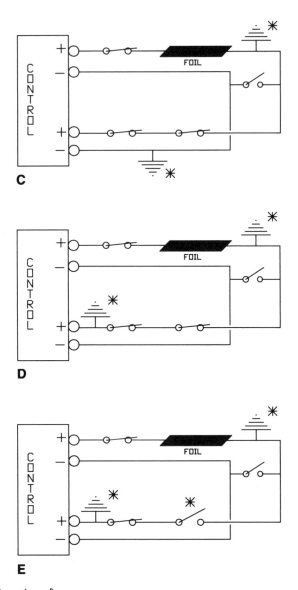

Figure 4–26   (continued)

first ground fault (Figure 4–26B), no corrective action would likely be taken. At some later date, a second ground fault could occur (Figure 4–26D). Again, no indication is received, so the loss of protection (Figure 4–26E) would go unnoticed. This could lead to an undetected break-in. This problem is corrected by an intentional ground, discussed in the next section.

4.5   DOUBLE CLOSED LOOP, GROUNDED

To prevent possible undetected loss of protection, the procedure is to intentionally ground one side, usually negative, of the loop (Figure 4–27). The first ground fault on the positive side (Figure 4–28A) will give an alarm condition. Thus, corrective action is taken immediately. This avoids double ground faults and lost protection as described in the previous section. A ground fault on the negative side (Figure 4–28B) will not cause an alarm, nor will it affect normal operation. Closed circuit devices should never be installed in the grounded (negative) side, because they would be bypassed if they were located between the intentional and any other possible ground. An exception to this rule is when double circuit lacing is used. Lacing, however, is rarely used any more.

4.6   DOUBLE CLOSED LOOP, SUPERVISED GROUND

An intentional ground connection is often made to a cold-water pipe or other location where moisture condenses or collects. This leads to corrosion and a possible loss of the desired ground connection (Figure 4–29). Unfortunately, there is no alarm or other indication of this loss. We now have an ungrounded system with its potential problems as previously explained under the double closed loop.

To correct this shortcoming, a supervised ground is used (Figure 4–30). This is done by cutting the negative wire and connecting each cut end to a separate ground clamp on a cold-water pipe (do not use it on plastic pipe) or other earth ground source. If a ground wire now opens due to corrosion or any other cause (Figure 4–31), an alarm calls attention to the problem. The supervised ground thus provides a better level of security.

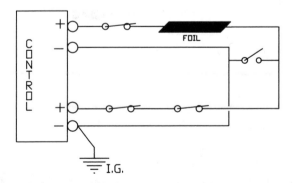

Figure 4–27   Double closed loop, with an intentional ground (IG) connected to the − side, secure condition.

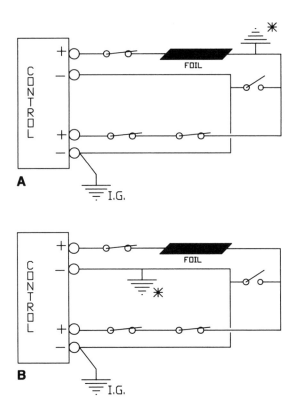

Figure 4–28   Double closed loop. (A) Ground fault on + side now causes an immediate alarm condition. (B) Ground fault on − side causes no alarm nor other problem, so long as no detection devices are connected in the − side. If there were, a ground fault could bypass them, as in Figure 4–26D.

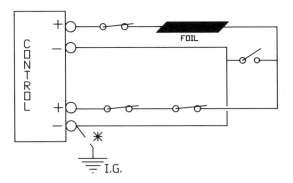

Figure 4–29   Double closed loop. If a break were to occur in the ground connection, no alarm would result to draw attention to the loss. The circuit would then be the same as Figure 4–19.

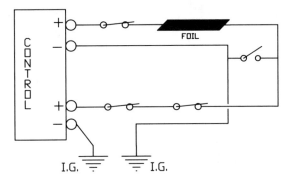

Figure 4–30 Double closed loop, with supervised (double) ground connections.

A ground or supervised ground can usually be located anywhere in the loop. Many transmitters, however, use the same ground, so it should be located close to the transmitter or control, rather than at some distance from it. Usually the negative side is grounded, but this is not always true.

4.7 END-OF-LINE RESISTOR (TERMINATOR) LOOP

The E-O-L resistor loop (Figure 4–32) uses a resistor at the far end to pass a limited current. Opening either wire, as in the operation of a closed circuit device Figure 4–33A) or from a wire break, drops the current to zero, signaling an alarm. Shorting the wires (Figure 4–33B), as when an open circuit device closes or when an accidental short occurs, bypasses the E-O-L resistor. This causes loop current to increase, which also signals an alarm.

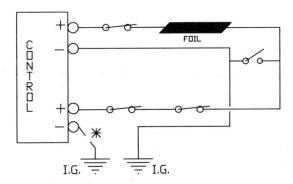

Figure 4–31 Double closed loop, with supervised ground, with a break in one ground wire, now causes an alarm condition.

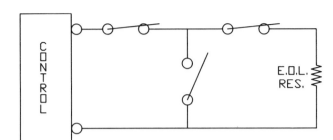

Figure 4–32   E-O-L resistor loop, secure condition.

The E-O-L loop provides all the advantages of the previously described double closed loop. As with the E-O-L battery, it is not necessary to run the end of the loop back to the control. This can save wiring. Since a simple resistor is used, no battery or power supply with power source and standby battery are required. This further simplifies wiring installation and eliminates the cost for the battery or power supply

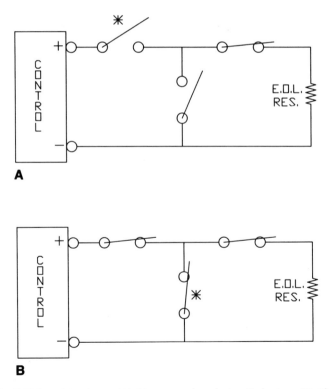

Figure 4–33   E-O-L resistor loop. (A) Alarm on closed circuit device. (B) Alarm on open circuit device.

with standby battery and their associated maintenance. Because of these advantages, this kind of loop is by far the most popular today.

There are a number of precautions to take when wiring the E-O-L loop if full loop supervision is to be maintained. The resistor belongs at the far end of the loop. If desired, the wire loop can be returned to the control and the E-O-L resistor physically located there. If this is done, the resistor must be connected to the far end of the loop. Do *not* connect the resistor at the feed end of the loop, that is, at the control terminals. If the resistor is connected in *series* with the loop at the feed end (Figure 4–34A), there will be no loop supervision against shorts. If a short were to occur, the protection beyond this point would be bypassed, with no indication of this loss (Figure 4–34B). Also, any closed circuit devices would not work, regardless of where they were in the loop or whether an accidental short had occurred. If the resistor is connected in *parallel* with the loop at the feed (control) end (Figure 4–34C), there will be no loop supervision against opens. If a break in either wire were to occur, there would be no alarm or other indication of the loss and, of course, any open circuit devices beyond

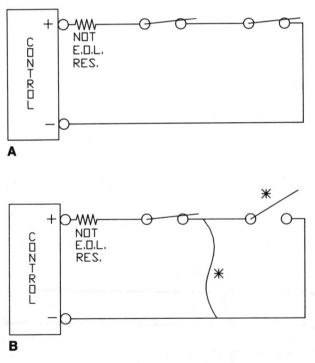

Figure 4–34 E-O-L resistor loop. (A) Wired incorrectly with resistor at control location, wired in series. (B) Short in wiring is not detected; part of protection is bypassed and an intrusion goes undetected. (C) Also wired incorrectly with resistor across loop at the control. (D) Break in the wire does not cause an alarm, yet it disables part of the protection beyond the break. *Continues on next page.*

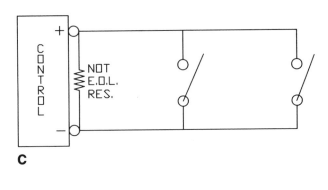

C

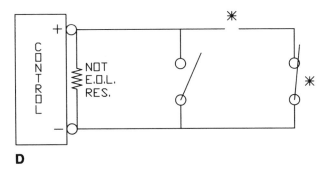

D

Figure 4–34 (*continued*)

the break would no longer work (Figure 4–34D). Closed circuit devices would not work at all regardless of where they were in the loop or whether an accidental break had occurred.

The value of the E-O-L resistor will vary depending on the manufacturer of the control or transmitter and is typically a few KΩ. The correct value must be used. These resistors are usually furnished with the equipment. Also, resistors do not have polarity, so they can be connected either way at the end of the loop. A ground or supervised ground can usually be used, usually in the negative side; however, check the manufacturer's specifications before doing so on multizone systems. On microprocessor-based controls, most manufacturers require the use of a good system ground. This will ground one side of each zone's loop. Don't forget that detection devices should not be wired into the grounded side of any loop.

The explanation of ground faults and intentional ground connections are the same as for the double closed loop and will not be repeated here. If the control uses a common ground for the entire system, it may not be possible to use a supervised ground.

Some E-O-L control units are able to distinguish between an open and a short on an E-O-L loop and to display these conditions as though they were separate zones. By proper choice of open loop and closed loop devices and choice of NO or NC contacts on motion detectors, it is possible to have two zones on one loop. Obviously, all devices have to be correctly wired. Unless accurate records are maintained, confusion will result during troubleshooting. Equally important, the subscriber must know what protection is on which loop. Many of today's controls permit the subscriber to manually bypass zones in trouble. Without this knowledge, he cannot make an intelligent decision as to how much coverage he is giving up in return for convenience of immediate arming, that is, for not having to wait for repairs to be made.

There are a number of potentials for misusing (miswiring) an E-O-L. Some installing companies wire each opening or device as a home run. That is, a separate wire is run from the control to each opening or device. The wires are appropriately connected together at the control to form a loop. The advantage is that, when troubleshooting, the trouble can be isolated to just one opening or device just by testing at the control location. This is true only if the wires are correctly tagged and records maintained. The problem is this: of the many wire runs, on which one do you install the resistor (Figure 4–35)? You can't put one on the end of each run, as you can use only one resistor. All those runs without the resistor have no supervision. Some installers, thinking to solve this dilemma, place the resistor at the control terminals (Figures 4–34A and B). As explained previously, this leaves all loop wiring without supervision. Either way, you have defeated one of the prime advantages of the E-O-L resistor loop: supervision. In essence, you have reverted to a single open loop or a single closed loop, depending on how you have wired it.

The solution is to wire each home run with quad (four-conductor) wire. Now the wires at the control location are connected to form a logical loop. Figure 4–36 shows how to do this correctly. Even this method is not 100 percent foolproof. It is possible that the positive wire going out and the positive wire returning could get shorted, as

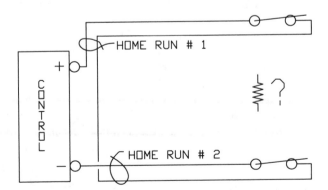

Figure 4–35   E-O-L resistor loop. Systems wired with multiple home runs leave unanswered the question, "Where do you place the E-O-L resistor?" Placing it at the end of any one run leaves all of the others unsupervised, as shown in Figure 4–34A and C.

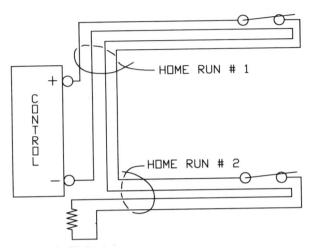

Figure 4–36 E-O-L resistor loop, with a better way to wire multiple home runs using quad (four-conductor) wire. Even this is not foolproof as, for example, a staple driven through the wire and shorting the two + wires but neither of the two − wires would bypass part of the protection without causing an alarm. The resistor can be placed at the last detection device, which can be wired with two-conductor wire.

with a staple driven through the wire. This would bypass any devices beyond the short, rendering them inoperative.

With the correct method, just described, the resistor physically goes at the control location but is at the logical end of the loop. You still maintain the convenience of troubleshooting from the control location but now you have correct supervision of all the wiring. With the advent of multiple zone systems, some with forty or more zones, it is often possible to assign each detection device or set of a few devices to a zone. This method allows the use of two-conductor wiring with the terminating resistor at the far end, and maintains the advantage of easy troubleshooting. Each device or set of devices not only has its own home run but its own zone and zone annunciator.

Any taps off the main wire will also cause loss of supervision. For example, a closed loop tap can be made (Figure 4–37A) but will not be supervised against shorts (Figure 4–37B). An open loop (OC) tap (Figure 4–37C) can also be made, but it will not be supervised against opens (Figure 4–37D). In neither instance will you have any indication of the loss of protection. Taps should be made as shown in Figures 4–37E and F using quad wire or two two-conductor runs. Again, these are not 100 percent guaranteed.

4.8 MAKE-AND-BREAK LOOP

The make-and-break loop is also known as the open-and-short loop or the break-and-cross loop (Figure 4–38) and is used only on direct wire service. It uses single-pole, double-throw (SPDT) switch contacts and relays in motion detectors and other sensors. These both open or break the hot side of the loop and short or cross it to the ground side (Figure 4–39).

This type of loop is the only one in which there is no alarm control unit, in the conventional sense, at the protected premises. The control function is located at the

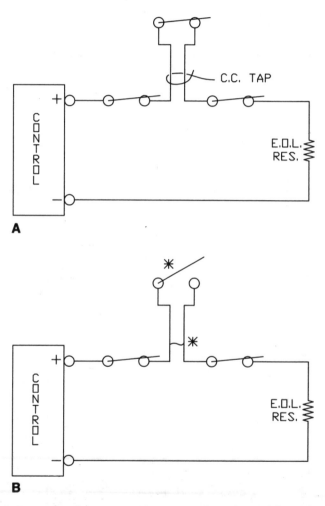

Figure 4–37 E-O-L resistor loop. (A) With a tap made in the middle of the run to pick up a closed circuit device. (B) A short in the tap wiring bypasses that part of the protection, yet does not cause an alarm. (C) A similar tap to pick up an open circuit device. (D) A break in the wire disables part of the protection, yet does not cause an alarm to indicate a problem. (E) A better way to make an open circuit tap, using quad wire. This is an improvement, but not foolproof. (F) A better way to make a closed circuit tap, again, not foolproof. *Continues on next page.*

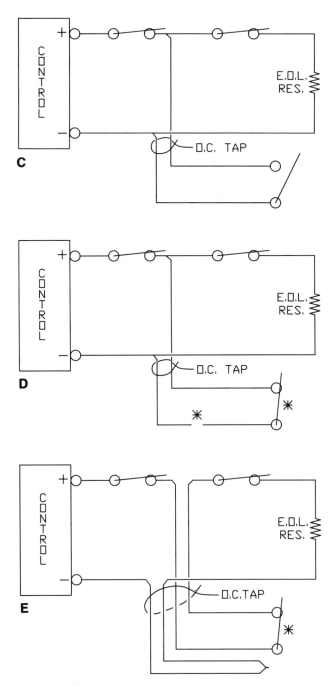

Figure 4–37   (continued)

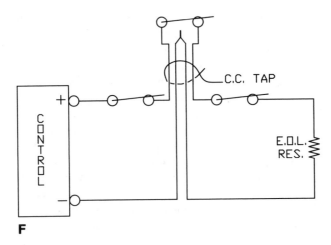

Figure 4–37   (continued)

alarm central station. The phone line can be thought of as being a part of the protective loop. Sometimes only one side of a phone line is used, along with an earth ground return. The second side of the phone line can then be used to secure another subscriber nearby. This type of loop is typically used for higher security applications. For very high security, a double system can be used in which the two are interlocked. Tampering with either circuit will alarm the other. Another high security feature is to add an AC signal at the subscriber's premises. If this signal is lost, as in an attempted compromise of the line, an alarm condition is registered at the central station.

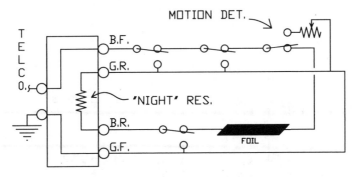

Figure 4–38   Break-and-cross loop, secure condition. Trace this circuit and convince yourself that it is, in fact, an E-O-L resistor loop with the resistor located at the control (day-night switch) location, using a four-wire circuit. The day circuit, day resistor, and day-night switch have been omitted for simplicity.

At the subscriber's premises there is a day-night switch. This is referred to as a direct wire control; its only function, however, is to switch the night loop into service when closing and out of service when opening for business. There is usually a day loop and a night loop. Both can be wired to the day-night switch box. Sometimes the day loop is connected between the telephone terminal (cable head) and ground, and the switch box. In the switch box are two adjustable resistors, one for day and one for night. Although the loops look quite different, they are actually E-O-L resistor loops. For more information, see section 8.5 on ring back. By the way, "ring back" is another name sometimes used for this loop because the central station operator can buzz or ring back the subscriber. In the following description only the night circuit is shown. The day circuit and the day-night switch have been omitted for clarity.

In the night position, the loop is completed through the night resistor, and a night current flows (Figure 4–38). This value will depend on the make and model of equipment being used at the central station. Because specific current levels are used to indicate different conditions, it will generally be helpful to do troubleshooting with a milliammeter instead of with a voltmeter.

If there is an intrusion through a door, the door contact will break the battery feed (BF) line and will short the line to ground (Figure 4–39). If you trace the circuit in Figure 4–39 you will see that the resistor has been bypassed. This produces a higher, cross current. An open in one loop wire (Figure 4–40A) or in the other wire (Figure 4–40B) will produce zero current because the entire circuit will be open. An open in the phone line or loss of a ground connection will also produce zero current. A short across the loop (Figure 4–41) will produce a cross current. A ground on the BF side or on the phone line will also indicate a cross. A ground fault on the ground side will not affect operation but detection devices must not be installed in the grounded side of the loop. Exceptions are double circuit lacing. This system uses a supervised ground. In this case, one earth ground connection is at the subscriber's premises. The other is at the alarm central station.

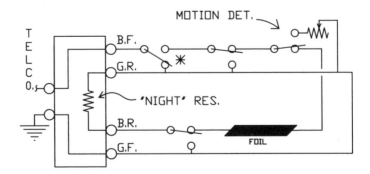

Figure 4–39   Break-and-cross loop, alarm condition. Note that the switch, or relay contact, not only breaks the battery side but also crosses the battery side to the ground side, hence, one of the names for this kind of loop.

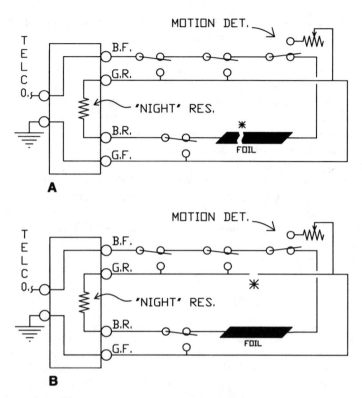

Figure 4–40   Break-and-cross loop. (A) Break in wire or foil in the battery side causes an alarm. (B) Break in the ground side also causes an alarm.

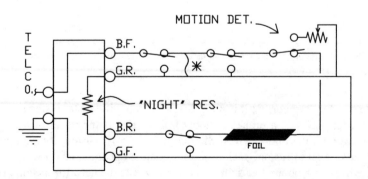

Figure 4–41   Break-and-cross loop. Short across battery side to ground side also causes an alarm.

An SPDT contact, as used in this type of loop, has three terminals and must be wired correctly. The lower contact in Figure 4–39 is actually wired incorrectly. Tracing the circuit, you will find the switch would open the loop (which would signal an alarm) but it would not cross the circuit as it should. The common, or armature, of the switch must always go to the BF terminal.

The motion detector (Figure 4–42 upper right) uses an SPDT (form C) relay contact. It produces a cross current but through an adjustable resistor of its own. This produces a current that is set to be slightly less than the usual cross current and identifies the alarm as originating from the motion detector system. This can be a big asset in troubleshooting.

In general, a day current or a night current establishes a secure condition. A switch at the central station is set to match the day-night switch position at the subscriber's premises. A deviation from one of these currents, either an increase or a decrease is sensed by relays or electronic circuits at the central station to initiate an alarm. The operator then reads the loop current on a meter. The current reading indicates the nature of the condition as follows:

Current	*Indication*
Zero	Open loop wiring, foil, or phone line
Night	Day and night loops secure
Day	Day loop secure
Cross	Door contact operated, loop wiring or phone line shorted
Motion*	Motion sensor alarm

*Several different current values can be used for different motion type sensors.

Note that for zero current it is not possible to know if the alarm signal is the result of an intrusion, such as a broken window foil, or if it is the result of a broken wire or a problem with the phone wires. Similarly, for a cross current it is not possible to know if there is an intrusion, such as a door contact operated, or if there is a short in the loop wiring or a phone line short to ground. Due to the need for metallic telephone lines, this kind of system is seldom used today.

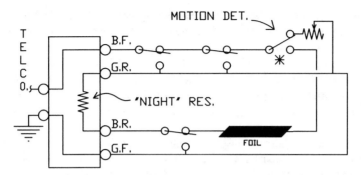

Figure 4–42 Break-and-cross loop. This motion detector is equipped with an adjustable resistor to set the current to a unique value so that the central office can tell which device the alarm is originating from, a big help in troubleshooting.

4.9 DISTRIBUTED RESISTANCE LOOP

A distributed resistance loop provides very high security. It somewhat resembles an E-O-L resistor loop, but instead of having one resistor at the end, it has smaller value resistors built into each contact. In foil circuits, a second set of foil takeoffs is used and is located on the window opposite the set of takeoffs used to connect the foil into the loop. A resistor is connected across this second set to complete the circuit (Figure 4–43). Thus the resistance is distributed among each intrusion-detecting device, be it a door contact, foil, or motion sensor.

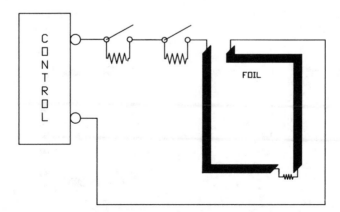

Figure 4–43 Distributed resistance loop, secure condition.

These systems require a very special control, designed specifically for this type of loop. They are sensitive to small changes in loop resistance and are much more sensitive than E-O-L controls. Once adjusted, a change of just a few ohms up or down will initiate an alarm. For this reason, the loop must be installed with meticulous care. All connections must be made very carefully. Sloppy workmanship, even that acceptable in normal alarm work, will soon result in false alarms. Although such sensitivity may seem a disadvantage, it is what enables this type of system to provide high security against tampering.

Several general points are in order. The distributed resistance loop system is not often used. Also, a standard E-O-L resistor system is not sensitive enough to do the same job. The loop should be installed with two or four zones, each having about equal resistances. This balances out temperature changes. There is a limit to how many detection devices can be placed in each zone. If too many are used, the system may fail to alarm or may be prone to false alarms.

In the secure loop, (Figure 4–43), the resistors inside the contacts complete the circuit. During an intrusion (Figure 4–44), the contact closes and shorts out the resistor. The loop current increases and triggers an alarm. A wire break anywhere in the loop drops the current to zero to trigger an alarm (Figure 4–45A). A short across any portion of the loop (Figure 4–45B) or any attempt to jumper out even one detection device (Figure 4–45C) will short out one or more resistors to trigger an alarm. A single ground (Figure 4–46A) will not affect system operation unless the system is grounded via the control unit. Two or more grounds (Figure 4–46B) will again short out one or more resistors to trigger an alarm. If you do have to work on a system like this, study and follow the manufacturer's instructions carefully.

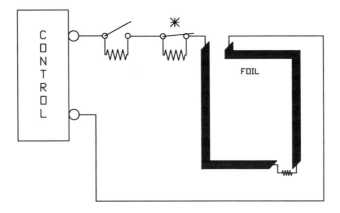

Figure 4–44 Distributed resistance loop, alarm condition.

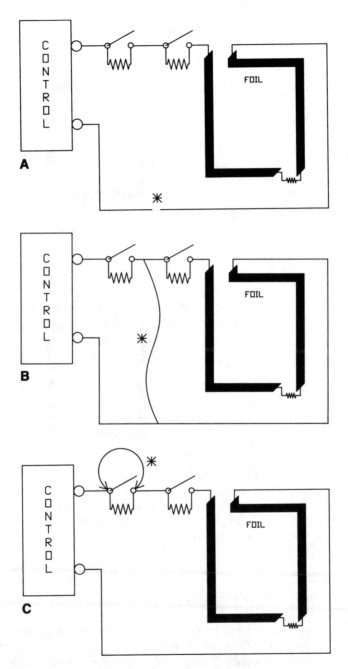

Figure 4–45 Distributed resistance loop. (A) Broken wire causes an alarm. (B) Short across the loop causes an alarm. (C) Short across a single device also causes an alarm, as the special control is sensitive enough to detect the small change in loop resistance.

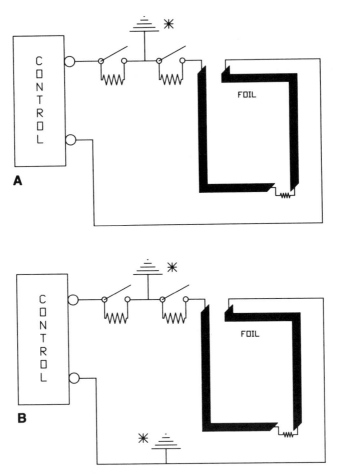

Figure 4–46 Distributed resistance loop. (A) Single ground fault causes an alarm if the system is intentionally grounded; otherwise it causes no alarm and no problem. (B) Multiple ground faults bypass part of the circuit, changing the total resistance, and causing an alarm, whether or not the system is intentionally grounded.

4.10 ON-PREMISES MULTIPLEXING

With the advances in electronics, we now have available various systems to transmit alarm signals via multiplex. These are often used to send signals from the subscriber's premises to alarm central stations. Multiplex systems are also available for use within large building complexes. These are typically used for lighting control, temperature control, and other functions and sometimes include security functions, too. In the first edition of this book, I wrote, ''Someday, with further advances in integrated circuitry and increased use of computer-based systems, we may see multiplexing used for local protective loops. These will offer the advantages of identifying the exact point of intrusion by individual contact or other devices and will provide a high level of security on the loop, all without the need to wire each device as a home run. The trend, for now, seems to be to use multiple zones.'' That ''someday'' has arrived. The microprocessor-based controls now have the ability to add zones by connecting zone expansion modules to the system keypad wiring, which is multiplexed.

4.11   ON-PREMISES WIRELESS

Short-range (on-premises) transmission of alarm signals has been around for many years. Its main advantage is that wiring is reduced. It can replace wiring to some or all detection devices. Still required is the wiring to obtain power for the control panel, bell or siren wiring, and phone line connection.

Wireless devices typically have a range of 150 to 300 feet (45 to 90 meters). They are available with built-in magnetic contacts or with pigtails (short wires) for connecting to a separate detection device, or, increasingly, they are being built into detection devices. If they are not built-in, detector manufacturers will often allow space inside their detector to permit easy mounting and wiring of a wireless module.

Wireless transmitters are battery powered, typically by a 9-volt transistor battery. Most transmitters now include battery supervision by detecting low battery voltage and by transmitting a signal, separate from an alarm condition. This signal can be connected to a separate zone to notify the user or alarm central station of the problem.

Receivers are typically mounted next to the control panel and connected to it by short wires. Multiple receivers can be used for multiple zones. Some receivers have built-in multizone capability.

Wireless units are also very convenient for panic or for medical emergency reporting. In such service these functions must be connected to separate zones so that the correct emergency response can be summoned.

Servicing includes the regular replacement of transmitter batteries and the periodical check of signal transmission and reception. False alarm problems can result if a neighbor gets a wireless system that uses the same frequencies and codes. If this happens, it will be necessary to change one system or the other. An inquiry with neighbors will be necessary to determine if they have recently had a wireless system installed or codes changed.

5   Seven Steps in Troubleshooting

Sometimes we can't see the forest for the trees; that is, we get so close to a particular troubleshooting problem that we lose the overall perspective of how the problem fits in the alarm system and, therefore, how best to approach the troubleshooting job. Before getting down to details, let's establish a perspective; let's look at the big picture. If we don't, we'll waste a lot of time and effort taking the long way around to get to the problem. The following seven steps will enable you to establish the proper perspective.

5.1   THE SEVEN BASIC STEPS

1. Know what kind of equipment or system you are working on.
2. Know how that equipment or system is supposed to operate.
3. Find out the symptoms that indicate the equipment or system is operating incorrectly.
4. Determine what kinds of failures could cause such symptoms to appear.
5. Divide and conquer: isolate the problem by dividing the equipment or system into segments or possible causes, check each, and eliminate those that are OK.
6. Repair the trouble.
7. Verify that the equipment or system now operates properly to insure that repairs were made correctly and that no additional problems remain.

5.2   APPLICATION OF THE SEVEN BASIC STEPS TO ALARM SYSTEMS

Know the kind of equipment you are dealing with. The make and model number can usually be found on the equipment and should also be available from your job records (assuming you or your company keeps such records). Your company may have standardized only one or a few models of, say, control instrument, so you have only one or a few kinds to worry about. Eventually, though, you will expand your line to newer and more flexible models. You will run into other models if your company buys out existing systems or if you change jobs to another alarm company. So know for sure the make and model number of the equipment you are working on.

Know how the equipment or system is supposed to work. Your past experience will usually provide you with this information, but you can be tricked. If you don't know for sure, study the manufacturer's instructions. If you don't have any instructions available, talk to a fellow worker or to your supervisor. If you can't find out from them, make a quick test of an identical unit that is known to work properly. If all else fails, call the manufacturer or distributor of the equipment. Before calling, make a list of all questions you want to ask and include the model number. It's best to have your supervisor make the call or get the supervisor's permission to make the call. Follow your company's established procedure in this matter.

Let's take an example. Usually, you expect a bell to ring when a local system is tripped. Suppose you tripped a system you were testing and the bell did not ring. You could waste a lot of time trying to find a nonexistent problem if you did not know the system was equipped with an entry delay that delays the ringing of the bell. It could be the prealarm was not working.

Find the Symptoms. The symptoms will generally be obtained from the subscriber or his representative. Your source for this information may be from your central station personnel or service dispatcher; thus, you are getting it second or third hand. If your supervisor does not object to your talking directly with the subscriber, and supervisors generally don't, you can often get additional, helpful information from the subscriber, particularly by asking the right questions. First, be sure you are talking to the person who knows what the trouble is. Don't be afraid to ask if he or she can tell you for sure what the problem is or if you should talk to someone else. You might also ask who first discovered the problem, as that person might be better able to tell you what was wrong and to give you helpful clues. A little judgment must be used, as you can't expect to spend several hours trying to find the original discoverer of the problem. When you do ask, don't take the person's first statement as the total truth. Subscribers seldom understand the detailed operation of alarm systems, so ask if there were other symptoms or possible causes of the trouble or troubles reported. For instance, a comment from the subscriber that the red light (walk test light) usually comes on when the new air compressor starts up could save a lot of time troubleshooting an ultrasonic system when the original complaint was only about false alarms. Asking the right questions will usually get the answers you need.

Make a list of possible causes. The necessity for this step may not be apparent at first. If after checking a defective system you don't find the trouble, it's a safe bet you didn't think of all the possible causes and, therefore, have not looked far enough. Usually you have at least a mental list of possible causes, based on experience. When you run into a "can't find" situation, make a written list of all possibilities and try again. A few minutes spent thinking and writing a list can often save a lot of time spent blindly chasing down the problem when the real trouble is somewhere else.

Let's try an experiment. Look at Figure 5–1 of a double closed loop (E-O-L battery) alarm system. Assume the subscriber's complaint is "The system will not arm." Make a list of all the possible causes you can think of. We will assume that

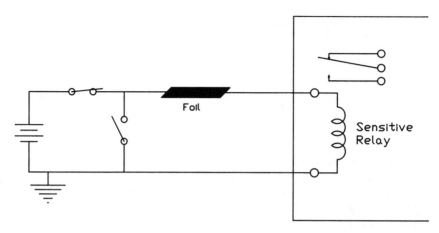

Figure 5–1 Typical alarm protective loop. How many possible faults can you identify?

this is an existing system that was formerly working. Also note that this is a continuous fault and not a swinger (intermittent) problem. Now compare your list to Table 5–1.

As you can see, there are probably more possibilities than appear on your list. You may have come up with possibilities that I have overlooked. This exercise will give you an idea of the procedure. Once the list is made, you can check off possibilities as you test for each one. Some manufacturers thoughtfully provide a list of typical symptoms, possible causes, and the proper corrective action for each.

Divide and Conquer. Some servicepeople begin troubleshooting at one end of a system and go all the way through, hunting for a problem. The wise serviceperson will isolate the problem to a certain area, starting first at the spot that experience has taught is the most likely cause. For example, a likely trouble source might be run-down batteries. A quick look at the date installed, if recorded on or near these batteries, would provide the first clue. If a quick meter check showed healthy batteries, the next step might be to make a quick walk check, looking for open doors or windows or obvious damage to foil, contacts, or wiring. If there was nothing obvious, the next step would be to check if the trouble was in the control instrument or in the protective loop. If the loop was at fault, the serviceperson would only then take time to check the loop carefully from one end to the other. If the loop was long, it would be best to check it somewhere about the middle to isolate the problem to one half or the other. There is no use in checking the good half, as might happen when starting at one end. The bad half can again be divided in half, and the process can be repeated as often as necessary. This would soon result in a lot of walking back and forth each time the bad segment was isolated. From a practical standpoint, it is best to isolate the problem to a reasonable size segment and work from one end of the bad segment to the other until the fault is finally located. Large systems are sometimes divided into zones with separate indicator lights to indicate the faulty zone. This saves the troubleshooter the time it would take to check the good zones.

Table 5–1   List of possible causes

1. Low or dead battery.	(O, S, G, ?)
2. Corroded battery terminal	(O, R)
3. Broken or cut wire	(O)
4. Grounded wire	(G)
5. Door or window open	(O)
6. Foil broken	(O)
7. Object on mat switch	(S)
8. Short in mat switch line	(S)
9. Corroded, burned, or broken door or window switch.	(O)
10. High resistance or open wire splice	(O, R)
11. High resistance or open screw terminal on switch or control instrument	(O, R)
12. Bad solder joint inside control instrument	(O, R)
13. Open sensitive relay coil	(O)
14. Sensitive relay stuck	(O)
11. Mat switch permanently damaged (shorted)	(S)
16. Corrosion of mat switch (unsealed type) causing leakage of current	(S, R)
17. Magnet broken off door or window	(O)
18. Iron particles in armature gap of sensitive relay (relay not physically jammed) .	(O)
19. Door replaced, magnet not transferred to new door (particularly true with recessed contacts)	(O)
20. Wires in damp or wet location causing leakage currents.	(S, G, R)
21. Foreign potential (voltage) on alarm system	(O, S, G, R, ?)
22. Mounting bracket for magnet or contact bent out of position	(O)

KEY: O = Open, S = Short, G = Ground, R = High (Low) Resistance, ? = Not sure

Repair the Trouble. Once the problem has been located, the repair needed is generally obvious. Replace a dead battery or broken contact; patch broken foil; resplice broken, cut, or corroded wire; unstick or replace a stuck relay; insulate shorts or grounds, etc.

Check for Correct Operation. Don't simply assume the system works properly after a repair has been made. There may be several problems, or you may have repaired something that was on its way to causing trouble but wasn't the cause of the present problem. Make as many repairs as necessary to get the system to work as it should. A little preventive maintenance is in order at this time, too. Replacing batteries now that will soon be due for replacement will save a service call in the near future. Loose wires can be refastened; foil that is nearly broken can be patched; contacts that have come loose or mounting brackets that have been bent out of position can be secured or repositioned.

6 Specific Troubleshooting Procedures

If you have not had previous experience troubleshooting, you may find you're not quite ready to begin. All of the information presented up to this point has been either general background or has presented a particular type of problem first and the effect on the circuit second. In real life, you won't know in advance what kind of problem you will have. You will first have to find out and proceed from there. Finding out is part of troubleshooting.

Let's try following through on some typical problems to learn what the detailed procedure is. We'll assume a few things for the sake of simplicity. Trying to consider all possibilities at once, trying to learn everything at one time, only ends up causing confusion. So, for the sake of learning one step at a time, let's assume we have a system with a permanent trouble. Later we will deal with intermittent type troubles. Let's also assume that you will be using a good V-O-M or DMM meter. Later we can try other kinds of test instruments. Finally, assume that you will be using the correct voltage range on the meter. Later we can talk about using a milliamp range or an ohmmeter range. We can assume that, being a good troubleshooter, you eyeballed the system when you arrived and spotted no obvious troubles and that you have followed steps one through four and are now at step five: divide and conquer.

6.1 THE PROTECTIVE LOOP OR THE CONTROL

The first act of dividing and conquering is usually to determine if the problem is in the protective loop or elsewhere. Just because most problems are in the protective loop does not mean that you should ignore all else and possibly waste hours testing the loop, especially when a very quick test will tell you if the problem is in the loop or not. Just disconnect the protective loop wires, then connect a jumper across the protective loop terminals of the control or transmitter to set up a secure condition. This can be done with short pieces of wire, but test jumpers with clips are more convenient. Then see if the alarm system will set up properly and finally, verify operation by lifting a jumper to break a closed loop to see that the system trips. You should also be able to trip the system by shorting the open loop terminals if the system has an open loop function. If the system fails to work with the correct jumpers in place, or if it fails to trip when they are not, you now know the control or transmitter is defective. Review Section 3.1, "Equipment Troubles," for possible ways to fix it. If these don't work, replace it. If you find instead that the control or transmitter does work, you now know for sure that the problem is in the protective loop, so you can start troubleshooting it.

Before going into the protective loop, let's look at just how you use jumpers to simulate a secure loop. This depends on what kind of protective loop your system uses. For instance, a single closed loop system wants to "see" a single closed loop with no grounds. First remove both loop wires to remove any possible grounds. Then add a jumper between the two terminals to provide a closed loop, which is what this kind of control or transmitter wants to "see" in the secure condition. Lifting that jumper should trip the system. See Figure 6–1.

Refer to Table 6–1 for the procedures for different types of protective loops. Find the type of protective loop on which you are working in the left column and then follow instructions as you move right one column at a time. The first step is to remove the loop wires as indicated. Next, set up a secure condition with jumpers. Then arm the system and trip it by removing a jumper or shorting the loop. Then silence the system, rearm it, and trip it again as indicated in the right hand column. If you are working on an E-O-L loop, you will have to substitute the correct value of resistor instead of using a jumper.

If the control works correctly, you now know for sure the problem is in the loop. The next step is to determine the nature of the fault. Is it an open, a short, a ground, or a foreign voltage? A foreign voltage can be the most dangerous and the most damaging to equipment and can give the most unusual symptoms. Specific procedures for this rare problem are covered in Section 6.6.

Before we can do any testing with a voltmeter (or a milliammeter, for that matter) we must have a source of voltage. Some controls or transmitters have a voltage present on the loop terminals at all times, even when the unit is off; others do not. You need a voltage for the meter to work, so check first as illustrated in Figure 6–2. Set the voltmeter to the 6- or 12-volt or next higher range, and check the terminals as indicated in Table 6–2 for the type of loop being used.

Some controls or transmitters have loop voltage present at all times, assuming it is properly powered up and is not malfunctioning. On other units, turning the system off also removes power from the loop. Thus, you have no voltage to make your test meter work. If this is the case, you have two choices: You can test the loop with an ohmmeter or use a continuity tester, as both of these have their own built-in battery, or you can turn the system on (with any bells or outputs disconnected so as not to have false alarms while you are testing) and proceed with your voltmeter.

Once you become familiar with the types of equipment you have to work on, you will soon remember if voltage is available or not with the system turned off. Then you won't have to repeat this test every time. This part of the procedure may sound like a minor point, but I once wasted over an hour on a very small loop only to find out later that there was no voltage available with the system turned off.

Having established that we do have a source of voltage to make the meter work

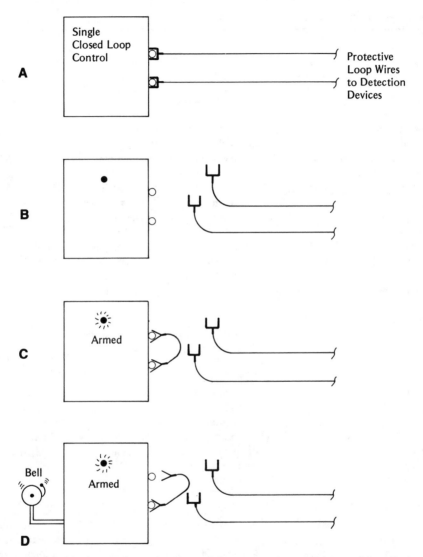

Figure 6–1   Typical steps in testing a control or transmitter. (A) Normal installation of single closed loop system. (B) First, remove wires to clear any possible loop problems. (C) Then add test jumper and set (arm) the system. (D) Finally, lift jumper (with system set). If alarm occurs, control is functioning and problem is in the loop. If it fails to trip, the problem is in the control, power supply or battery, or output device (bell or transmitter).

Table 6–1 Testing the control or transmitter

With This Type of Protective Loop	Disconnect These Loop Wires	Add These Jumper(s)	Trip System By	Also Trip System By
Open loop	Both	None	Shorting loop	–
Single closed loop	Both	Across the two terminals	Lifting jumper	–
Open and closed loop	All 3 (or 4)	NC to common	Lifting jumper	Shorting NO to common
Double closed loop, no ground	+ in and + out	+ in to + out; and – in to – out	Lift one jumper; then replace and lift other jumper	Shorting + to –
Double closed loop with ground or supervised ground	+ in and + out	+ in to + out; and – in to – out	Lift one jumper; then replace and lift other jumper	Short + to earth ground
End-of-line battery with or without ground	+ only	Use substitute battery of correct voltage; connect + battery to + control; and – battery to – control	Lift one battery wire	
End-of-line resistor loop, ungrounded	Both	Use substitute resistor of correct value; connect to loop terminals of control	Lift one end of resistor	Short across resistor
End-of-line resistor, grounded	Ungrounded side only	Use substitute resistor of correct value; connect to loop terminals of control	Lift one end of resistor	Short from ungrounded terminal to earth ground
Make and break loop	Battery feed, ground feed, battery return	Battery feed to battery return, ground feed to ground return	Lift one jumper	Short from battery to ground

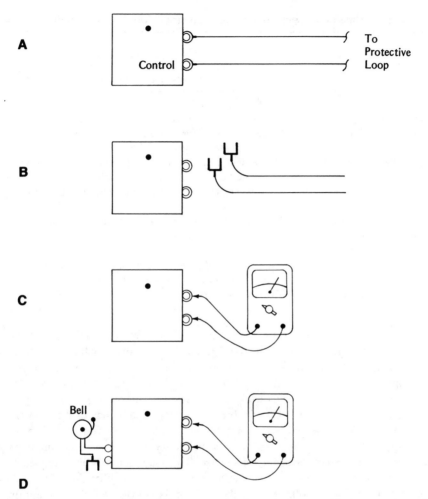

Figure 6–2 Checking control for presence of voltage before troubleshooting loop with meter. (A) Typical installation. (For E-O-L battery loop, check at E-O-L battery or power supply.) (B) Disconnect loop. (C) If voltage is present, proceed with loop testing. If voltage is not present, go to next step. (D) Temporarily disconnect bell or other output device(s) and turn system on. If voltage is now present at loop terminals, leave system on and proceed with loop testing. If voltage is still not present at loop terminals, control is defective or there is no power (battery or line supply).

Table 6–2 Testing for presence of voltage at control before troubleshooting the loop

If You Have This Kind of Loop	Check for Presence of Voltage Across These Two Terminals with Loop Wires Disconnected
Open loop	The two loop terminals
Single closed loop	The two loop terminals
Open and closed loop	NC and Common (or NC and NC)
	NO and Common (or NO and NO)
Double closed loop (with or without ground)	The + and − feed terminals (If you don't know which pair are the feed terminals, test both pairs of + and − terminals. The pair that has the voltage is the feed, or out, pair.)
End-of-line battery loop	The end-of-line battery or power supply terminals
End-of-line resistor loop (with or without ground)	The two loop terminals
Break-and-cross loop	Battery feed and ground return (or earth ground) (may require 150-volt meter range or higher)
Distributed resistance loop	The two loop terminals

for testing, we will establish a convention as follows: we will call this voltage the "source." The opposite end will be the "far end." Knowing which end is which will be important, as it will tell us during testing in which direction the problem lies. On single open loops, single closed loops, and end-of-line resistor loops, the source will always be the control. On loops using an end-of-line battery (or power supply), this will be the supply end. On other, double closed loops, both ends of the loop will go to the control. Only one end will supply the voltage which, of course, will be called the supply end. In this case it will also be necessary to know how the premises are wired, that is, clockwise or counterclockwise. This may require a bit of physical wire tracing. It can also be done by testing at the first opening on either side of the control. If neither side shows a voltage, then the problem is between the control and one of these two openings.

6.2. OPEN, SHORT, OR GROUND ON THE LOOP

When you have voltage available for testing, you are ready to determine if the problem is an open, short, or ground. The type of fault may be obvious or not, depending on the type of loop the system uses. For instance, if a single closed loop system is in the alarm condition, the problem must be an open because this is the only thing in the loop that will cause an alarm condition. On the other hand, with a double closed loop system, the problem could be an open in one wire, an open in the second wire, a short between the two wires, or a ground on the hot wire (if the loop has one side intentionally grounded). By knowing which of these conditions applies, you can more quickly locate and repair the problem. See Figure 6–3. Obviously, the procedure used to identify

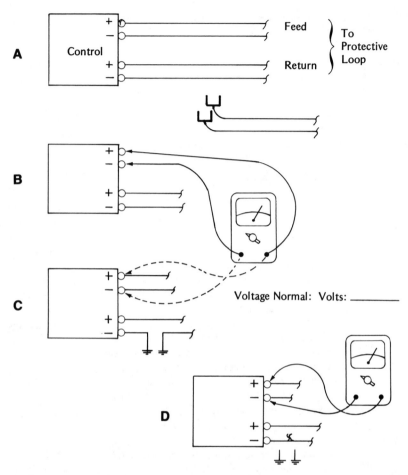

Figure 6–3 Identifying type of problem (open, short, or ground). (A) Typical installation of double closed loop. (B) Disconnect feed (supply) wires and measure the voltage. If the voltage is zero or nearly so, either the battery is dead, there is no power, or the power supply is defective. (C) Reconnect loop wires. If voltage remains the same or drops less than 1 volt from the previous, normal reading, the problem is an open. If the voltage drops to 0 or to less than one-half of normal, and one side is intentionally grounded, the problem is a short or a ground on the hot side of the loop. (Or the battery is very weak.) (D) Disconnect ground wire or disconnect both ground wires and twist together to complete the loop without a ground. If the voltage is less than one-half of normal, the problem is a short. If the voltage returns to normal, the problem is an accidental ground on the hot side (usually the + side) of the loop.

Table 6–3 Determining if problem is an open, short, or ground

Type of Protective Loop	Test For	Problem Is
Open or closed loop	Is voltage present at loop terminals with loop connected?	
	• Yes	Open
	• No	Short
Double closed loop (see Figure 6–3)	What is the voltage at the E-O-L battery or at the loop feed or supply terminals with the loop wires disconnected?	
	• Voltage is zero or well below normal	Battery is dead (or nearly so), or power supply is disconnected or defective
	• Voltage remains the same when wires are reconnected	Open
	• Voltage drops more than 1 volt when wires are reconnected	Short (or ground on hot side of a grounded system)
	If this system has an intentional ground connection, disconnect this wire (or disconnect both wires and temporarily connect the two ends together if a supervised ground is used)	
	• Voltage remains low	Short
	• Voltage returns to normal	Ground
End-of-line resistor loop	What is voltage at terminals with loop disconnected?	
	• Voltage drops to about 50% when wires are reconnected	Loop OK
	(Note: the percent drop will depend on the manufacturer's design. Determine the normal drop using a known control. Allow 20% tolerance either way or use manufacturers published limits.)	
	• Voltage remains the same or nearly so when wires are reconnected	Open
	• Voltage drops to zero or nearly so when wires are reconnected	Short (or ground)
	If system has one side of loop intentionally grounded, either via the loop itself or via a common system ground, temporarily disconnect this wire. (Note: omit this step if it causes other system problems or if not recommended by the manufacturer.)	
	• Voltage remains at zero or nearly so . . .	Short
	• Voltage returns to about 50%	Ground

Table 6–3   (continued)

Type of Protective Loop	Test For	Problem Is
Make-and-break loop[a]	What is voltage between battery feed and ground return when battery feed wire is disconnected?	
	• Voltage is zero or much lower than normal . (Note: The phone line is actually a part of the protective loop, as is the earth ground return.)	Phone line trouble or bad earth ground
	• Voltage normal	Proceed with testing
	When the battery feed loop wire is reconnected, the voltage	
	• Remains high (near normal)	Open
	• Drops to zero or nearly so	Short or ground
	Disconnect ground return wire and	
	• Voltage goes high (near normal).	Short
	• Voltage remains at zero or nearly so . . .	Ground
Distributed resistance loop	Testing must be done with a very accurate ohmmeter or with a Wheatstone bridge. Loop resistance must match exactly the resistance when installed within 1 or 2%	
	• Resistance now infinite or much higher than normal; resistance now higher; resistance now lower	Open, short, or ground depending on manufacturer's design. Follow manufacturer's instructions. (Note: This kind of loop is seldom used and is limited to high-security applications.)

[a]Make-and-break loops typically use a high voltage, such as 130 volts, so beware of shock hazard.
Some loops may use a + ground, so watch meter polarity.
Some equipment has a built-in meter jack on the day-night control box, making it more convenient to troubleshoot using a milliammeter with a matching plug.
Both day (24-hour) and night loops must be tested. Some systems feed the day loop directly from the phone line, before the day-night control box.

the type of fault will vary depending on the kind of protective loop used. Table 6–3 has been prepared as a guide for quick reference.

6.3 PROCEEDING ALONG THE LOOP

Now that it is known that the trouble is in the loop and what kind of trouble it is, you can proceed to locate and repair it. Sometimes it is convenient to proceed from one end of the loop to the other until the problem is found, providing the system is small.

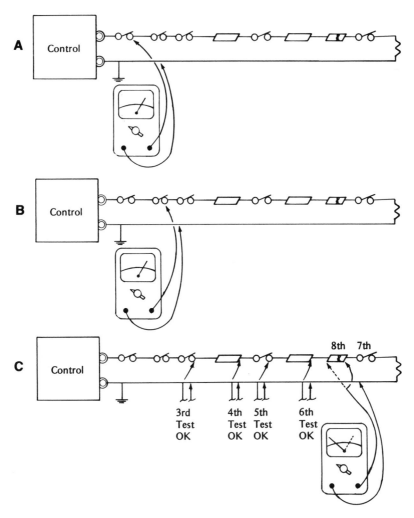

Figure 6–4 Progressive testing along the loop from one end to the other is OK but is time-consuming on long loops. (A) The first test is at the first contact (switch). The presence of voltage indicates the loop is good from the control to this point. (B) The second test is at the next contact, with the same results. (C) The seventh test is at the last contact. Lack of voltage indicates you have gone past the problem. The eighth test is at the left side of the foil and shows voltage, but the right side shows no voltage. Therefore the foil is open. Move meter probe along foil to find break if not visible.

See Figure 6–4. If, however, the system is large, it would take a long time to get to the far end of the line if that's where the trouble happened to be. To save time, go to about the middle of the loop, some place that is relatively easy to get to, and make a test. The results of the test will tell you whether the trouble is toward the control or transmitter, or towards the far end. Divide the defective half into half again and test until you get it narrowed down to a small section that can be checked end to end. See Figure 6–5.

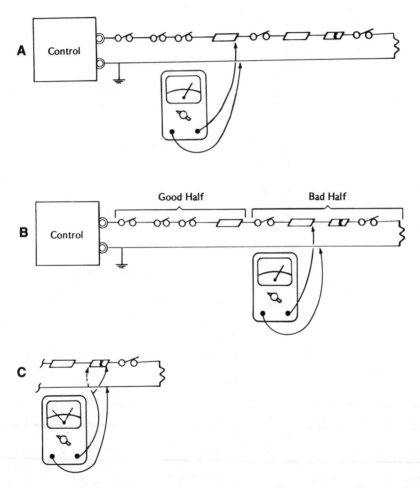

Figure 6–5   Testing by halves. This method saves time on large systems, compared to the linear method in Figure 6–4. (A) Make the first test at approximately the middle of the loop. The presence of voltage indicates the half between the control and this point is OK. (B) Make the second test at about the middle of the bad (right) half. Again, voltage indicates the left one-quarter is OK. (C) Make the third test in the middle of the remaining bad section. Again, you will find the problem in the foil, but with many fewer tests.

Let's take an example of a single closed loop system and proceed along the loop. (See Figure 6–6.) One method is to place the voltmeter leads across the terminals of each switch, foil, or other detection device, one at a time (Figure 6–6A). An open is found when the meter reads system voltage (Figure 6–6B). There are several reasons not to use this procedure:

1. There is no way to divide the system in half.
2. It will not work if there is more than one open (Figure 6–6C).
3. It will not detect broken wires (Figure 6–6D).
4. It won't work on foil if the takeoff terminals are too far apart to reach.
5. It is inconsistent with the technique used on other kinds of loops.

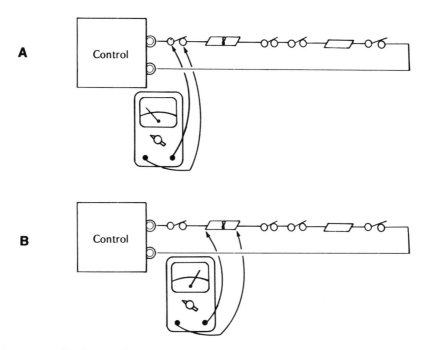

Figure 6–6 The danger of testing across switches, compared to testing across the wires. (A) Typical single closed loop. Meter reads 0 volts, so this contact (switch) is OK. (B) Meter reads normal voltage across foil, so foil is open. So far, so good. (C) In this case the meter reads 0 volts across the foil, failing to detect the break, because there is a second open in the circuit. This could very easily happen due to an open door or window or motion detector in alarm. (D) In this instance the meter will also read 0 across each contact or detection device, indicating each is OK, but it will fail to locate a broken wire. (E) Preferred test method is to place one test probe on one wire of the loop (insulation-piercing test probes or clips are great for this) while testing on each side of each detection device with the other probe. Additional opens don't affect this test method. Repair first problem found and continue testing. (F) Continued testing reveals open contact. Repair it and proceed to find an open wire, too.

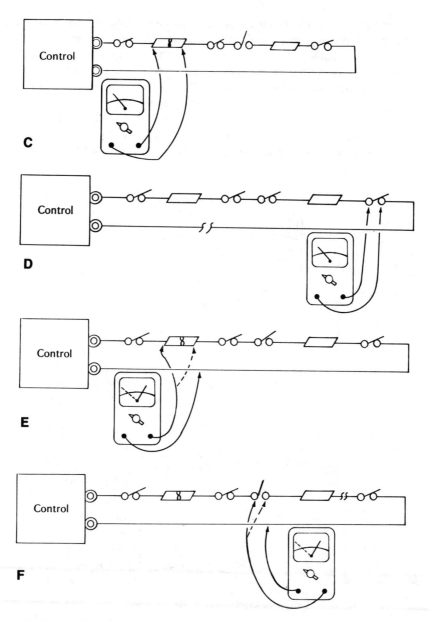

Figure 6–6   (continued)

A much better technique, and one that will work on any kind of loop, is to measure across the two wires as shown in Figures 6–6E and F. Usually alarm systems are wired with two-conductor parallel or twisted wire. The wire may or may not have an outer jacket. That doesn't matter. It may even have other conductors in a cable. That doesn't matter either, so long as you know which color wires you are interested in and so long as some careless installer did not cross colors at a splice or junction point. Once in a great while you may find a loop wired with one, single conductor run all around the premises. You now have several choices: You can take your chances with the meter leads across each switch, foil, etc., as shown in Figure 6–7A. You can

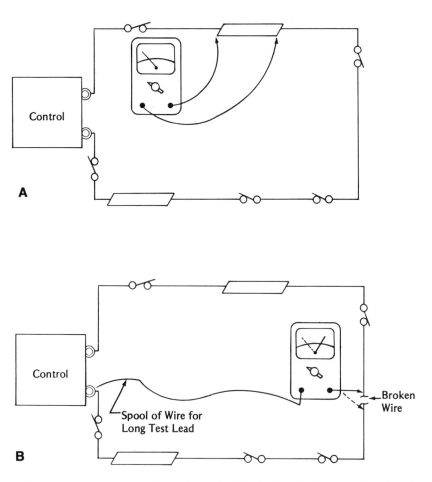

Figure 6–7   Testing a one-conductor loop. (A) Single closed loop wired with only one conductor. Try testing across each contact or detection device. (B) If you cannot locate the problem, try using a spool of wire that is long enough to reach from the control to each point in the loop as a test lead.

rewire the system. You can get a spool of wire and make a temporary test lead long enough to reach from the control to any point in the loop, as shown in Figure 6–7B. The test cable reel, described earlier, will serve this purpose nicely.

Even assuming a two-conductor loop, there are several possible physical arrangements of which you must be aware. It depends on who installed the system. Let's look at each. Generally, you will find the wires have been run from the control, past each protected opening, with the loop physically ending at the last opening where the wires are connected to the two terminals, as shown in Figure 6–8A. This presents no problem. Another method is where the loop pair has been continued past the last opening and around to the control. Here the two ends are simply connected together inside the box (but not to any terminals), as shown in Figure 6–8B. The extra wire back to the control box serves no useful purpose, but neither does it cause any problems in testing.

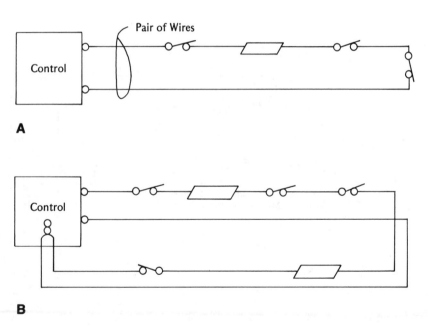

Figure 6–8 Different ways a single closed loop can be installed. (A) The last contact or detection device is at the physical end of the loop (right). (B) The far end of the loop is physically returned to the control, where the two conductors are connected together, but not connected to anything else. (C) One conductor of a twisted or parallel pair is used; the second conductor is not used at all. Troubleshooting is the same as in Figure 6–7, with the following exception. (D) Connect both ends of the unused wire to one terminal (not both terminals) to provide a built-in test wire. If an ohmmeter shows continuity, you will have no problem using this wire for loop testing. Note distinction of supply end and far end on the diagram for test purposes. *Continues on next page.*

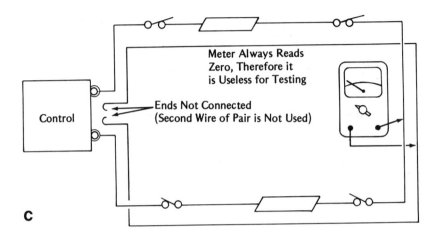

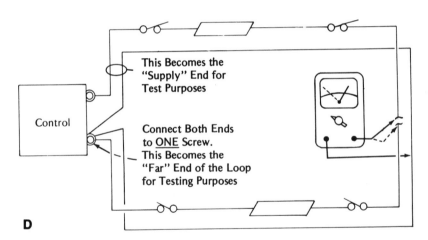

Figure 6–8 (continued)

Once in a while you may find a two-conductor loop running all the way around the premises and back to the control, in which only one conductor is used. That is, one wire on each end is connected to the control. Both ends of the other conductor are disconnected. The second conductor is dead. Trying to use it for testing won't work. (See Figure 6–8C.) To make it work, simply connect both ends of this extra conductor to one of the two loop terminals as shown in Figure 6–8D. Now testing can be done just as in the other two arrangements already mentioned. Just remember the end of the loop with the two conductors shorted (connected to the same terminal) represents the far end of the loop. This is important so that you know in which direction to proceed as you test.

If it seems strange that someone would have wired the loop in this manner (that is, with one wire dead), remember it could have been installed by somebody who is more accustomed to putting in double closed loop systems. Or the wiring may have been left over from a previous double closed loop type of system. At any rate, be glad that extra conductor is there because, with the extra connection, it sure simplifies testing. Also note that if the extra wire has two or more opens in it, then testing will not be successful. Test it for continuity first. If you don't have continuity, then use the long-wire method shown in Figure 6–7B.

Now that we have all the if's, and's, and but's out of the way, let's proceed with our example of troubleshooting a simple closed loop. Let's say we are looking for an open and that we do have voltage available to the loop from the control. Go to the middle of the loop and connect the meter leads across the two wires. You can do this most easily at a door contact or window foil. At least one wire is usually bare (that is, the screw terminal). You will either have to strip the other conductor or, better yet, get a test probe or test clip with insulation-piercing needles. These are available at better electronics parts distributors, or you can make your own. With the test leads connected, the meter will indicate either system voltage or 0 volts. If it indicates a voltage, then you know the loop from the control to this test point is complete and that the open is toward the far end of the loop. If your meter indicates 0 volts, the open is back towards the control. Go to the middle of the bad half and test again to determine which is now the bad quarter. By repeated testing you will eventually locate the problem. One hint: when testing at a door or window, keep one probe through the insulation while you try the other probe at each terminal of the switch, foil, etc. You may find you have a bad door contact (assuming you aren't holding the door open) or that you have open foil. By doing this you can avoid going down the line only to later find yourself back where you have already been. It saves time. (See Figure 6–10.)

Suppose now that we have to find a short instead of an open. Again, the meter leads are placed across the two wires in about the middle of the loop. Now we have a short, and the voltage across a short is zero. So it will be necessary to open one wire. You can cut a wire, but it is much easier just to open a switch by opening a door or lifting one wire at a foil takeoff block. Note that the meter has to be on the control side of the opening to see a possible voltage. If the wires are twisted together so that it is impossible to tell, simply check both sides. If opening the loop causes the meter to read approximately the system voltage, then opening the loop has removed the short. Therefore, the short is toward the far end of the loop. If, on the other hand, opening the loop leaves the meter reading 0 (or if it reads 0 on both sides of the opening, and you can't tell which side is which), then the short must be back toward the control. Again, repeated testing will locate the trouble. You will eventually, however, reach a point where you know the short is between two openings (switches, foil, etc.), and you will have run out of convenient ways to open the loop for testing. At this point, you can make a close visual inspection of this section of wire in the

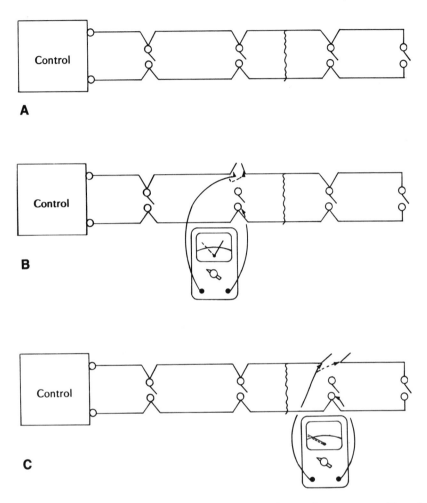

Figure 6–9   Testing an open loop for shorts. (A) Typical open loop system with a short. (B) Lift wires from one side of a switch, separate, and test the control (supply) side for presence of normal loop voltage. If it is uncertain which of the two wires is the supply side, test both. Since one side does read system voltage, reconnect the wires and proceed toward the far end (right). (C) Repeat the process. This time there is no system voltage on either side of the switch. Therefore the short is towards the control (left). Repair the wire if you can visually see the problem, or else replace the shorted wire. If the wire is a long one, you can cut one conductor near the middle and test again to narrow down the trouble. Splice and insulate the cut wire when done.

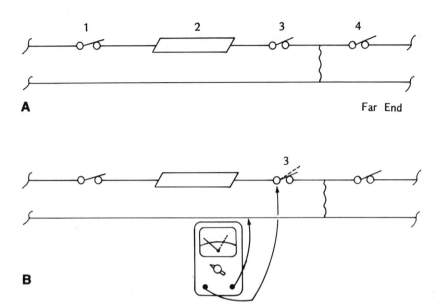

Figure 6–10 (A) Any typical loop using closed circuit devices, with an unwanted short in the wiring. (B) With the switch closed, the meter reads 0 volts, or nearly so. Therefore the short is still in the circuit. Now open the switch (dashed line) and test on the supply (control) side. Meter now reads system voltage, indicating that the short has been removed and that it lies towards the far (right) end. If it is unclear which wire is the supply side, test on both switch terminals with the switch open. Normal voltage on either terminal indicates trouble is towards the far end. (C) Testing at this point shows no voltage on either side of the switch when it is open. Therefore the problem lies towards the supply end. Continue testing at convenient points such as a contact (switch), which can be opened, at foil, where one wire can be lifted, or at a motion detector, which can be put into alarm condition or have one wire lifted. If the problem is not right at a detection device, you will eventually narrow the trouble to a wire run. Repair the problem if you can spot it visually. If necessary, replace the wire run. (D) If the wire run is long, cut one conductor in about the middle and test again. Here the meter reads system voltage on one side of the cut, indicating that the short is towards the far end. Splice and insulate the wires when finished. If necessary, the wire can be cut repeatedly in about the middle of each bad section to further narrow down the problem. (E) A time-saving alternative is shown. Measure the resistance to the short from the nearest contact or detection device on either side of the short. In this example we get 6.2 ohms and 3.1 ohms. The sum is 9.3 ohms. Using a simple ratio, the short is $3.1/9.3 = 0.33$, or 33% of the distance from switch four. This is an approximation, as the short may not be a dead one (i.e., it may be something higher than 0 ohms), and poor-quality splices in the wire could add several ohms to one reading or the other. This method, however, will usually get you very close to the short. *Continues on next page.*

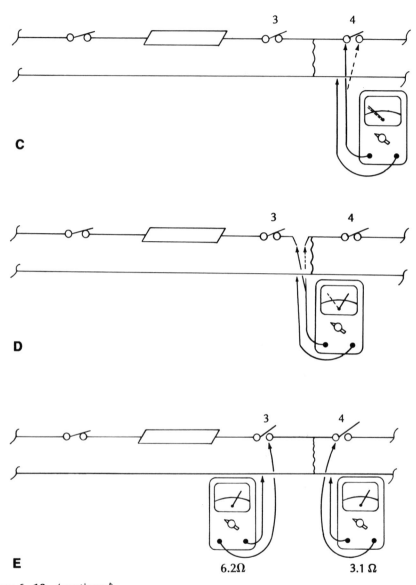

Figure 6–10   (continued)

hopes of finding the short and repairing it. You can replace that section of wire or, if the wire run is too long, you can go to the middle, cut one wire and test there, then splice the cut wire. By repeatedly narrowing down, you will eventually find that short. One hint: when testing double closed loop systems for grounds, test at both ends of foil, as you could easily have a ground at a crossover, that is, where the foil crosses over a metal window divider or frame. On wire shorts, look for staples driven through the wire's insulation.

Rather than provide a written description of the actual procedures for each kind of problem on each kind of protective loop, the information has been condensed into Table 6–4 for convenient reference. The procedure is the same as outlined for the single closed loop example. The meter readings, too, always indicate the direction of the trouble, and it is always the same, regardless of the kind of loop or fault. A reading of 0 volts means trouble is toward the supply end. A reading of supply volts or nearly so means the trouble is away from the supply end, that is, towards the far end. See Table 6–5 for a definition of the supply end.

When testing E-O-L resistor loops, you will be dealing with three possible voltages, rather than two. Zero volts or nearly zero, indicates an unsecured condition. Maximum system voltage, typically about 12 volts, indicates an open, which is also an unsecured condition. A normal, secured loop will register some midvalue voltage. The secure voltage, actually a range of voltages, will depend on the particular manufacturer. This range will be specified in the instruction manual. Some manufacturers thoughtfully post this information inside each control box.

6.4   MILLIAMMETER METHOD

A milliammeter can be used instead of a voltmeter for any of the preceding test procedures, providing the correct meter range is used. There are two important cautions:

1.   Some solid-state controls use a loop current of only a few microamps, so a meter with a sensitive enough range must be used. Cheap meters often will not serve the purpose.

Table 6–4   Loop-testing procedures

1. Test at middle of loop or of bad section.
2. Put meter probes across the two wires or across one wire and a switch or foil terminal.
3. When testing for an open, check at both terminals of a switch or magnetic contact (with the door or window closed) or at both ends of a foil, as the switch, contact, or foil may be defective.
4. When checking for shorts or grounds, open the loop by opening a door switch or lifting wire at foil terminal or by cutting one wire (the hot wire in a double closed loop system). Always test on the supply side of opening (or on both sides if the supply side is unknown).
5. Read meter. It will usually be "0-volts" or "supply-volts" or close to one of these (except end-of-line terminator loops where an OK loop will read about ½ of the open loop supply voltage).
6. If meter reads "supply-volts," the trouble is toward the far end, away from the supply end.
7. If meter reads "0-volts," the trouble is toward the voltage supply end.

Table 6–5 Definition of voltage supply end of a loop

Type of Loop	Voltage Supply End
Open loop	The control or transmitter
Single closed loop	The control or transmitter
Open and closed loop	The control or transmitter
Double closed loop	The ''supply'' or ''feed'' pair of terminals of the control or transmitter
E-O-L battery loop	The E-O-L battery or power supply
E-O-L resistor loop	The control or transmitter
Distributed resistance loop	The control or transmitter
Break-and-cross night loop	The night battery and ground feed terminals
Break-and-cross day or 24-hour loop	The day or 24-hour battery and ground feed or supply terminals or the phone line and earth ground

2. When testing double closed loops and end-of-line battery loops for shorts or grounds, very high currents can be drawn, especially when testing close to the source (with very low wire resistance). The meter can be burned out if care is not used in selecting an appropriate range.

For these reasons, it is best to stick to the use of a voltmeter for loop trouble-shooting. An exception would be break-and-cross loops (direct wire systems), which often have milliammeter test jacks built into the subscriber day-night control.

6.5 OHMMETER OR CONTINUITY TESTER METHOD

Protective loops can also be tested with an ohmmeter or any of several types of continuity testers. Any of these instruments has its own built-in voltage source, usually a battery, for correct operation. Therefore, all other voltage sources must be disconnected from the loop before testing. If you don't do this, you are likely to damage the meter or tester or, at best, get a false reading or indication. Generally, it's best to completely disconnect the loop from the control or transmitter and from the end-of-line battery or power supply, if there is one.

A check with an ohmmeter or continuity tester will quickly indicate whether the loop is open or closed or if there is a short between the two wires of a double closed loop system, provided of course that neither end has been shorted. If one lead of the meter or tester is connected to an earth ground, it can be used to detect any grounds on the loop wires. It can also be used to detect the absence of such a ground if a ground is supposed to be present.

When looking for an open, first short the wires together at only one end. Then, proceed to test the loop by halves. Follow the same procedure as for the voltmeter and think of the shorted end as the supply end. If you see the short, the open is the other way. If you don't see the short, then the open is toward the end you have shorted. (See Figure 6–11.)

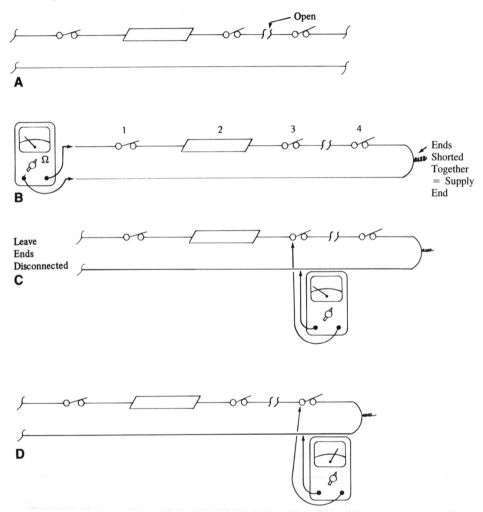

Figure 6–11 Ohmmeter or continuity tester method of locating an open. (A) Typical loop using closed circuit devices. Note that, for proper testing, the loop has been disconnected from the control and that the other end has been temporarily shorted together (if not already shorted). (B) Ohmmeter reads ∞ (infinity), indicating problem is an open. (C) Ohmmeter again reads ∞, so the open is still towards the temporarily shorted end. (D) Ohmmeter now shows a low ohms reading so open is away from the temporarily shorted end. Continue testing along the wire by piercing the insulation until the break (open) has been found.

When looking for a short or ground, an ohmmeter offers one advantage. You can read the actual ohms to the short. For example, if you get a reading of 20 ohms and you know the original loop resistance was 80 ohms (total for both conductors), you would know the short was about ¼ of the loop length away. You could then go directly there for your next test. This is only a rough guide because the ohmmeter reading represents electrical length and not physical length. The problem is that foil, if used, has a much higher resistance than copper wire, which makes it a little harder to judge distances. Poor connections can also have resistance. Still, the ohms reading can be used as a rough guide, and successive tests will indicate how fast you are closing in on the short. If, however, your readings start increasing again, you have passed the short. If in doubt, open a door switch and test to see which side has the short on it. (See Figure 6–12.) If you don't know the original loop resistance, you can judge it using Table 6–6.

Remember that certain earlier alarm controls had loop resistance limits of only 100 ohms or so. When using an ohmmeter, remember that a reading of 150 or 200 ohms, even though it has continuity, is sure to cause trouble on such a system. By comparison, most continuity testers will show continuity up to several thousand or tens of thousand ohms, depending on their design. Thus, a 200-ohm loop would show continuity even though such a loop would be unsuitable for a control having a 100-ohm loop limit. This situation won't be encountered very often, which is all the more reason to remember this little point. So if your continuity tester ever says "yes," but the alarm says "no," haul out your trusty ohmmeter to check actual resistance. Then compare this value to the manufacturer's published resistance limit. This value should be in the instruction manual.

Continuity testers do have advantages, such as giving both aural and visual indications. They can also have a latching function, but we'll save that until we get to intermittent problems.

6.6   FOREIGN VOLTAGES (POTENTIALS)

The term "foreign potential" is borrowed from the phone company. It is used to indicate that some potential (voltage) is present on the phone lines that does not belong there. The same thing can happen on alarm systems. For example, alarm circuits could get connected to door bells, intercoms, control circuits, audio or stereo systems, unrelated alarm systems, and various other things. Although it is unlikely that alarm company personnel would make such "foreign" connections, remember that many other people have access to subscribers' premises, including subscribers' employees. Many of these people do not understand electricity and even fewer understand alarm systems. Some of them may unwittingly or uncaringly interconnect other circuits to alarm circuit wires simply because they are handy and serve their purposes. Such foreign connections could also be the result of damage to alarm wires running close to other, also damaged, wires. In either case, the problem could exist where it is not

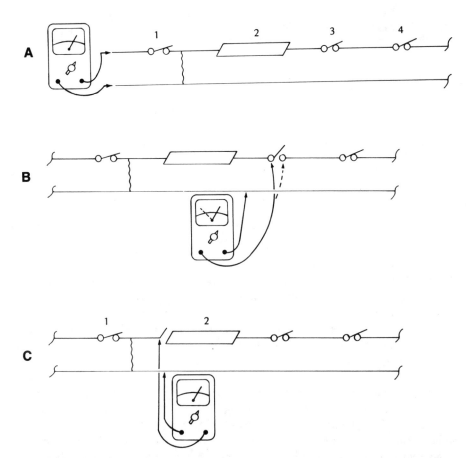

Figure 6–12 Ohmmeter or continuity tester method of locating a short. Note that loop has been disconnected from the control and that the other end has been temporarily opened, if it is normally shorted. (A) Continuity reading indicates that problem is a short. (B) Continuity reading on left of switch with switch open indicates that short is on left. A reading of ∞ (infinity) on right of switch (dotted line) indicates there are no additional shorts to the right. (C) Continuity reading at the lifted wire of the foil connection shows that short is to the left. Another test at switch one would indicate the short to be to the right. The wire can be visually inspected or cut in the middle for further tests. If an ohmmeter is being used, relative resistance readings can be taken, as in Figure 6–10E.

readily observable, such as in attics or crawl spaces, above suspended (drop) ceilings, and behind boxes or other warehouse stock.

Fortunately, foreign voltages are rare. They deserve coverage in this book because they can present a serious shock hazard, can seriously damage alarm equipment, and can cause problems that are very difficult to diagnose.

Table 6–6   Resistances of copper wire and lead foil

Wire Gauge	Ohms per 1000 Loop Feet	Foil Type	Ohms per 1000 Linear Feet (Approximately)
16	8.0 Ω	⅜″ × .001″	300 Ω
18	12.8 Ω	⅜″ × .0015″	200 Ω
20	20.2 Ω	⅜″ × .002″	150 Ω
22	32.2 Ω	1″ × .0025″	50 Ω
24	51.4 Ω		
26	81.6 Ω		

If you find melted or charred insulation, arcing or sparking or evidence that they have occurred, or melted foil or fused (melted) wire, you should suspect a foreign voltage and probably a high voltage. If so, approach the system cautiously and check for the presence of a voltage with a voltmeter set to a high AC range (150 volts AC or higher). An AC range is preferred because on AC, the meter will generally (but not always, depending on DC polarity) respond to both AC and DC. Digital meters will usually not respond to DC when set to AC, so test for both AC and DC if you are using a digital meter. Test between both conductors of each alarm circuit and between each wire and earth ground.

If alarm equipment has failed, even without the presence of the previously mentioned symptoms, you may still have a foreign voltage. This may be true particularly if replacement equipment also fails. Again, check for the presence of higher-than-normal voltages or the presence of AC where only DC should be. Remember though that equipment can be damaged repeatedly by incorrect installation or by the use of the incorrect supply voltage. Alarm equipment sometimes fails simply because components wear out, so don't always blame failures on foreign voltages. One equipment manufacturer related a case in which six control modules were returned to him as "no damned good." A quick look at the printed circuit board revealed physical destruction of parts and burned printed circuit traces. From the location of the damaged area it was obvious the alarm installer connected 120 volts AC to the power input terminals, which were clearly marked 12 volt DC. When the first control didn't work, the installer tried the second, then the third, fourth, fifth, and sixth. At this point, he ran out of replacements and sent them all back. This is more an example of incorrect installation (wrong power source) than it is of a foreign voltage, but the destruction was the same. All six were replaced for free. Some manufacturers will stand behind their products, even beyond what it is reasonable to expect. Hurrah for V.B.Ross & Company, El Monte, CA.

Even if a foreign potential is low enough in voltage to avoid damage, it is still likely to cause malfunction of the alarm system. It is impossible to predict the nature of the problem because it would depend on the type of alarm equipment, the nature of the foreign voltage (volts, AC or DC, resistance, etc.), and where it was entering the alarm system (protective loop, bell circuit, remote control circuit, phone line, etc.). Even a foreign connection that does not have any voltage present could still have a low enough resistance to short out part of the alarm system.

As though these problems are not bad enough, consideration must be given to the operation of the foreign voltage's source. For example, a doorbell circuit connected to an alarm system might only cause problems when the doorbell button is pushed. Other sources might work off of wall switches, timers, or other automatic controls, such as thermostats. This would be like a swinger and could be very difficult to locate.

Your best bet, when dealing with foreign voltages or connections, is to thoroughly understand how the alarm equipment is supposed to work. This is step two of the seven basic steps of Chapter 5. If you find a system that is not behaving as you know it should, and cannot find the difficulty by other troubleshooting methods, look for a foreign connection.

One final note: Some direct wire circuits use voltages as high as 130 volts DC in their normal operation. The presence of such a voltage should not be confused with a foreign potential, but it can still give a shock.

6.7 INDUCED AC

Alarm wiring will, at some point, run close to other wiring in the building. This can cause pickup of AC, most often from 60-Hz power wiring. Pickup can also result from motors, generators, transformers, and other electrical devices. This induced AC can cause malfunctions of the system if too great. To check for its presence, set your meter to a low AC range and measure between the wires and from each conductor to a good earth ground.

Digital meters will normally read only AC and ignore the presence of any DC. This is just what you want. Some analog meters (V-O-Ms) will measure DC even when set to an AC range. Thus, if DC is present, and it very likely will be, you will not get an accurate reading. To test your meter, set it to AC, then measure a battery. Reverse your leads and test the other polarity. If either gives a reading, set your V-O-M to "output." This places a capacitor in the meter circuit that will block DC. On DC you will get a brief meter deflection, but it will settle to a steady reading within a second or so.

The maximum acceptable AC will depend on what part of the alarm circuit it occurs on, such as loop wiring, bell wiring, or control station wiring. It will also depend on the make and model of equipment you are using. You will probably be safe if you have less than 0.1 volts AC, although higher limits may be acceptable. Consult the manufacturer's specifications.

If you do encounter excessive AC, there are a number of possible corrective actions, listed here in increasing order of difficulty or cost of implementation.

1. Check for presence of a good earth ground on the alarm system.
2. Find out which wire is picking up the AC, then reroute it.

3. Replace parallel conductor wire with twisted pair.
4. Replace wire with shielded wire. Ground the shield at one end only.
5. Have subscriber remove, relocate, shield, or discontinue the use of offending electrical apparatus. This will most likely be very difficult or impossible.

When testing for induced AC, it is important to know which wires in the system normally have some sort of AC on them. A good example is system keypad wiring. These circuits are multiplexed, so will have an AC component. Become familiar with your kinds of systems so that you don't mistake these normal signals for unwanted, induced AC.

6.8   RADIO FREQUENCY PICKUP

Alarm system wiring can act as an antenna to pick up radio, TV, ham radio, two-way business radio, police radio signals, or any other radio frequency transmission. Such reception can also interfere with proper alarm system operation. These frequencies are usually too high to be measured with a meter. You can check for the presence of such reception by connecting a telephone installer's test set (butt-in) across the wires and from each wire to ground. Any sound heard in the test set, clear or garbled, indicates you have some sort of pickup. Corrective actions can consist of items 1, 3, 4, and 5 above, plus an inspection for quality. That is, make sure all connections are tight and are free of corrosion and moisture. As with AC pickup, make sure you know what parts of the system have multiplexing, such as system keypad wiring, as these can produce audible sounds and can mislead you.

6.9   SWINGERS (INTERMITTENTS)

Swingers can be the most aggravating type of troubleshooting problem because they often disappear before you get there to work on them. When the trouble disappears, you can't find it. Unfortunately, swingers are all too common. Rather than trusting to luck to find the source of a malfunction or throwing your hands up in despair, there are some things that can be done to solve swinger problems.

The first thing to do is to remember that they are a time-related problem. Intrusion detection devices such as ultrasonics, microwaves, and photo beams can certainly be the cause of swingers, too. Such problems will be addressed in Part Four of this book. Right now, let's look at swingers occurring in wiring, foil, and switches.

6.9.1   Quality

Before trying to find swingers, it will be helpful to understand what causes them. Almost invariably, they are caused by poor quality, that is, by shoddy installation or repair efforts. Some common examples are screw terminals that aren't tightened snugly, splices that are not soldered or on which a crimp connector was not used or not properly installed, splices that are not insulated, poor foil splices, foil takeoff connections that are not properly reinforced, and door cords that are too short. These are just a few examples. The list could go on and on.

6.9.2   Why They Swing

Any of the examples given could be permanent troubles as well as swingers. Then what makes them swing? There are three general answers. The simplest answer is direct mechanical motion such as wind, drafts from heaters, furnaces, air conditioners, ventilators, earthquakes, the rumble of traffic, trains, airplanes, or elevators. All of these can jiggle loose connections, causing a false alarm.

Another cause is varying temperatures due to day-to-night changes, differences in seasonal temperatures, heaters or furnaces, ventilators, air conditioners, or sunlight. These changes cause thermal expansion and contraction, which is a type of motion. Again, motion and loose connections spell trouble.

The third cause is moisture. Examples are condensation, leaky roofs, rain on equipment or wires located outside, flooding, use of a hose to wash area, or leaky pipes. Moisture will cause an electrical leakage path that can easily cause trouble. While pure water will not conduct electricity, there is usually enough dirt and impurities present to make the water a fairly good conductor.

Not only will moisture cause an electrical leakage path, it will also promote corrosion, particularly of copper wire. Eventually the wire can be eaten through, or the surfaces of a connection can become covered with corrosion if they are not soldered, crimped, or screwed tight. When the corrosion material is damp, it conducts electricity. When it dries, it no longer conducts.

Swingers can be, and often are, a combination of these three factors. They can be the result of physical damage to the system, but then the damage can often be spotted visually. More often they are the result of poor-quality installation or of previously made repairs.

6.9.3   Quality Inspection

One way to approach swingers is to inspect for quality. For example, you can tighten all screw connections in the system; scrape, twist, and solder all previously unsoldered connections; replace door cords that look worn (especially if too short); tape or insulate all connections; relocate wires away from damp or wet areas; carefully inspect for and repair physical damage; repair questionable foil splices or takeoff connections; or refoil poor foil jobs. This could be time-consuming, and, unfortunately, it does not give any guarantee that you have not overlooked one or more problems. This is particularly true when the circuit runs in places that are hard to get at or are inaccessible.

This technique, taken to the extreme, would end in complete replacement of the protective loop or even the entire system. This is sometimes done on old or particularly troublesome systems. Often, at least part of the reason for complete replacement is to update the system.

After a number of false alarms in my own service van, I finally resorted to a complete system replacement, only to find that the 6-volt dry cell battery had an internal intermittent. At first, I suspected the high afternoon temperature of about 140 degrees Fahrenheit (60 degrees Celsius) inside the van. But the false alarms occurred in the morning and evening when the temperature was changing most rapidly. Cutting the batteries open revealed cell leakage and corrosion. This, plus the temperature change, caused the problem.

6.9.4 Using Force

Another technique in locating swingers is to cause the problem to appear. In the military, this is known as "brogan maintenance," or, literally, kicking the equipment. Although a boot is usually not appropriate, it is sometimes possible to cause a problem to appear by rapping on windows, wiggling door cords, or tapping or pulling on wires. Done judiciously, this method will work, but care must be used to avoid damaging the system. New damage could be mistaken for the real problem.

The foil zapper is a kind of electrical brute force device. The high voltage, high current will burn open bad splices and hairline cracks in foil. The damage is then easily located and can be properly repaired. Good foil and splices will not be damaged. For more detail on this device, see Section 2.8.

6.9.5 The Time Factor

Since a swinger is a time-related problem, the most effective method of troubleshooting is to get time on your side. The simplest way to do this is to use a latching tester described in Section 2.5. Depending on the type used, a momentary open or a momentary close will cause the tester to latch and give a continuous indication (buzzer or light) until manually reset. Such a device, plus the brute force method described in the preceding section, makes an effective troubleshooting approach.

An even better method is to use the Exor-System® or Loop-Sticks® described in Section 2.9. They are superior because of their sensitivity and fast response. They are more convenient to use because they automatically reset themselves every second, and they are wireless in operation.

6.10 RESISTANCE FAULTS

Most of the faults we have considered so far were dead shorts (essentially 0 ohms) or clean breaks (essentially infinity ohms). These conditions are not always met and can confuse the troubleshooter. This section explains how to deal with resistance faults effectively.

6.10.1   Resistance Buildup

Resistance faults are often related to swingers, but not always. One example is a resistance buildup. This is usually related to poor or loose connections. Often the loose contact area becomes oxidized or corroded. As this happens, the resistance gradually increases. This is likely to happen at unsoldered or uncrimped wire splices or at loose screw terminals. When the resistance builds high enough, perhaps a little bit at each of several different places along a loop, the loop will eventually appear open.

This type of problem may be hard to locate when using a continuity tester, which simply indicates whether or not the system is functioning. If the resistance limit of the tester happens to be higher than that of the control, the tester may say "OK" when the control says the loop is "not OK." The best method is to use an ohmmeter to compare the present loop resistance to the resistance when the system was first installed or last serviced. That is one reason why it is important to record the original resistance for each loop. I write the loop resistance, the date, and my name on a piece of tape stuck inside the control box lid. Then it doesn't get lost. An advantage of using an ohmmeter is that you can check the reading as you work along the loop correcting problems. You should see the loop resistance decrease and approach the original installation value as you progress.

Sometimes a wire can be completely corroded through. The circuit is then completed through the corrosion material itself, which will usually have a high resistance. Further, this resistance will vary depending on the amount of dampness or moisture in the air. This can lead to swingers. I had just such a problem when a fine, lacing wire corroded all the way through, next to a soldered splice, but where the enamel insulation had been scraped away. Careful use of an ohmmeter led me to the problem.

6.10.2   Leakage

On the other side of the fence we can have resistance shorts or grounds. This is often the result of the loop wire being in a very damp or flooded area. Even though the wire is insulated, the insulation is often not perfect, so a current leakage path forms through the water. Leakage paths can also form from foil to ground where foil is improperly varnished or where crossovers are poorly insulated and the windows become wet. There is more likely to be such problems when the windows are dirty, because dirty water is a better conductor than clean water.

6.10.3   Consequences

It is impossible to make a general statement as to what the result will be of either a resistance buildup or a leakage path (short or ground). Obviously, if the resistance builds up sufficiently or if the leakage path resistance drops low enough, the result will be a false alarm or a loss of part of the protection. Either way, the resistance values at which difficulties occur depend on the make and model of control, the type of protective loop, the condition of the end-of-line battery if any, the voltage of the power supply or standby battery for the control, the length of the protective loop, and where a leakage occurs in the loop. Understanding what is happening will enable you to locate and correct such problems.

6.11 CONCLUSION

Troubleshooting procedures are not simple because there are so many possible problems. The seven basic steps should have given you a big picture to keep things in perspective. This chapter provided specific procedures for generalized troubleshooting and some specific guidance for special problems. To sit down and read it all may be confusing. As you put these ideas to practice they will make much more sense and will become second nature to you.

A good way to become familiar with these procedures is to set up alarm equipment and systems on the workbench and check them out. Have somebody else put in a problem without telling you what or where. Then practice finding the problem and solving it.

When I presented my troubleshooting seminars at the International Security Conferences, I designed and built a working alarm system that could be plugged into a variety of demonstration boards. Each board demonstrated a different type of loop: single open loop, single closed loop, double closed loop, E-O-L battery loop, E-O-L resistor loop, and break and cross loop. Each board had a row of four-position slide switches. Each of these introduced a particular problem (open, short, ground) at various points in the loop. In addition to ''clear'' and ''trouble,'' the two extra positions were used for two levels of resistance faults. One of these gave enough resistance to provide an immediate alarm condition while still providing continuity with a continuity test device. The remaining switch position provided some resistance but not enough by itself to cause an immediate alarm condition. Nevertheless when it was used in combination with the same position on several other switches, an alarm condition did result.

This demonstration equipment proved very effective in my seminars in teaching troubleshooting methods. You can build your own for your organization. To simplify construction, you can use a standard alarm control unit, and the loop need only be the same type (or types) that you use. Very heavy, 12 gauge wire can be used to make the loop. This makes it very easy to use insulation-piercing test probes, and it conceals the small wiring that goes from the trouble locations through the back of the board to the slide switches. Cover the switches so as not to reveal what troubles are present during training.

This chapter does not cover every type of problem nor every troubleshooting technique. Many people have developed their own methods—some useful, others less so; some safe, others dangerous; some shared, others kept secret. My purpose is to offer usable techniques that will enable you to get the job done and also to stimulate your thinking. By all means, expand on these ideas and develop your own techniques. If you find better ways, share them. By doing so you will be helping the industry progress. Maybe you'll be the inventor of that better mousetrap.

PART THREE

Part Three delves into the simple alarm hardware used in all systems. Chapter 7 explains the various types of alarm controls. Since it is impossible to cover every type of control on the market, various features are explained. Actual equipment will use various combinations of these features. Chapter 8 covers the various types of silent alarm signal transmission methods, as well as local bells and sirens. A battery or power supply of some sort is needed in every system. Some systems use several. These essential items are covered in Chapter 9.

7 Controls

A thorough understanding of controls is essential for two reasons. First, controls sometimes become defective. Therefore, the serviceperson must know how to correctly diagnose the problem so that the control can be replaced or repaired. Secondly, without a thorough understanding, the serviceperson will not be able to correctly diagnose the source of the problem and may spend endless hours looking in wrong places.

Before going any further, let's define a control. To many, it is just a box, a piece of hardware. It might be called a control, a control box, a control module, a panel, a control panel, or any of several other names. Basically and most simply, it provides a means of monitoring the protective loop and, when it detects an intrusion, of maintaining a continuous alarm even if the protective loop is restored. It also provides a means of turning the system on and off and a method of activating some sort of alerting device such as a bell or transmitter. A power supply or battery is usually included, too. In fact, the control function may be combined in the same package with a transmitter, a dialer, or some other device. Early controls were built with relays and were generally limited to these basic functions.

Increasingly, new designs are using solid-state devices such as transistors and integrated circuits. Generally, these take less space, draw less standby power, and offer enhanced operating features. Examples are a bell cutoff timer, an entry-exit delay, a multiple zone operation with selectable day-night or instant-delay operation, multiple remote key station operation with system status indication, and push-button combination arming-disarming. Most recently, manufacturers are designing alarm control units around microprocessors. These devices are the heart of microcomputers, and some types are available today for less than the cost of a relay. True, other devices such as memory chips and other circuitry are required to make an operating control. But once the commitment is made to use a microcomputer, there are tremendous potentials opened for a wide variety of features that would not be practical otherwise. Microcomputers can offer multiple zone operation, adjustable time delay on any zone, selection of night or 24-hour operation for any zone, and programmable digital communicator with multiple alarm functions.

Physically, a control unit is available as a simple module or as a unit in a lockable box with space for batteries, wiring, and possibly accessory modules. Also available are separate modules that can be attached to controls to add features, such as a bell cutoff timer for a control not originally equipped with this feature. Such expansion modules should not be confused with controls.

A thorough understanding of any control is essential. Some years ago, when I was installing a system, I could not make it trip on intrusion although the panic circuit worked fine. After a few puzzling moments, I decided to call the manufacturer. After hearing the symptoms, he asked, "Did you wait for the exit and entry delays?" All I could say was, "Oh. . . ." I had forgotten that this particular control had no "instant" zone; it all operated under an entry-exit delay. As soon as I realized the problem I rechecked the system. It worked exactly as it was supposed to. The moral of the story is to read those instructions.

Alarm control units are available from a sizable number of manufacturers and with a wide variety of operating features. There are so many that it would be pointless to try to describe them all. Instead, I will take a much more practical approach, that is, to explain the dozen or so features that make up the various controls. Since each feature does the same or nearly the same thing no matter whose control it appears on, it will be much simpler to explain it only once. After you understand the features, it will be up to you to determine which is provided on any particular system on which you happen to be working. Remember also that manufacturers are constantly introducing new features and sometimes change the operation of existing ones. That's why this book can't provide a complete listing of every possible feature. Read those instruction sheets!

7.1   SIMPLE CONTROL

Early controls provided only the basic functions. They had an on-off switch on the control box, a sensitive relay to detect whether the loop was secure or not, and a drop (latching) relay (which remained "locked-up" or "sealed-in" through its own contacts) to ring a bell until manually turned off with a key or until the batteries ran down. In this way, restoring the protective loop (such as closing the door through which an intrusion was made) would not silence the bell.

A sequence of operation of a simple control is shown in Figure 7–1. Although relays are shown here, many of today's controls use solid-state devices to accomplish the same results. Study these diagrams to see what is happening.

Refinements to a simple type of control include a meter to indicate loop status and an on-off switch with a test position to test the bell and battery by briefly ringing the bell.

Not to be confused with the control switch is the shunt switch. The shunt switch is mounted on or near the door where the proprietor enters the premises. It bypasses the door contact so that when the proprietor enters, the alarm will not be set off. The proprietor then turns the entire system off at the control. Sometimes the shunt switch is keyed alike (KA) to the control switch. If motion sensors or other interior detection devices are used, the shunt switch may also have to disable these to avoid false alarms. Rather than do this, it is generally preferable to locate the control close to the point of entry. Then the proprietor can enter far enough to turn off the system without disturbing interior sensors. This way, if the proprietor forgets to turn off the shunt at

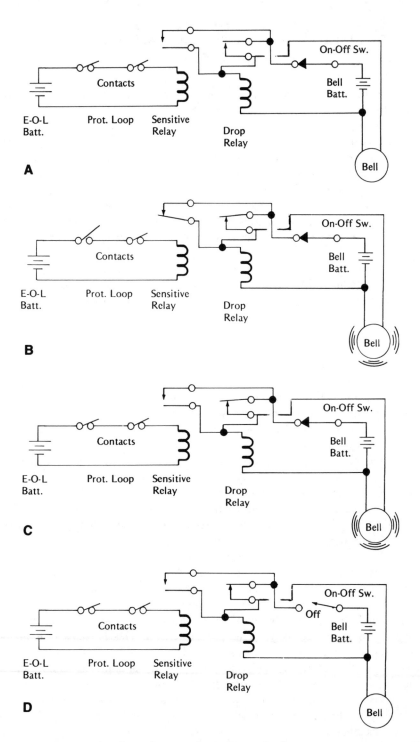

Figure 7-1 Operation of simple control. (A) Protective loop secure, system on. (B) Intrusion occurs, bell rings. (C) Loop restored but bell continues to ring. (D) Manually silenced with on-off switch.

closing time, the motion sensors or other interior sensors are still in service and only the entry door remains shunted out (bypassed).

It is quite common for silent-only alarm systems to use neither an on-off switch nor a shunt switch. When the proprietor enters in the morning an alarm signal is transmitted. At the alarm central station, this signal is interpreted as a normal opening or as an intrusion according to a prearranged time schedule. This method avoids the problems of lost or stolen alarm keys or picked or forced locks. It does require adherence to the time schedule for openings and closings, and the alarm company must be notified in advance of any schedule changes. In this type of system, the system is switched to the "day" position to prevent a constant stream of unwanted alarm signals during business hours.

While some systems use the shunt switch or control switch arrangement, other systems use only an on-off switch at or near the point of entry. This switch controls the entire system. Thus, use of a lost or stolen key or an attack on the lock would disarm the entire system.

7.2   DAY-NIGHT FEATURE

With only a single protective loop in the simple alarm just described, the entire system is off during the day. If, for example, window foil is damaged during the day, the damage most likely won't be discovered until closing time when the system won't set up. This means the proprietor must either wait until the alarm serviceperson arrives and finds and fixes the problem or go home without any alarm protection for the premises. It can also mean a rash of service calls for the alarm company to handle at typical office or store closing times.

To prevent this problem, some controls are equipped with a day, or 24-hour, circuit. Window foil, wall foil, lacing, screens, and unused openings such as trap doors and certain windows are wired into this circuit. Doors, windows, motion sensors, and photo beams that are used during the day are wired into a separate night circuit. When the system is turned to the night position, the entire system works like a regular system. An intrusion in the day or the night loop will signal an alarm. When the system is set to the day position the night loop is turned off. The day, or 24-hour, loop can sound a buzzer locally, usually right in the control box. The proprietor can then notify the alarm company for immediate repairs. This prevents waiting for a repairperson at closing time and spreads the service load for the alarm company during the day. In this type of system, only the buzzer sounds. Alarm bells do not ring, and no silent alarm is transmitted. In some types of silent-only alarm systems the day circuit will transmit a silent alarm. The alarm central station will know such a signal indicates system damage if it is received during the business hours that have been previously established.

In such a direct wire (not the polarity-reversing kind) system, the subscriber's premises are equipped only with a day-night switch. The control function is performed by equipment at the central station. The telephone line, in essence, becomes part of the protective loop. This is the only type of silent alarm system that functions in this manner.

On local bell or combination local-silent systems the off position of the four-position control switch usually becomes the day or 24-hour position. Other systems may use a separate day-night switch. A day-night system should not be confused with a perimeter-interior type of control or with a multizone type of control, as they function differently. These will be explained later. Some multizone systems may have 24-hour operation available on some zones, or this feature may be selectable by the installer. This will also be covered later.

7.3   MULTIPLE ZONES FEATURE

As systems become larger and use more advanced detectors, things can get out of hand. For example, although it is beneficial to know an intrusion has taken place in a large complex, it is of little benefit to have police and alarm company guards searching one end while burglars finish their caper and escape from the other. A more important example is the problem of trying to isolate a malfunction in a large complex. The serviceperson has the entire system to troubleshoot. Intermittent problems are particularly nasty in this respect. The practical answer to both problems is to divide the system into multiple zones and use a zoned control. On existing systems, it is sometimes possible to add a zone module.

Some thought must be given to zoning a system, that is, how the premises is to be divided into zones. In a multiple story building, a logical approach would be to assign each floor to its own zone. In a large, one-story building, one zone might be assigned to the north wall, one to the east wall, and so on. Depending on building layout, it may make more sense to divide zones according to areas, functions, or departments, such as office area, warehouse area, manufacturing area, etc. High-value areas should usually be put on a separate zone. If there is more than one, they may each deserve their own zone. Motion sensors should usually be placed on a separate zone or zones. This is particularly important since these devices are subject to their own causes of false alarms, as outlined in Part Four of this book. Some motion detectors now have their own built-in zoning. With this feature built in, it is not essential to assign such a motion detector to its own control zone.

Perhaps, ideally, every detection device should have its own zone. With advances in microprocessor-based controls, this is now possible. Some tradeoff must be made of the extra costs of zoning versus the extra benefits of simplified servicing and pinpointing intruder activity for responding police or guards. The simplest type of multizone control places all the zones on the night circuit. More sophisticated types of controls, particularly the microcomputer type units, permit greater flexibility. For example, zones can be assigned to the day or the night circuit; they can be assigned to provide instant alarm or entry-exit delay operation; and they can be assigned various functions such as intrusion, fire, holdup, and medical alert. (Some systems provide four, eight, or ten functions and transmit a distinct alarm identifier for each.) Not all multizone controls offer all these features, but the microcomputer units tend to offer the most flexibility. Rather than having a multitude of switches or cut-wire options, the desired options are selected by pushing buttons on a programming unit that is temporarily plugged into the controller by the installer. The control remembers these instructions after the programming unit is disconnected. The operating instructions can be changed at any time through the programming unit.

The terms "microcomputer" and "programming" may conjure up thoughts of complexity, but don't worry. Using such units is relatively simple, certainly much simpler than conventional computers. For one thing, microcomputer-driven alarm controls are dedicated specifically to alarm work. This makes their use and their programming surprisingly simple. If you understand various alarm operating features, as discussed in this chapter, just follow the step-by-step instructions provided by the manufacturer. After a practice session you should find programming straightforward. In addition to portable programmers, many of the newer control units can be programmed by downloading the required settings from a computer (usually a PC) located at the alarm central office via the telephone line. All reputable manufacturers provide security measures to prevent unauthorized changes, although some provide more measures than others.

One of the often-advertised advantages of multiple zone systems is that zones in trouble can be manually bypassed. Repairs can then be made the next regular work day. In fact, some of the newer controls employ forced arming in which nonsecured zones are automatically bypassed. Some systems may not even indicate this fact to the user. These features must be used with caution. Always remember that part of the protection, perhaps a major portion of it, is out of service. Also, the bypass may be forgotten about and intended repairs never made. In fact, several bypasses could accumulate until no protection is left. In an attempt to get the system operating, even good zones could be bypassed by the user. Some controls warn when this happens. They should all do this.

7.4   LOW SPEED FEATURE

Early controls used relays and operated at relay speeds. Typically this was in the range of 10 milliseconds or ten one-thousands of a second, which is usually just fine. Electronic controls, by comparison, could operate thousands, even millions, of times faster. To do so would leave electronic systems far too susceptible to false alarms due to static, electrical noise, and radio interferences picked up by system wiring. Instead, good electronic controls are intentionally slowed down to avoid these problems. Some controls offer extra loops or zones that are designed to respond very slowly, even much slower than relays, typically 0.5 seconds. This equals 500 milliseconds, perhaps 50 times slower than standard. The idea is to reduce false alarms due to bad loop wiring such as poor connections, damaged foil, or defective contacts. In my opinion, this approach treats the effect. What often happens is that the problem continues to worsen until you are faced with repairs anyhow. It would be far better to correct the cause by finding and repairing the problems. The best tool to find these problems, that I am aware of, is the Loop-Sticks® discussed in Section 2.9.

Particular attention must also be paid when using fast-responding sensing devices. The two prime examples are vibration contacts and certain glass break detectors that are connected directly into the protective loop. Certainly a slow response control would not work. Even a normal control may not respond fast enough to detect the brief signals from these devices. The best advice is to thoroughly check a system containing such devices for proper operation. If there is any difficulty, it will be necessary to use detection devices with built-in electronics that provide adequate signal time. Another method is to wire such devices in a separate loop that is connected to a pulse stretcher. The pulse stretcher output is then wired into the protective loop. When using electronic pulse stretchers, it is wise to have several of them on large jobs, and connect only a few sensing devices to each. This keeps wiring to the input of the pulse stretchers short and reduces chances of electrical noise pickup. The pulse stretcher is just as happy to stretch noise pulses into an alarm signal as it is to stretch those pulses generated by detection devices.

Other electronic detection devices such as microwaves, ultrasonics, and photo beams usually have enough alarm duration built in. Once triggered, they will trip even a control with a slow loop. There is always the exception, though, so test a system thoroughly after installation, modification, or major repairs.

7.5   BELL TIME-OUT FEATURE

With the rapidly growing number of alarm systems in use and the high false alarm rates, many cities are passing ordinances regulating alarms. A typical regulation limits the amount of time a local bell can ring. Even without an ordinance, bells in or near residential areas should be time limited. Early bell time-out devices were all built as separate modules that were connected between an existing control's bell terminals and the bell. Today many controls have this feature built in. This is referred to as a bell time-out feature or a bell cutoff timer. Some have continuously adjustable time settings. Others permit selecting from among several preset times. These settings are selected by cutting a wire loop sticking out of the control, by cutting one end of a designated resistor, by a switch setting or by placement of a jumper, depending on the manufacturer. Time intervals typically vary from a few minutes to as much as 30 minutes, again depending on the manufacturer. There are four modes of time-out operation:

1.   Bell times out, entire system goes dead until manually reset. This is highly undesirable unless a silent alarm is also transmitted that will summon someone who can promptly reset the system.
2.   Bell times out and, if the loop is still unsecured, the bell immediately reactivates. Under this condition the bell never really shuts off. This is highly undesirable

unless used with a system containing only self-resetting detection devices, such as motion sensors or mats. Foil, contacts, traps, and lacing are not self-resetting. This type would probably not meet ordinances calling for bell cutoff timers.

3. Bell times out. System rearms itself if loop is restored. Otherwise, system goes dead. Some systems will rearm themselves if loop is later restored.

4. Another mode, used on multizone systems, works the same as number three as far as the tripping zone. Other zones continue normal protective service after bell time-out even if the tripping zone remains out of service. A variation on this type is a residential control that automatically arms a backup (interior) zone when the perimeter system is tripped, even if the backup zone was not originally in use. This method and its variation both provide a second line of defense in case the tripping zone remains out of service. The latter method would not be desirable if, for example, pets were left in areas covered by motion sensors.

Whatever the mode of operation, an indication is desirable to let the user know that the system has been tripped. If the indicator is visible from outside, it warns a returning occupant that an intrusion has taken place. This could prevent a confrontation with an intruder who might still be inside. In my own system I provide an exterior light, visible from the street, that remains on even after bell time-out. It must be manually reset. I also included lock-in zone lights to pinpoint the tripping zone or zones. These are located inside the control box.

7.6   REMOTE, MULTIPLE KEY STATION FEATURE

The simple types of alarm controls, described at the beginning of this chapter, work fine for most businesses, but they don't work for residences. With a control switch on the control box and a shunt switch outside, it is difficult to provide complete perimeter protection for the user inside the house at night. Many systems are available today that use remote control stations. These are wired to the control and provide a momentary type (spring-return) key switch.

Momentarily turning the key alternately turns the system on and off. It also usually silences a ringing bell. An indicator light tells if the system is on or off. Interior remote control stations often include a second indicator light of a different color to denote if the protective loop is secure or not. The second light may be on or off to denote that the system is secure and, if on, may or may not go off when the system is armed. This depends on the particular make and model of control used. Early systems used incandescent bulbs, but LEDs are preferred because they last much longer and take less current to operate.

Systems can accommodate up to some maximum number of remote control stations. A typical limit is four, although some can take more. The limit is the number of indicator lights. The more stations there are, the more lights. This, of course, puts more drain on batteries during standby operation.

Some indoor remote control stations are furnished with push buttons instead of key switches. This may save a few dollars but should be avoided. Any intruder who knows or can find the location of these buttons could very easily break in and deactivate the system before the entry delay time expires.

A combination type push-button can be used instead of a key-operated switch to arm and disarm the system. This is not to be confused with a single push button, mentioned in the preceding paragraph. The combination push button, often called a key pad, sometimes resembles a touch-tone telephone keypad. This device requires the user to push the correct sequence of buttons, usually three or more, to arm or disarm the system. Sometimes a limited number of tries is permitted. If this limit is exceeded, the keypad can be disabled for a time to prevent guessing on the part of a would-be intruder. Sometimes different codes are used for different arming modes or to send a duress signal.

Remote control stations can be located at one or more points of entry and at convenient points inside. When located outside, they should be equipped with tamper switches. Tampers should be connected to the panic circuit to provide 24-hour tamper protection. Be careful though. Some tamper loops do not function with the bell cutoff timer. If this is so, then use the regular protective loop to meet bell time-out ordinances.

A distinction should also be made between stand-alone keypads and system keypads. A stand-alone unit replaces a conventional key-operated switch. The keypad itself is programmed for the desired code, usually by setting small switches or jumpers on the back. Pushing the correct combination momentarily closes a switch that serves the same function as a key-operated switch. On other types, the switch may alternately open and close with each correct combination entry. System type keypads, by comparison, only send code signals back to the control that represent the depression of a particular button. In fact, the same tones can be used as are used for push-button phone keys. All combination programming is done at the control, which is usually a microprocessor type system. The combination is also decoded at the control, so gaining access to keypad wiring does not allow compromising the system, as it would with a stand-alone keypad or key-operated switch. System type keypads are often combined with alphanumeric displays to show system status and usually offer a number of functions using different keypad combinations.

7.7 AUXILIARY FUNCTIONS

Many controls today offer a number of auxiliary functions in addition to the intrusion or burglary function. A panic circuit is a common one. The panic circuit usually accommodates normally open, momentary push buttons. The circuit is on 24 hours a day and will function regardless of whether the burglary circuit is on or not. The panic output usually drives the same bell output that is used for the burglary alarm. A panic alarm is a local noise alarm and should not be confused with a holdup alarm, which is always silent. A panic alarm is fine for a householder who wants to scare away a prowler heard or seen outside. A local bell holdup alarm could easily result in an already nervous holdup man shooting someone. Therefore, it is generally best to use no local noise on holdup. Some panic alarms are silenced the same as is the burglary function. Others require separate resetting at the control box. Some panic alarms time out the same as burglary alarms, others don't.

A fire or auxiliary function is often included in today's burglar alarm controls. This usually uses open circuit detectors and is usually unsupervised. If the burglary loop uses E-O-L resistor supervision, this feature may also be used on the fire or auxiliary circuit, too. If some sort of supervision is provided, a buzzer or indicator is needed to indicate trouble on this circuit. The alarm output is usually separate from the burglary output. A separate, distinct warning device can then be used. The fire or auxiliary circuit must be on 24 hours a day. Some systems use the burglary control to silence the fire or auxiliary alarm. Others use a separate switch at the control box. These systems may be suitable for residential use. Any fire alarm system must meet all local, state, and national code requirements for commercial or industrial installations.

Alarm systems can also be used to signal medical emergencies. This function requires a 24-hour loop and must have remote monitoring to summon medical help. On-premises wireless transmitters are ideal for such service, although cord-connected pendant (hand held) type switches by chair or bedside can be used. Some means, such as a horn or buzzer, should be provided to let the user know that the alarm has been activated.

Some burglar alarm controls include auxiliary output contacts that work at the same time as the burglary bell output. These can be either dry contacts, which are simply relay contacts with no voltage applied by the control system, or voltage outputs. Such contacts can be used to actuate auxiliary devices, transmitters, etc. The load that is switched must be within the voltage and current ratings of the relay. Consult the manufacturer's literature for these ratings. Similar auxiliary relay outputs are also sometimes furnished for fire, medical alert, or other types of loops.

7.8   ENTRY-EXIT DELAY FEATURE

Traditionally, either shunt or key-controlled switches have been mounted outside the protected premises. This exposes the switch to the weather and to attempted defeat. Unfortunately, today, picking tools are readily available even for round key switches. In addition, there are a number of tools made especially for attacking key switches. Installation requires time and wiring too. On-off switches, in particular, have to be wired back to the control.

With entry-exit delays, it is now possible to locate the on-off switch inside the protected premises. It is then protected from the weather and from attack. In some installations only one key switch located on the control box is sufficient.

When using an entry-exit delay, the user arms the system with an inside key switch or keypad. The user then has a preset amount of time, that is, the exit delay time, in which to leave without triggering an alarm. Later, upon returning, the user enters and has another preset time delay during which to turn the system off. A small warning horn or buzzer usually is used as a reminder to do so. If not turned off within the delay period, the alarm will sound or a silent signal will be transmitted, or both.

Many of the controls that have entry-exit delay also accommodate remote control stations. Although one key switch may be sufficient, such systems can use several conveniently located inside the premises. Some multizone systems provide one zone with entry-exit delay for entry door or doors, and one or more zones for instant alarm for the rest of the system. Some systems permit the installer to select delay or instant operation for each zone. This is usually done by a jumper connection, a switch setting or a cut-wire option. Microcomputer systems use a programming unit for this function.

Here's another way to foil a burglar. Install a remote control station outside but connect the key switch (momentary type) to the 24-hour panic input. If no panic input is available, connect it to the protective loop. The alarm user never bothers with the outside switch. In fact, it should be keyed differently from those inside to prevent its use. Anybody attacking the outside key switch gets a surprise: the alarm goes off.

7.9 MICROPROCESSOR-BASED CONTROLS

In the early days, an alarm control consisted of a box with a few relays, a switch, and a few dry cells. Along came solid-state controls with more features. In 1977 Radionics™ introduced the first alarm control unit that was built around a microprocessor chip similar to that used in a home computer. Few people realized at the time what a quantum leap forward this was for the alarm industry. Today, all of the major alarm companies offer controls that are built around a microprocessor.

Previous to the use of microprocessor-based units, any feature that was wanted had to be designed into the hardware, that is, the control unit. With the new units, many features could be programmed in via software and required little or no change in the hardware.

For example, in the late sixties I designed an alarm control for my own use that featured nine zones; automatic bell time-out with automatic bypass of zone or zones not secured at the end of bell time-out; three bell output circuits, each separately fused and supervised; three floodlight circuits, each separately fused and supervised; three direct wire-reporting circuits, each separately supervised (for annunciators in nearby neighbors' homes); a panic circuit; push-button combination arming-disarming and access control; and a host of other features. Every design change required changing the circuitry, and some required starting from scratch with a bigger box. To handle all of this logic required fifty-four relays and some solid-state circuitry. Today, one microprocessor can handle all of these features and much, much more. That microprocessor will cost less than one relay will today. True, more is required than just the microprocessor, such as memory, input-output, and display, so don't expect a new control to be priced the same as an old two-relay control. Once the microprocessor is designed in, however, features can be added much more economically. More importantly, features can be changed from a remote location, a process known as uploading-downloading. This has had a tremendous impact on the alarm industry and how we run our business.

A microprocessor is a digital logic device. It does what it is told to do via a set of instructions, called a software program, that is stored in memory. It can do only one thing at a time, but it can do things in very rapid sequence. In fact, it can do millions of things per second. Changing its operation is just a matter of changing the set of instructions, rather than redesigning the hardware. The basic program is built into permanent memory by the manufacturer and seldom changes, say, when a new model is introduced. The installing company can change the programming by turning features on or off or by selecting among several available options. An example would be to enable zone 31, designate it as an entry-exit delay loop with a 30-second exit delay and a 40-second entry delay, specify that it have a 250-millisecond response time and that it is a burglary loop with a steady bell output, and show the zone as "front door" on the system keypad's display.

These controls offer a myriad of features. For example, twenty, thirty, fifty, or more zones are possible, conceivably enough to have a separate zone for each detection device. New features include such things as digital status display that reads in English; stored history of recent alarm events such as armings, disarmings, alarms, restores, and manual zone bypasses; multiple user codes to indicate which user took what actions; system keypad wiring that requires only four conductors; built-in digital communicator that can handle a variety of formats to match different brands of receivers; alternate telephone numbers for dialing out in case it can't get through on the primary number; automatic battery test under load done once or several times a day with low-battery condition reporting; provision for use with derived channel telephone line reporting; and ability to connect zone expander modules to the system keypad wiring. (Remember, all of these signals are being multiplexed, something I predicted in my first edition.) The list goes on and will continue to grow as each manufacturer tries to outdo the other.

Some of the benefits to the alarm industry besides the increased flexibility are those features designed to help reduce the false alarm rate. Some of these are programmable loop response time, surge protection for field wiring inputs, manual zone bypass capability, multiple zones (which helps narrow down the source of alarms), and automatic zone bypass on swingers.

By far, the most significant change is the ability to upload and download. Uploading is the ability to transmit system status and system feature settings from the control to a computer (usually a PC) at the alarm central station or at some other location via the dial-up telephone line. Downloading is the ability to transmit instructions from the computer at the central station to the control at the subscriber's premises to change the status or to change feature settings. For example, suppose your subscriber called you from three states away saying, "I left on vacation and I think I forgot to arm my system. Would you run over there and turn it on?" You can now check the system's status via uploading and, if it isn't on, change the status via downloading, by having your computer call the control. This allows you to save on service calls.

8 Silent Alarms and Local Bells

When an intrusion is detected, some action has to be taken. This could be the sounding of a local device, such as a bell or siren, or the transmitting of an alarm signal by wire or radio to a remote location such as an alarm central station or police department. In a proprietary system, the signal is sent to a guard station on the premises. A combination of a local bell and silent signal can also be used. In this chapter, we will look at various forms of silent transmissions, then briefly at local sounding devices.

The most often used transmission path for silent alarms is telephone lines. Alarm service personnel are not responsible for maintenance of phone lines. Alarm people, though, do have to understand the various transmission methods, including telephone lines, to be able to service their own transmitting and receiving equipment. They also have to be able to accurately diagnose problems as being either in their own equipment or in the telephone company lines or equipment. Most telephone companies now charge alarm companies for wasted service time when no problem is found in their lines or equipment. I understand some alarm companies have successfully charged phone companies for their own work when the phone company denied blame for the problem and it was later found that the problem was with the phone lines or equipment after all. I strongly urge that you develop a cooperative rather than an adversarial relationship with the telephone companies. The best way to do this is to thoroughly understand your own equipment and to do your testing thoroughly. The intent of this chapter is to start you on your way to that understanding. We will also look at alternatives to phone line transmission, primarily long-range radio.

8.1 HISTORICAL PERSPECTIVE

At one time alarm companies were almost totally dependent upon phone companies for the transmission of alarm signals. Two major changes have come about. One is the disappearance of the metallic, or copper, pair. The other is the availability of alternate means of transmission.

Originally all alarm signals were sent over metallic phone lines using the presence and absence of voltage, voltage with polarity reversal, specific current level, or pulse coding (McCulloh loop). All of these required DC continuity, that is, a continuous, metallic path between the subscriber's premises and the alarm company's central office. (Since wires were often made of copper, they were also referred to by that name.)

141

This was fine when the telephone companies used wires to carry telephone conversations both within a telephone exchange and between exchanges. As the cost of installing and maintaining copper cable increased, and as the cost of electronic carrier equipment, digital multiplexing equipment, and fiber optic cable decreased, the phone companies switched over to these technologies. At first these new methods were economical only for long-distance circuits. Today they are used extensively for interoffice (phone exchange-to-phone exchange) circuits. Increasingly, phone companies are using these methods for intraexchange (phone exchange-to-phone subscriber) circuits as well. Suffice it to say that these methods do not require DC continuity, so they are not suitable for the old alarm signal transmission methods that require DC continuity. Also, for the most part, copper wires are no longer available for alarm transmission use.

Alarm companies have had to adopt signal transmission methods that are compatible with the new phone circuit methods. Most of these use tones that fall within the frequency band covered by standard telephone circuits and are therefore compatible with their carrier and multiplexing methods. Even digital alarm signal transmission methods usually encode the digital signals using such tones via a modulator-demodulator (modem) on each end.

To avoid the cost of a telephone line dedicated to alarm service, there has been a trend toward using the regular dial-up telephone circuits. Since regular dial telephone lines already exist at most alarm subscribers' premises, they can be used within limits. One exception to the use of frequencies in the standard telephone range is the use of a derived channel. This method uses a subcarrier to transmit the alarm signal over a subscriber's regular phone line, without interfering with normal telephone service.

One of the major alternatives to the use of telephone circuits is the use of long-range radio. This technology has been in use for over twenty years but has only recently become popular. Alarm companies can install their own receiving equipment or, in the larger metropolitan areas, can lease radio services. In either case, they install transmitters at the protected promises.

Cable TV can sometimes be used for sending alarm signals. This does require two-way capacity cable systems. Unfortunately, most cable TV systems are only one-way, that is, from the cable company head-end to the TV viewer. So far this method is more likely to be found in specific housing, building, and apartment complexes.

8.2   SIMPLE CURRENT SIGNAL

The simplest method of sending an alarm signal to a remote location is to have the alarm control apply a voltage to a phone line when the system is tripped. At the monitoring location, a relay is energized that alerts the operator. This type of system requires a metallic phone circuit, that is, one that has DC continuity by using metallic wires all the way. This system will not work with repeaters or carrier systems. The shortcoming is that a shorted or cut phone wire disables the silent alarm. This method is similar to an open circuit protective loop.

An alternative is to have the control apply a continuous voltage and to remove that voltage when in alarm. The relay at the monitoring end remains operated but drops out to signal an alarm. Cutting or shorting the phone line signals an alarm. This is similar to a closed protective loop. Unfortunately, there is no way to distinguish a line problem from an intrusion. These systems are rarely used today.

8.3 POLARITY REVERSING

The polarity-reversing method of signal transmission does distinguish between intrusion and line trouble. In the secure condition, a voltage is applied to the line. When an alarm is detected, the polarity is reversed. This can easily be done with a double-pole, double-throw (DPDT) relay.

At the monitoring (receiving) end, one relay is operated through a diode to indicate a secure condition. When the polarity is reversed, the first relay drops out, but another relay operates through another diode with the opposite polarity. This relay signals an alarm. If the line is cut or shorted, neither relay is operated. The relay contacts are arranged to signal a trouble condition. Instead of two separate relays with diodes, one polarized relay can be used. A polarized relay is a special unit that closes one set of contacts with one polarity applied to the coil and a second set of contacts when the opposite polarity is applied.

Some manufacturers use a meter with one relay. The meter is labeled ''alarm'' on one side, ''trouble'' in the middle, and ''normal'' on the other side of the meter scale. One regular relay with a diode is held in the operated condition. It drops out in either trouble or alarm position. Its contacts are used to sound a local annunciator. The operator must look at the meter to determine if the signal is an alarm or a trouble. Polarity-reversing systems require a metallic phone line and are seldom used any more.

8.4 McCULLOH TRANSMITTERS

The McCulloh transmitter has been in use for many years. It is like an alarm party line. All subscribers are connected in series, and each subscriber's alarm is transmitted by a coded signal. The code is generated by a toothed wheel that rotates to send the signal. Teeth are removed in a pattern so that the remaining teeth generate the desired code. For example, one code might be 3-1-3, and another on the same line could be 3-2-1. Note that all subscribers and the alarm central office must be wired in series. This is unusual for the phone companies as they are accustomed to connecting everything in parallel. Except when a transmitter is running, the phone circuit is completed through closed contacts at each transmitter and through a receiver at the alarm central office. Voltage to operate the loop is supplied at the alarm central office and typically runs from 45 volts to 130 volts.

Originally the code wheel was rotated by a spring-wound motor. A contact in the spring assembly created a trouble signal, indicating it had wound down. Later transmitters used code wheels powered by a small electric motor. Later still, transmitters were all electronic. They avoided the mechanical works that can cause repair problems. Codes are set with switches or jumpers since there is no code wheel and no teeth to remove.

Signals are transmitted by "rounds." Typically, an alarm signal is transmitted by sending three rounds. This means the code wheel (or its electronic substitute) completes three revolutions, sending the code sequence three times. Two rounds are typically sent as a closing signal when the proprietor arms the system and leaves for the night. Some units do not send opening and closing rounds. Some units transmit one round when the control is reset after sending an alarm. A few units send five rounds as a holdup alarm. Some transmitters are slaves that attach to existing controls. Others have the McCulloh transmitter and the control function built into one unit.

With all subscribers connected in series, a single break in the line would disable the entire loop. To prevent this, the McCulloh transmitter sends pulses, both by breaking the loop and by shorting each conductor of the line to ground. A single break in the phone loop will not disable alarm transmission and will register a trouble signal at the receiver. Systems by different manufacturers use slightly different pulsing techniques. Refer to the manufacturer's instructions for correct adjustment of the code wheel and brushes (contact springs). Follow these directions carefully, as the adjustments are often critical. The electronic versions do not use mechanical code wheels and thereby avoid these adjustments.

As already mentioned, McCullohs are a party line type system. This can result in problems if two or more transmitters run at the same time. This is called "clash" and results in a garbled message at the monitoring point. A good operator can sometimes sort things out, but not always. Because of this shortcoming, it is wise to limit the loop. For example, Underwriters' Laboratories (UL) listed installations must be limited to no more than 15* subscribers. Some newer McCulloh transmitters include an anticlash circuit. This circuit checks the line before transmitting. If the line is busy, it waits until the line is clear. This permits putting more subscribers on the line. This feature is also important when a computer is used to monitor the McCulloh circuits. Computers usually cannot untangle garbled signals resulting from clash. UL permits up to 45 subscribers per line when anticlash is used. Since McCulloh circuits are DC, they require metallic pairs and are seldom used today.

8.5   DIRECT WIRE METHOD

The name for the direct wire system is, unfortunately, not standardized. I tend to think of it as a milliamp method of alarm transmission. The term most often used in the industry is "direct wire." It is also called "ring back."

This system is unusual in that the alarm transmission circuit becomes part of the protective loop. Sometimes only one side of the telephone pair is used. In this case,

---

*Check current UL 611 standard.

an earth ground completes the circuit. This also permits serving two customers over one phone pair if they are located close together. Another possibility is to provide a double system to one subscriber. The two systems are interconnected. Tampering with one will alarm the other, providing a high degree of security.

The alarm control function is at the central station. The only equipment at the subscriber's premises is a two-position, day-night switch and a buzzer, although this is often referred to as a direct wire control. Two adjustable resistors are used to set the day current and the night current. The central station supplies the DC power, typically 120 volts DC. Special relays detect a decrease or an increase in the loop current to signal an alarm. A meter indicates actual current. One current level represents a secure night condition, while a different current level represents a secure day condition. A third current represents an intrusion, while zero current represents a break in foil or lacing (or an open phone line). A fifth current could represent a motion detector alarm. Actual current levels depend on the make and model of equipment used. Thus, the operator has some idea of what is happening. This is why I suggest the term "milliamp method." Some people use the terms "direct wire" and "direct line." These terms, however, are both used for the voltage, voltage removal, polarity reversal, and even sometimes for the McCulloh methods. With some systems, the alarm company operator can also send an AC signal to the subscriber to sound a buzzer. This is used to acknowledge proper opening and closing signals to the subscriber, hence the term "ring back." In troubleshooting this type of system you should, as always, ensure that the problem is not in your system before calling in the phone company.

As a measure to improve line security, an AC signal can be superimposed on the DC signal at the subscriber's end. This signal is monitored at the alarm central office. Loss of this signal indicates an attempt to compromise the line and is treated as an alarm.

If the current at the central station end is zero, make sure the system is not switched to the out-of-service position. If it is not, check to see that the correct voltage is being applied to the phone line at the central station end. If not, the problem is at the central station. If the voltage is correct, test the voltage at the subscriber end. If the voltage is correct, then the wiring at the subscriber's premises is open. If no voltage is present, the phone line is open or there is a short at the subscriber end.

If the current at the central station is at or above the maximum for that make and model of system, then check the current at the subscriber's end. If they are the same, any problem is in the subscriber's wiring. If the current at the subscriber's end is zero, the phone line is grounded. If the subscriber's reading is less than that on the central station end, the phone line has leakage to ground, assuming the test meters are accurate.

An explanation of the correct setup of this type of system should help you to understand the procedure just described. In setting up a normally working system, a temporary short is placed across the phone line at the subscriber's premises. If only one half of a pair is used, place the short to earth ground. A variable resistor at the central station is adjusted for the correct current. This is called the cross current. During an alarm, this current value represents an intrusion through a door or window or the operation of a photo beam or motion detector. SPDT contacts must be used. The current value could also represent a short or ground in the protective loop or phone line.

Next, the day current is set by the day adjustable resistor at the subscriber's day-night switch box. This must be done with the day or 24-hour protective loop in the secure condition and the switch set to the day position. Finally, the night current is set by adjusting the night resistor in the same box. Both the day and the night protective loops must be in the secure condition and the switch set to the night position.

In operation, a switch at the central station is set to the same position as the subscriber's day-night switch. A special relay at the central station then senses any change from the correct loop current to signal an alarm. Alarm signals are sent when the subscriber opens in the morning and closes at night. Openings and closings must therefore be in accordance with preestablished time schedules. Alarm signals at any other time are considered an intrusion at night or as circuit damage during the day. This kind of system requires a metallic pair, or at least one metallic conductor, and is seldom used any more.

8.6 TAPE DIALER

Voice dialers have been around for many years. They became popular because they do not need a metallic phone pair, nor do they require a separate phone line dedicated to alarm service. Instead, they are connected to a standard dial type phone line. This avoids the hard-to-get metallic pair and eliminates phone line charges, both initial installation and monthly, since a regular phone line is usually already available.

The dialer uses an endless loop of audio recording tape. The telephone number of the monitoring point is recorded as a series of tone pulses. This is followed by a voice message stating the nature and location of the alarm and what response is desired. When the alarm system is tripped, it in turn triggers the dialer, which starts the tape running. The tone pulses actuate the dialing sequence followed by the audible message. Often the dialer is programmed to call the police department, eliminating any monitoring charge. This, and the elimination of phone line charges, yield a comparatively cheap system.

The advantages of the tape dialer resulted in a proliferation of dialer installations. Many dialers were connected to cheap, poorly installed systems, resulting in false alarms. Also, many early machines were poorly designed and would often self-trigger. These three factors—proliferation, poor systems, and poor dialers—resulted in large numbers of false alarms that plagued police departments and tied up their emergency phone numbers. Today, many cities have ordinances regulating the installation and use of all types of alarms, and many prohibit the programming of dialers to call directly to police departments, particularly to emergency numbers. The National Fire Code prohibits dialers calling fire department emergency numbers anywhere in the United States.

Tape dialers have improved in design to the point where most of the self-tripping has been eliminated. The reliability of the alarm system is up to the installer and the installing company. Knowledgeable installers can greatly reduce false alarms by using good equipment, good installation practices, and correct application of detection devices. In the foreseeable future, alarm systems will continue to proliferate. This means we are going to have to do twice as good a job just to keep up and four times as good a job to get ahead. For the most part, tape dialers have been superseded by digital devices.

8.6.1   Servicing Tape Dialers

Although tape dialers are seldom used today, service information is included here because most of it applies equally well to digital communicators (dialers) and to other systems that use dial-up phone lines.

First, the dialer must have the correct power supplied. If batteries are used, they may need replacement. Check also for the correct triggering signal from the alarm control if a separate one is used. Sometimes the control function may be built into the dialer. The triggering can be a dry contact closure (auxiliary contact) in the control, or it can be a voltage, such as from a bell output. Some dialers will accept either, but different terminals must be used in the dialer.

Since tape transport mechanisms seldom get exercised, the tape may tend to stick. The tape can also jam or break. Generally, the best corrective action is to replace the tape with the correct type of cartridge for the dialer. Be sure to program the replacement tape. Other than a few minor adjustments that may be outlined in the service manual, this is about the extent of service that you can do.

Unless you are well-versed in electronic servicing, with an accurate schematic knowledge and the necessary test instruments and spare parts, it is generally preferable to send defective dialers back to the manufacturer for repair. By the way, this advice applies to all electronic equipment.

If the dialer seems to be working but the message is not getting through, the problem may be in the phone line. This assumes that you have checked the tape and that it is correctly programmed. One problem may be that someone else is using the phone line or that a receiver has been left off the hook. Although not essential, a telephone test set makes testing easier. These are also referred to as telephone hand sets or as "butt-ins," so named because they can be used to butt into someone's telephone conversation.

If you do suspect phone line trouble, it is wise to first disconnect the dialer. Then, check the line for normal operation (i.e., dial tone, correct dialing, disconnect) using your test set or a regular telephone. If the line still does not work, call the phone company for repairs or have the subscriber do it. If, on the other hand, the problem disappears when you disconnect the dialer, the dialer must be either repaired or replaced. Don't overlook the wire connecting the dialer to the phone line.

At one time there was a legal requirement in most areas of phone company service to use a coupler between the dialer and the phone line. This device was furnished for a sizeable initial installation charge plus a monthly rental fee. Couplers also required

18 volts DC, which is nonstandard in the alarm industry. This usually meant adding a special power supply. This legal requirement was not always followed. Today, couplers are not required, provided that the dialer has been certified for safety and phone system compatibility.

Dialers are often connected to the phone wiring at any point along the wiring. It is generally preferable to connect the dialer first, then wire to the phones. When the dialer operates, all phones are disconnected. This prevents an intruder from lifting an extension phone to block the dialer's call or from listening in on the dialer's message. Not all dialers have this feature. Dialers should be connected to the phone line using a special plug available from the phone company. This plug routes the phone line through the dialer. A telephone serviceperson working on the phone can disconnect the plug. The matching jack then completes the circuit to the phones. This provides a quick, easy method of isolating the trouble should the dialer be at fault. These are known as RJ-31 jacks.

When installing dialers in businesses or other locations having several phone lines, the first number should not be used. Instead, use the last or next-to-last number in a rotary group. A rotary group is a series of phone numbers accessed in sequence—for example, XXX-7211, -7212, -7213. At one time these had to be in numerical sequence, but this is no longer true in newer phone exchanges. If available, use an unpublished or unlisted number. These steps reduce the likelihood of an intruder's dialing an incoming call (from outside, of course) to busy the line to block the dialer. Many dialers can be programmed to provide a brief answer signal and then a 30–45 second hang-up signal before dialing their own emergency message. Although many dialers can be programmed this way, it depends on the particular phone system as to whether the dialer will, in fact, break an attempted blocking call placed by an intruder or accomplice. At any rate, always use an unlisted line or the last or next-to-last number in a rotary group.

Some private branch exchanges (PBXs) used by businesses use what is called a "ground start." This requires grounding one side of the phone line momentarily in order to start the call. If the subscriber has such service, you will have to have a compatible dialer or communicator in order to be able to call out.

8.7   DIGITAL COMMUNICATORS

Digital dialers are much like tape dialers. So much so in fact that they are now often called digital communicators to avoid associating them with the earlier tape dialers and the bad name some of the tape dialers developed.

Communicators, dialers, call them what you like—the digitals share the advantage of using standard dial phone lines. Thus, they too avoid the need for a metallic pair. They also share the same shortcoming: neither has line security. The best that can be done for either digital or tape dialers is that an accessory line-cut monitor can be added. This device can be used to enable a local bell or to switch to a second phone line if it senses that the primary phone line has been cut. Unless phone lines that enter from different directions are used, all lines could be cut or damaged simultaneously. In spite of the lack of supervision, dialers of both kinds have enjoyed considerable popularity. There are no line charges and metallic pairs are not required.

What are the differences that set digital dialers apart from tape or voice dialers? There are several important ones. Digitals are all electronic. Thus, they have eliminated the tape and the mechanical tape transport mechanism. This is an important step in improved reliability. Another difference is that digitals are programmed digitally, usually by multiple position (ten or more) slide switches or by jumpers. This includes the number to be dialed and the subscriber's account number. Multiple tripping inputs are available to signal from four to eight distinct types of alarms on some models (fire, intrusion, medical alert, etc.). This eliminates voice messages, which may be unclear or incomplete. There is the story about the tape dialer that was programmed, "Help, burglary. Help, burglary," but never identified the location. This, of course, was the fault of the installer and not of the tape dialer. Needless to say, an incompletely programmed digital dialer would have been no better. Remember that the account number identifies the location.

A digital dialer must send its message to a matching receiver at a central monitoring location. The receiver decodes the message and displays or prints out the account number and the alarm condition code for the operator. Some also display and print the time and date. The receiver also sends an acknowledgment or "handshake" signal back to the dialer when the call first comes into the station. It also tells the dialer that a correct message has been received. Correctness is determined by comparing several successive transmissions, which takes less than one second. These two features also improve reliability. First, the dialer can hang up and redial if it does not get the handshake signal within a preset time limit. Second, it can continue to transmit its digital message until a good comparison is detected and acknowledged by the receiver. If it is not acknowledged, a time limit will cause the dialer to hang up and redial. Although a tape dialer can send several messages, it has no way of knowing if it has reached the correct destination or if the message was accurately received. One step a tape dialer can take is to call several different destinations. The person monitoring a digital dialer usually takes care of notifying as many or as few destinations as are needed. Changes are easier to make as there is no need to reprogram a tape. Of course, how a digital dialer works will vary with the make and model of machine.

Virtually all the comments regarding servicing of tape dialers and their phone line connections also apply to digital dialers. The obvious exceptions are the comments applying to the tape and its transport mechanism. A telephone test set is handy, but you won't be able to decode the digital signal to see if the correct data is being transmitted. Some companies have portable decoders to serve this purpose.

In the newer alarm panels, particularly in the microprocessor-based ones, digital communication is built-in. These units often use standard computer modem technology, although some use a proprietary protocol. Most of these systems can send alarm signals that uniquely identify eight, sixteen, or more zones. Some also can report when a zone has been restored.

8.8   MULTIPLEX

Multiplex, or MUX for short, is a relatively new technology in the alarm industry that transmits digital signals that are encoded as tones. Actually, the McCulloh loop and the ring-back circuit are both forms of multiplexing as several signals could be sent over the same circuit and separately identified at the receiving location. McCulloh is an example of time-division multiplexing. It uses time pulses. Ring back is an example of analog multiplexing. It uses different current levels.

There are many forms of multiplexing but, in general, they all communicate with a large or potentially large number of users. Signals are usually sent in some form of digital code using tone pulses similar to those of a touch-tone phone. Telephone circuits dedicated exclusively to alarm service are required and must be voice-grade circuits. Because only voice frequency tones are used, there is no need for DC continuity. That is, a metallic pair is not needed. Phone companies can transmit voice-grade signals just like regular telephone calls. They can use wire, carrier, microwave, or whatever they wish. It makes no difference to the alarm MUX system. Since this is true, there is usually no difficulty in getting circuits from the phone company. This is in sharp contrast to interoffice metallic pairs, which are seldom available in many areas and are getting harder to come by in a growing number of other areas.

One type of MUX is a polling system. The receiver queries or canvasses each subscriber in turn. Each subscriber's unit then responds with its status, such as secure, intrusion (by zone), or fire. Several hundred subscribers can be polled in a few seconds. Complex digital coding can be used to provide very high security.

MUX systems are more complex than the other types of alarm transmission. There are also several different kinds of systems. Because of the cost, their use is generally limited to high-security accounts or to areas where metallic pairs for McCulloh, polarity reversal, or ring-back circuits are just not available and where dialers are not acceptable. If you are involved in servicing MUX systems, study the manufacturer's literature and manuals very carefully. Attend a manufacturer's training seminar on the equipment if possible. Also, make sure you have, and know how to correctly use, any special test equipment. As with most electronic alarm equipment, servicing will generally be limited to replacing defective equipment. Even to do this intelligently, you will have to know how it is supposed to work, how it is to be connected, what power is required, what adjustments you can make, and how to make them.

8.9   WIRELESS TRANSMISSION

Another alternative to metallic pairs is to use wireless or radio transmission. This equipment has an approximate range of 5 to 15 miles (about 8 to 25 kilometers), although greater range can be achieved. For short ranges, the antenna can be mounted directly on top of the transmitter box. For increased range, it may be necessary to extend this antenna to a higher location. This kind of signal transmission should not be confused with the on-premises wireless, which has a range of 100 to 300 feet (about 30 to 90 meters).

A wireless system has a radio transmitter connected to an antenna via coaxial (RF) connectors and a coaxial antenna lead-in. I mention this since alarm people generally do not work with coaxial cable. An alternative is to use cable already made up with connectors in predetermined lengths. An RF power meter and a voltage standing wave ratio (VSWR) meter will be useful for testing transmitter RF output and adequacy of the antenna and its lead-in. These instruments must cover the frequency band at which your radio operates. You will also have to develop a feel for the radio's transmission path. The signal can be blocked by tall buildings, hills, etc. On the other hand, they can bounce off of hills and large buildings, which could help you get around another obstruction.

Sometimes extra antenna height can help to get the signal through. Moving the antenna a short distance may be all that is required. Another alternative is to try locating the antenna in the attic or on a higher floor of the building. For security reasons, it is preferable to locate the antenna inside the protected premises if possible. If all else fails, it may be necessary to locate the antenna on a roof or on a mast. When locating an antenna, remember that radio waves will normally penetrate wood, glass, and drywall, but they will be shielded (reflected) by metal such as metal roofing, siding, or metallic "wallpaper." For wireless systems, study and follow the manufacturer's instructions carefully.

The system just described is a one-way system. A newer system uses two-way transmission with a transceiver at the protected premises. This system uses a polling technique similar to the wired type multiplex systems. It offers more security than the one-way system.

8.10 LOCAL BELLS

Although the purpose of any silent alarm is to summon appropriate guard or law enforcement response to a detected intrusion, the purpose of a local bell system is to scare the intruder away. When conducting surreptitious activities, that is, breaking in without being seen or heard, a sudden loud noise is very unnerving. In one of my own residential installations, the homeowner called to report finding a pillowcase full of valuables that had been dropped when the burglar stepped on a mat switch. Directly over that mat switch, concealed behind a cold-air return grill, was the inside bell. I wish I could have been there to see the burglar's expression!

Originally, local bells consisted of just that—one or more loud bells, typically 10 inches in diameter. Sometimes a motor-driven siren was used. Since these were typically powered by 120 volts, no back-up power was available. Electronic sirens became popular as these operated from the 6- or 12-volt alarm battery. They consisted of a siren driver module and a suitable horn type speaker. Some of these imitated a conventional siren, although many produced a raucous, warbling sound. The general goal is a loud, attention-getting noise.

Whatever type of sounding device is used—bell, siren, or electronic device—the item is usually mounted high on an outside wall, typically 10 to 12 feet (about 3 to 4 meters) but not over 4 stories high. The device should be located where it will be visible (and audible) from the street. As I mentioned before, interior sounding devices can also be used in addition to exterior ones. When choosing sounding device types and quantities, remember to stay within the power limits of the control or driver device. Don't overload the standby battery either. More is not necessarily better if you overload things.

A bell is typically mounted in a bell box to protect it from tampering and from the weather. A cheap box has a single lid and a few louvers for the sound to get out, with no extra tamper protection. A better box has a tamper switch that will trigger the alarm if the lid is removed. A step better is to provide an inner lid to physically protect the bell from tampering even if the outer lid is opened. Tamper switches detect opening of the outer lid and also detect attempted removal of the box from the wall. A class A bell box consists of a double box with tamper switches. The inner box is electrically insulated from the outer box. The two boxes are connected to a double closed loop or E-O-L resistor loop. Attempting to drill or cut through the outer box would short the two boxes together via the drill bit or saw blade, thus sounding an alarm. Tamper switches are also used to detect removal of the bolts or screws that secure the outer lid. The class A box is typically used only for high-security applications because of cost and size. By comparison, typical siren boxes are often cheap affairs and may not even have provision for tamper switches.

An alternative to using a bell or siren box is to conceal the bell, siren, or siren speaker behind an attic louver. Since the device's presence is concealed, there is little probability of tampering, and no box is needed. The louver itself will also provide protection. This technique is more applicable in residential installations and is generally not acceptable in commercial ones.

Whatever type of sounding device is used, it is important to protect the wiring to those devices. If an intruder can get to the wiring, even during business hours, and cut the wires, then the alarm system can be disabled. Wiring should be run inside walls or through conduits. Wires should enter the bell box from behind, directly through the wall it is mounted on. Since sounding devices draw a relatively high current, heavy wires must be used to avoid excessive voltage drop. For a single bell, 18 gauge wire is suitable for up to about 75 feet (23 meters) and 16 gauge wire up to about 150 feet (46 meters). Each bell should have its own wire run from the control location. If you wish to calculate your own voltage drops, remember that for a bell with an average current of .5 amps, the peak current will be about four times that amount and is the value that should be used.

As an additional attention-getting device, a flashing strobe light is sometimes used, along with a bell or siren. These are often mounted on the front of the bell box. The wires must come through the inner cover of the bell box. This permits easy access to the wires by opening only the outer cover and permits disabling the bell circuit by shorting the wires. For this reason, I prefer to run a separate wire to the strobe, with an in-line fuse in the control box that is just heavy enough to carry the strobe. A short then blows the fuse rather than disabling the bell circuit. Strobes usually run on 12 volts DC. If you are using a siren (with the driver module in the control), you will have to run separate wires for the siren and for the strobe anyway. Also, do not overload the total output of the control.

9 Batteries and Power Supplies

Virtually all alarm systems today require electric power to operate. The main operating power is usually supplied from 120-volt house power that is stepped down by a transformer to typically 6 or 12 volts and converted to DC by a rectifier inside the power supply. To take over during a power failure, batteries must be provided. In this chapter we will look at both sources of electric power.

9.1 BATTERIES

Batteries are an essential part of just about every alarm system. In many early systems, dry cell batteries provided the only source of power. An E-O-L battery of one to four cells (1.5-6 volts) was used to operate the sensitive relay via the protective loop. In the control panel another battery (usually 6-volt) was used to drive the bell or McCulloh transmitter. Some systems later used one battery for both purposes, but this required running the protective loop back to the control. Later systems used 120-volt power to the control box. A transformer inside was then used to step the voltage down. Dry cells were used for back-up operation. The 120-volt portion of the wiring had to be handled per the National Electrical Code (NEC), at least in the United States.

Today most alarm equipment operates from low-voltage, energy-limiting transformers. These are usually referred to as Class 2 transformers per article 725 of the NEC. The advantage is that Class 2 wiring carries very few restrictions as to wire size, insulation material, or thickness, and fuses or circuit breakers are generally not required. (Note: fuses or circuit breakers may still be used and, in fact, may be desirable for alarm system integrity.) For example, the remote control status indicators can be fused at the control box. A short will blow the fuse. The indicators will be out of service, but the rest of the system will continue to function. In the United States, Class 2 transformers are usually equipped with prongs to plug directly into a standard 120-volt wall outlet. A screw through the tab on the transformer should be used to replace the screw holding the outlet cover plate in place. This will prevent the transformer from being accidentally unplugged, and it will hold the outlet cover plate in place. Always select an outlet that is not controlled by a wall switch or timer.

House power that is 120 volts should be backed up by some sort of battery. Dry cells are the cheapest initially but must be replaced often. This causes expensive service calls. Most of today's systems use rechargeable batteries.

155

Maintenance of batteries generally means periodic replacement. Even rechargeable batteries have a limited life. There are a great number of factors that affect battery life expectancy. A few of these are listed here:

1. Operating temperature
2. Temperature cycling
3. Charge-rest-discharge cycling
4. Rate of charging
5. Rate of discharging
6. Physical abuse
7. Deep discharging
8. Excessive overcharging
9. Shelf life
10. Cutoff voltage of powered equipment
11. Contamination of electrolyte
12. Memory effect
13. Loss of electrolyte due to venting or leakage
14. Thermal runaway
15. Cleanliness

To make matters worse, many of these factors interact with each other in complex ways. This makes it difficult to predict life expectancy with any accuracy because we don't know in advance what each of the above factors will be. As a rule, sealed type lead-acid batteries might last three to four years; sealed Ni-Cads might last four to five years; and dry cells perhaps one year. Under ideal conditions, any of these might last longer. Under adverse conditions, they might last much less time. Since dry cells are not rechargeable, they could be depleted the same day they were installed if a long power outage occurred that day. On local bell-only systems, no indication is given of dead back-up batteries. When power is restored the system would resume operation, but the batteries would probably never get replaced until the annual inspection (if any) a year later. In the meantime, the system would be nonfunctional during commercial power outages. At least rechargeable batteries get recharged after power is restored. A bell test position on the control switch (if it has a test position) would reveal a dead battery, but only if it switched the charger or power supply out of the circuit and tested the battery by itself.

The lithium battery is a relatively new item. It has a high output, approximately 3 volts per cell and has an extremely low self-discharge rate. Shelf life is therefore ten to fifteen years, far more than any other commonly used kind of battery. Unfortunately, it is not rechargeable. At least one manufacturer has designed a passive infrared detector that is powered only by a lithium battery. Thus no external power is required, which is an installation convenience. Through careful circuit design, the current draw of the unit is extremely low. This, and the long shelf life of the lithium battery, enable the manufacturer to guarantee this detector and battery for ten years. This guarantee takes into account the frequent alarm conditions that would be encountered during business hours. The walk test light must be turned on manually for testing but will automatically turn itself off after a few minutes to prevent needless battery drain. That's a good security feature, too; it prevents a would-be intruder from determining the extent of detector coverage during business hours.

9.1.1   Battery Testing

Determining when to replace batteries is an inexact science because there is no 100 percent reliable test method and also because battery serviceability is dependent on the load it must power. For example, a nearly dead battery might still provide enough power to operate a transmitter. The same battery in the same condition but in a different system might be inadequate to ring a bell or two. By "dead" I mean the loss of ability to deliver power either due to the state of discharge or due to loss of ability to store charge (generally due to aging).

Testing dry cells with a voltmeter is useless. Even a nearly dead cell or battery will show almost full voltage without any load applied. A high-current ammeter such as 0–35 or 0–50 amps can be used. This places a dead short across the battery and will drain it very quickly. If you use this method, take a quick reading and get off. I cannot tell you what reading indicates a good battery or a bad one. Different readings will be obtained from the same battery using different types of meters. Conversely, the same meter will give different readings from different types and sizes of dry cell batteries even though all batteries may be in equally good condition. These two facts are true due to the design of the meter, particularly to its sensitivity, its range, and its internal resistance. Even the test lead resistance is important. Short, heavy test leads should be used.

If you always use the same meter and test leads, you can develop experience for each type of battery you use. Test a number of new batteries or cells and note the typical readings. Discard batteries having readings that are significantly below the others. You may have defective new cells or batteries, which is not unusual. I have had several alarm companies tell me they make it a standard practice to test all dry cells immediately upon receipt. Also, test a number of batteries or cells that have been in service for various, known lengths of time in different kinds of equipment. Compare the results to new readings. Develop a feel for what is good and what should be replaced. Test for a few seconds (three to five) and pay particular attention to how fast the meter drops. A good battery should hold a fairly steady reading. A bad one will drop. This method is not perfect, but with some experience, it will provide a reasonable guide. A word of caution: never use an ammeter to check rechargeable batteries. Rechargeable batteries can deliver much higher amperages than dry cells, perhaps 100 amps or more. This could burn out the meter, damage the battery, or burn your fingers. The test leads will get hot very quickly.

The technique of using a voltmeter with a load can be used to test any kind of battery. Rechargeable batteries must be tested with the charger disconnected. The reason for this is to test the battery, not the charger. This method of testing measures the voltage while placing a load across the battery. In order to standardize things, I suggest a load of ten amps. This would be roughly equivalent to the load drawn by a microprocessor-based control, several system type keypad stations with displays, an assortment of motion detectors, and two bells ringing plus a safety factor. Although ten amps is somewhat arbitrary, it is a reasonably realistic measure. It won't seriously deplete a battery during a short test, yet it will provide reasonable results.

As with the ammeter test previously described, you will have to develop your own experience factor for each type and size of cell or battery. With this method, the test should be conducted for a time period such as one minute. You should see a relatively constant voltage reading for rechargeable batteries. If the voltage drops rapidly, the battery probably needs replacing. Note that batteries should not be checked immediately following a power outage. Such a battery could check defective because it did not have a chance to recharge. Figure 9–1 shows a diagram of a simple battery tester you can build.

The preceding methods are only quick checks of a battery's condition. To more thoroughly test a rechargeable battery requires a timed discharge. This requires a constant current (not constant resistance load) discharge. Then the time that it takes for the terminal voltage to reach some predetermined endpoint voltage must be measured. The discharge current in amps is usually set equal to the battery capacity in ampere hours. Although it can be done, such a test is time-consuming, requires special equipment, and is seldom used in alarm work.

9.1.2   Battery Replacement

Each battery must be replaced with its own kind. The new battery must be the kind (dry cell, Ni-Cad, or lead-acid) that matches the charger in the system. There is always the chance that somebody previously installed the wrong kind. The reason for this is

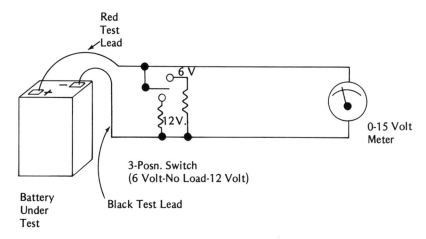

Figure 9–1   Battery tester with 10-amp load. For 12-volt load use eight 10-ohm 20-watt resistors in parallel. For 6-volt load use five 3-ohm 12-watt resistors in parallel.

that a dry cell accepts no charging. Trying to charge one can result in destruction of the battery, leakage of chemicals, and possible explosion. Nickel-cadmium batteries usually use constant current charging, while lead-acid batteries use constant voltage charging. Substituting the wrong kind of battery can easily result in undercharging or overcharging. Undercharging means inadequate power for standby use. Overcharging means destruction of plate grids inside and loss of water due to venting of the excess gases generated. Either will result in short battery life. Remember to connect batteries with the correct polarity.

Of course, batteries must be replaced with those of the correct voltage. Most batteries for alarm use are either 6 or 12 volts. Some systems, particularly fire alarms, may use 24 volts. Some burglar alarms may use one or two 1½-volt dry cells for end-of-line battery service, although this type of system is fast disappearing. When dry cells are used, either one 6-volt battery or four 1½-volt dry cells can be used to power 6-volt systems. Twelve-volt systems are usually powered by one 12-volt battery, although eight separate cells could be connected in series to do the job, as could two 6-volt batteries.

The rated voltages are nominal. A fresh dry cell will have an open circuit terminal voltage slightly higher than rated. A partially used or aged battery will be slightly below rated voltage. A freshly charged rechargeable battery will be slightly over the nominal (rated) voltage. A battery that is being charged will have an even higher voltage. In most alarm systems, the batteries are constantly being charged. In fact, lead-acid batteries should have their voltage checked periodically to see if the charger is working properly. A digital voltmeter is required to get accurate enough readings. As an alternative, you can build the battery float charge voltmeter described in Chapter 2 of this book. A table of correct float voltages is included in Figure 2–17. If you can't remember them, write them on a small piece of paper and tape them to your meter. Again, do not test a battery just after a power outage. They may need up to sixteen hours to fully recharge. As with dry cells, rechargeable battery voltage will be lower for partially discharged cells when measured without any charger or any load connected. Rechargeable batteries will generally have a steadier voltage with use than will dry cells. By the way, any battery will partially discharge when not in use, even when sitting on the shelf. For this reason dry cells should be used promptly. Rechargeable batteries must be allowed to charge fully when first installed, prior to testing.

When replacing Ni-Cad batteries, it is important to consider size (capacity). Due to the constant current charging, a Ni-Cad battery should also be replaced with the same size. In some equipment, the physical space available may limit you to the same size of replacement. At other times, you may have a choice. If so, use the same size, or at least a battery having a capacity of from ⅔ to 1½ times the original. You can deviate more than this if indicated by the equipment or battery charger manufacturer. The reason for this restriction relates to the constant current charging capability of the charger.

Since a lead-acid battery uses constant voltage charging, any sealed, lead-acid battery of practical size can be used. Capacities typically used for alarm work range from about ½ to 5 ampere-hours.

I would recommend against using a car battery. You might be able to do so if you use a sealed type and test to see that the alarm charger can properly charge the battery. That is, can it maintain the correct float voltage? If not, the battery will be undercharged and its large capacity will be unavailable. Allow several days to charge up before testing. Normally you will not need this much standby battery capacity.

Dry cell batteries use no charger, so any size battery can be used. A battery of adequate capacity should be used. A larger battery will provide longer standby operating time. Substituting one that is too small could provide insufficient operating time. For dry cell batteries in alarm work, always buy quality batteries from a reliable source. Cheap batteries are often cheaply made and don't last. Also, buy from a dealer that has a rapid turnover of stock. You don't want to buy dry cell batteries that have sat on a distributor's shelf for a year.

9.1.3   Power Requirement Considerations

Batteries or cells can be located in bell boxes in the Arizona sunshine or exposed to Montana blizzards. Both of these temperature extremes will adversely affect them. High temperatures lead to faster self-discharge rates for all batteries and to overcharge of rechargeables. Low temperatures decrease the available power for all batteries and for undercharging rechargeables. Lead-acid batteries can also be damaged by freezing when discharged. It is preferable to locate batteries of any kind inside where they will be protected from temperature extremes. The practice of installing a control module and batteries in the bell box is to be discouraged. If it is necessary to locate batteries where they will be exposed to temperature extremes, that is, over 104°F (40°C) or below 0°F (−20°C), it may be wise to seek help from the equipment manufacturer concerning batteries and charging equipment.

Batteries are added to most alarm systems both to prevent false alarms and to provide continued protection in cases of AC power failure. (A few systems are battery only.) Yet little consideration is given to how long the system will operate from the batteries. Some systems will last only a few hours. The manufacturer or the installing company can still say, "Oh, yes, our system has standby batteries!" From an installing company's point of view, bigger batteries cost more money, so why put them in? Also bear in mind that some control units today have power supplies only large enough to run the system during nonalarm conditions. They depend on the battery to ring bells or power electronic sirens and strobe lights during alarms.

9.1.4   Power Requirements

There are two sides to the question of how big is big enough for a battery. On the one side is the system's power requirements. On the other side is the question, How long is long enough? for standby operation.

System power requirements vary widely. Active motion detection systems (microwave and ultrasonics) take considerable amounts of power. The more detectors used, the greater the power requirements. Status indicators (LEDs) are also power gobblers. Systems with lots of remote control stations with indicators use lots of power. Those with incandescent bulbs instead of LEDs take even more. Liquid crystal displays (LCDs) take very little power. That's why watch displays use LCDs. On the other hand, simple relay-operated systems without motion sensors or status indicator lights take very little power in a secure condition. Such systems can and often do operate from batteries only. Simple solid-state control modules can operate on extremely tiny currents. Here, current drain on the batteries is so low that they will last essentially for their shelf life.

Although Ni-Cad and lead-acid batteries can be recharged, they will run down even on the shelf. That is why they are constantly being charged when used in most alarm service. Consideration must also be given to maximum power requirements. A battery that is nearly dead or discharged may be able to operate a system but be unable to run a transmitter or to ring one or more bells if an intrusion should occur. Such a system would fail to do its job.

There are several ways to determine how much standby battery time is enough. The minimum time to plan for is that which is required to keep the system operating through a typical power failure. The difficult part is to determine how long a typical power failure lasts. In metropolitan areas, this might be a few hours. In smaller communities or rural areas, it could last many hours. Two other possibilities exist. The first is that an unusual power failure could last several days. The other is that a potential intruder could turn off the power and wait for the batteries to run down. Many alarm systems will transmit an alarm or trouble signal when the batteries run down. As long as there is enough energy left to transmit a silent alarm (on silent systems), the potential intruder will be turning in the alarm. The alarm company response will bring a serviceperson who can get the power restored and replace the batteries with fully charged ones, if necessary.

The problem of a prolonged power outage (and that of intentionally turned-off power) can be answered by the use of larger batteries. This, of course, costs more money, but doubling the battery size costs less than double the price of the smaller battery. The cost of batteries must be balanced against the cost of service calls. For example, suppose your alarm company has several hundred silent systems, and there is a rather long power outage in your service area. What will be the cost of responding to, and of servicing, a large number of alarms as the batteries run down? How will this large number of calls be handled?

In addition to the capacity of a battery when new, consideration must also be given to aged batteries. New batteries usually can store the amount of energy as rated by the manufacturer. This is usually stated in ampere-hours at a specific rate, such as the 20-hour rate. For example, a battery rated at 1 ampere-hour at the 20-hour rate could power a load of $\frac{1}{20}$ amp (50 mA) for 20 hours. That same battery could not deliver 1 amp for 1 hour even though they both come out to 1 ampere-hour. As batteries grow old they lose the capacity to store and deliver their energy. If not replaced soon enough, they will have lost over half of their storage ability. When the power fails, batteries may last minutes instead of the hours they had when new. Batteries gradually lose their storage capacity while on float charge too. This is true even if the battery is called on very seldom to deliver energy during power outages. In addition to this slow aging, batteries will age faster the more they are called upon to power the system during outages, that is, the more discharge-recharge cycles they go through. For example, if we had an eight-hour outage every day, the batteries would age fast. This could very well happen if the alarm system (or part of it) were connected to a wall outlet that was controlled by a switch or timer and was turned off for part of each day.

Early alarm systems had an E-O-L battery and a bell battery. Later, one battery served both purposes. Today's motion and other detectors also require power, including standby power. Some of this equipment has built-in batteries. Many others have provision for built-in batteries but leave it up to the installing company as to whether to use separate batteries in each unit or to use one common battery for the entire system. Let's look at each method.

Individual batteries have a certain convenience. Equipment can be bought with batteries in place. The correct charger is built in. On the other hand, each unit requires its own transformer and wiring and eventual battery replacement.

The other method is to locate one battery, usually in the control, and power all equipment from it. The advantages are that only one battery is needed (one large battery is less costly than several smaller ones) and only one Class 2 transformer is required. One disadvantage is that DC power must be run to each user device. This is not as bad as it sounds, since two extra conductors can be run with the protective loop wiring that has to be run anyhow. Another disadvantage is that all user devices must operate on the same voltage. This may require alternate equipment types or brands so all units in the system will operate from the same voltage. Note that center-tapping a 12-volt battery to get 6-volt power is generally not a good idea. The extra load on the one side of the battery will unbalance it and leave it undercharged. If wire runs are long, there could be excessive voltage loss to other equipment.

9.2   POWER SUPPLIES

The main portion of this chapter has been devoted to batteries because of their importance and complexity. The AC power source deserves some attention, too. Most alarm systems and equipment used in the United States today are powered by low-voltage, Class 2, plug-in transformers. Both the voltage and the volt-amp rating are important. Typical voltages for alarm work are 6, 12, 16, and 24 volts. Sometimes the secondary voltage rating of the transformer will be higher than the battery voltage. For example, a 16- or 24-volt transformer is sometimes used with a 12-volt battery. Use the transformer voltage recommended by the equipment manufacturer. Using too low a voltage will result in undercharged or dead batteries and probably nonfunctioning equipment. Using too high a voltage may cause overcharging and destruction of batteries. It can also cause damage to equipment.

The volt-amp rating of the transformer must be sufficient to both power the system and recharge the battery. Again, the equipment manufacturer's recommendations should be followed. Typical volt-amp ratings are 5, 10, 20, 40, and 50 volt-amps for alarm use. If too low a rated transformer is used, the battery may be undercharged and the equipment may not work properly. A transformer with a higher than required volt-amp rating will cost slightly more than a smaller one but will work just as well.

Wire runs between transformer and equipment are usually short, typically less than 50 feet (15 meters). Twenty or 22 gauge wire is usually adequate. For long runs, it may be necessary to use heavier wire such as 18 or 16 gauge. As an alternative, use a transformer with the same voltage but with a higher volt-amp rating. These tend to have a slightly higher output voltage than smaller transformers. They also have better regulation, which means they will have less voltage drop under load.

Battery-only alarm equipment can often be converted to line-powered operation with the addition of a power pack. This is usually powered from a plug-in transformer. Some power packs provide for dry cell battery backup with automatic changeover upon power failure and power restoration. Other units provide for rechargeable battery use and include a charger circuit. The battery may be housed inside the pack or an external battery may be required, depending on the make and model of power pack. Also, different manufacturers may use their own name instead of the general term "power pack." Additionally, note that some power packs have limited capacity and are intended for such service as E-O-L power and transmitter power and are not capable of delivering high currents needed to ring a bell or power a siren.

9.3 FIRE ALARM SYSTEM BATTERIES

Commercial and industrial fire alarm systems are usually governed by more strict code requirements concerning equipment and its installation. Rather than the relatively small capacity, sealed construction batteries used in burglar alarms and residential alarms, large fire alarm systems may use large, vented batteries. These typically have a capacity of 30 ampere-hours or more and are often 24 volts. Because of their large size and vented construction, the batteries are usually housed in a box separate from the fire control. The charger is often fed from a 120-volt AC line. Legally such connection usually requires the services of a licensed electrician. Vented cell batteries also require periodic servicing, primarily the regular addition of water and possibly the application of periodic equalizing charges.

9.4 SUMMARY

Plug-in transformers, chargers, and power packs are long-lived and require little service. All batteries must be replaced periodically. Dry cell batteries must also be replaced after long bell ringing on battery-only operated systems having a local bell and after extended power outages on systems that normally rely on AC power.

As rechargeable batteries age, they lose their ability to store a charge. Eventually they must be replaced. A quick test involves a voltmeter reading with a load of about

10 amps applied. The test can be done over some brief time interval, on the order of one minute. Each serviceperson will develop a personal "experience factor" for each type of battery.

Replace batteries with the same type, that is, dry cell, Ni-Cad, or lead-acid. Do not substitute. Use the correct voltage. For Ni-Cad use the correct ampere-hour capacity.

Line power should be obtained from Class 2 transformers of the correct voltage and volt-amp ratings. Do not plug transformers into outlets controlled by wall switches or timers.

PART FOUR

Although Part Two covers circuits and simple detection devices and Part Three covers hardware, neither mentions the more sophisticated types of intrusion detection devices. These are the province of Part Four.

Each intrusion detection device has advantages and limitations. Each has problems unique to it that will cause false alarms and others that will cause failure when it should alarm. These points must be fully understood in both the application of these detection devices and in servicing them. Also note that these points are totally unrelated to the types of problems, such as opens and shorts, covered in Chapter 3.

10   Advanced Intrusion Detection Systems

The information in this section is mostly limited to things that are fixable in the field. This specifically excludes troubleshooting and repair of electronic circuitry because most alarm servicepeople are limited by one or more of the following:

1. Lack of knowledge of solid-state electronic circuitry
2. Lack of circuit schematics
3. Lack of specialized test equipment needed
4. Lack of spare parts
5. Lack of the time needed to make such repairs economical

Many of the problems resulting from the more advanced electronic type detection devices are related to how the device works and the location and environment in which it is located. Often the substitution of a new unit will not correct such a problem. This section of the book discusses these kinds of environmental problems.

10.1   PHOTOELECTRIC BEAMS

Photoelectric beams, also known as photo beams, PE beams, PEs, or just plain beams, operate on a very simple principle: a light source shines on a photo detector some distance away. An intruder, interrupting the beam path, produces an alarm. Mirrors or lenses are used to focus the beam to provide longer beam paths. They have been used for over fifty years.

Photo beams come in a wide variety of types and can be subdivided as follows:

- Visible versus invisible (IR) beam
- Steady versus pulsed beam
- Incandescent versus LED (IRED) versus laser

- Double ended versus single ended (bounce back) (Do not confuse with passive infrared, covered later)
- Combinations of the above

The earliest photo beams used visible, incandescent, steady light sources. This made it relatively easy for an intruder to spot and thus avoid the beam. Alternatively, the intruder could hold up (bypass) the beam with a flashlight by holding it in front of the receiver. The same thing could happen accidentally if sunlight or a bright light fell on the receiver. Incandescent lights also burn out, causing false alarms. They also draw relatively large currents, thus limiting standby battery-operating time in case of a power failure.

The first improvement was to place an infrared (IR) filter in front of the light source to make the beam invisible. The filament voltage was reduced to below the bulb's voltage rating to increase its life expectancy.

Another method was to use a pulsed, visible beam of light. The pulses detected by the receiver were compared to those transmitted, and any differences were detected as an alarm. Thus an intruder, attempting to defeat the system with a flashlight, turned in the alarm. Since the beam is still visible, however, it could still be spotted and avoided.

Most of today's photo beams use an infrared emitting diode (IRED), which is similar to the common LED except that its beam is invisible. Some long-range units use lasers, but they are generally limited to military use. The LED beam operates in a pulsed mode that provides longer ranges and security against flashlight defeat attempts and accidental bypass from sunlight or other light sources, which, by the way, can be direct or reflected (shiny floor, metal, glass, etc.). Most photo beams are double ended. That is, the transmitter and receiver are two separate units and are mounted at opposite ends of a room, as shown in Figure 10–1A. These units are available with maximum ranges of from 50 to 1000 feet (15 to 300 meters), depending on the make and model used. A mirror can sometimes be used to reflect the beam around a corner or to increase coverage, but not total beam length, as shown in Figure 10–1B.

Single-ended beams include both transmitter and receiver in one unit. They use a retro-reflector, similar to those used on a bicycle, to bounce back the beam to the transceiver, as shown in Figure 10–1C. They have a maximum range of from 75 to 250 feet (23 to 76 meters). They have gained in popularity because they require the installation and wiring of only one unit. The reflector can be hung or simply mounted on the wall, as reflector alignment is not critical. This can save considerable wiring.

A shortcoming of the single-ended photo beam is that a light-colored or reflective object, set close in front of the transceiver unit, either accidentally or on purpose, could reflect enough IR energy to complete the beam path, as shown in Figure 10–1D. In this case part of the protection is lost with no alarm condition to advise of the loss. Therefore, a double-ended beam provides a higher level of security than does a single-ended beam because any path obstruction will create an alarm condition. This is not to say a single-ended system is no good. Certainly all detectors have limitations and you must be aware of them in every installation. When photo beams are installed,

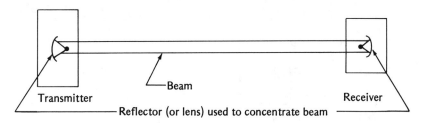

A Typical Double-ended System

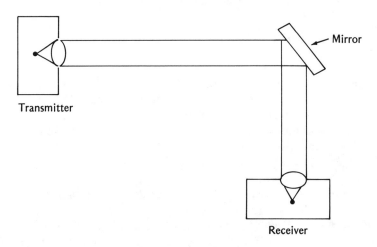

B Use of mirror to reflect beam around corner

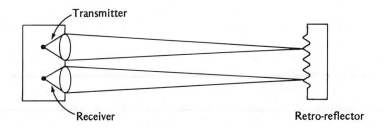

C Typical single-ended system using Retro-reflector

Figure 10–1   Photoelectric systems. (A) Typical double-ended system. (B) Use of mirror to reflect beam around corner. (C) Typical single-ended system using retro-reflector. (D) Light-colored reflective object close to PE unit causes undetected loss of protection. *Continues on next page.*

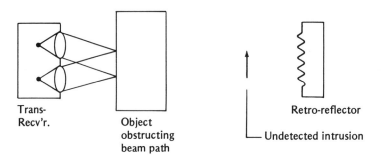

Trans-
Recv'r.

Object
obstructing
beam path

Retro-reflector

Undetected intrusion

D Light colored object close to PE unit can cause undetected
loss of protection

Figure 10–1   (continued)

the units must have a clear path and be rigidly mounted and carefully aligned. They must also be protected from bumps that might knock them out of alignment. Several manufacturers have optional guards available for this purpose. For heavy-duty protection, such as against forklift trucks in a warehouse, 4- to 6-inch (10- to 15-centimeter) steel pipe can be embedded in the ground or securely attached to the floor as a physical guard. The pipes themselves can be filled with concrete.

A common temptation with photo beams is to exceed their maximum range or to use too many mirrors. The former problem often results from an attempt to save money by using a cheaper, short-range unit or to use only one when two units are necessary to cover the distance. Mirrors can be used, but bear in mind that each mirror will make alignment more difficult and more critical. Each mirror will also reduce the maximum beam path by 20 to 50 percent. Use a 25 percent loss per mirror as a starting point. If a mirror is required, use no more than one. Mirrors must be given the same secure mounting and physical protection as the transmitter and the receiver. The mirrors, as well as all optical parts, must be kept clear of dust, dirt, and moisture condensation. Because of the added problems, the trend today is away from the use of mirrors.

Photo beam units are usually mounted on a wall or other rigid surface. Some smaller units, both single and double ended, are available for flush mounting, i.e., inside a wall. These provide a clean appearance and are relatively well protected from physical bumps. Some are disguised to look like regular duplex wall outlets.

An unusual mirror application is to mount the mirror on a door, thus triggering an alarm when the door is opened. This could provide coverage of a single door, say, at the back end of a warehouse, without the need to run a wire a long distance to pick up a magnetic contact. There are two precautions, however: (1) the door must be very solid and firmly latched, without play, or false alarms are sure to result; and (2) do not forfeit beam placement for best detection just to be able to aim at a door. The beam will be of little value if located where an intruder is unlikely to go.

Another unusual but legitimate application of a photo beam is as a wireless transmission path for an alarm signal. Suppose you have two buildings to be protected that are several hundred feet apart. Suppose also that no line is available between buildings and that it would be difficult and expensive to put in a secure line. The alternative is to locate the photo beam transmitter at the remote building, aimed at the main building. Adequate weather protection and a clear line of sight are, of course, required. The alarm control at the remote building is arranged to turn off power to the PE transmitter when an alarm occurs. When this happens, the PE receiver at the main building will go into alarm. The photo beam can be mounted high enough to avoid false alarms if the outside area is unsecured, or it can be mounted at the correct height to detect intruders if the outside area between buildings is to be secured. The latter idea might be a better substitute for the mirror-on-the-door technique mentioned earlier. Figure 10–2 shows how the system is arranged. Some photo beam manufacturers provide a unit in which their photo beam transmitter incorporates provision for a protective loop, thus eliminating the need for a separate control instrument at the remote location. Suitable power and a standby battery are required at the remote (transmitting) end.

Any photoelectric beam that is mounted outside requires several considerations. For example, in cold climates it may be necessary to use thermostatically controlled heaters to prevent condensation or frost on optical parts. Standby batteries should be maintained preferably no lower than 40°F (5°C) for reliable operation and recharging. Lower temperatures are possible but reduced capacity will result and cells may vent during recharge.

Adequate protection from weather and mechanical protection of alignment are obvious requirements. Care must also be used to avoid sunlight or other bright light sources falling on the receiver. Swapping transmitter and receiver locations and using

Diagram for Photoelectric beam

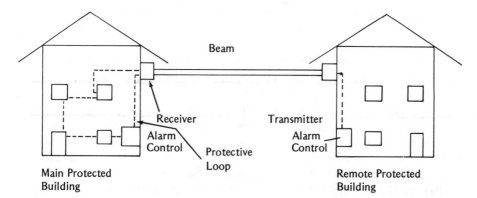

Figure 10–2   Use of photoelectric unit to transmit alarm signal between buildings without wiring.

light shields will usually solve stray light problems. Other things to be avoided include animals, birds, and wind-blown leaves, debris, and tree branches. Untrimmed weeds or shrubs can also cause problems.

Photo beams are usually well-behaved detection devices; they are relatively easy to apply and are relatively free from false alarm. Their detection, however, is along a straight line, as opposed to a volumetric type detector.

False alarms can stem from either beam interruption or bright, steady lights. The latter assumes the use of a pulsed beam type. Beam interruptions can result from cartons or other stock stacked in the beam path, vehicles parked in the beam path, falling cartons, animals, insects, birds, a burned-out bulb, a unit bumped out of optical alignment, or dirty or wet optical surfaces. Sunlight or other bright light, either falling directly on the receiver or reflected from a shiny surface, will false alarm a pulsed type beam.

On the good side, photo beams are rarely, if ever, set off by air turbulence; moving objects, fans, or machinery outside the beam path; hail or rain; two-way radios; bells, sirens, whistles, or other noises; fluorescent lights, and a host of other things that typically cause problems with motion type detectors.

The only likelihood of a failure to alarm is that already mentioned, namely, a reflective object placed close in front of a single-ended beam. Vigilance on the part of the user can reduce this shortcoming. On the older steady (nonpulsed) beam, a steady bright light could hold up the beam. If you suspect this, walk test all parts of the beam when suspected lights are on or when the sun is at a suspect angle. Also, looking towards the transmitter with the eye just in front of the receiver should help spot bright lights or glare that would provide a multiple light path to the receiver.

10.2 PASSIVE INFRARED DETECTORS

As the name implies, the passive infrared (IR) detector is a passive device. Unlike photo beams, ultrasonics, and microwaves, they do not transmit any energy. They simply look for changes in IR energy, which is heat energy. All objects at a temperature greater than absolute zero, which is minus 457°F (-273°C), radiate energy in proportion to their temperature. For example, a person whose body temperature is 98.6°F (37°C) radiates more energy than a wall at 68°F (20°C). Thus when an intruder passes through a protected area the difference in thermal (IR) energy is detected.

The question arises: what if the wall is 98.6°F (37°C)? To a certain extent, the detector's sensitivity is reduced as the background (wall) temperature nears body temperature, so the detection range will be reduced. In practice, not every part of the background will be at the same temperature. Also, note that while body temperature is 98.6°F, the outer temperature varies due to clothing. These reasons are why detection is still reliable even if the ambient temperature is 98.6°F.

Passive IR, or simply PIR, detectors are available with a variety of detection patterns. One is the wide-angle pattern, which typically covers 75° to 80° and a range of 25 feet (7.6 meters) to 40 feet (12 meters). When located in a corner, it can cover most of the room while avoiding potential false alarms caused by heat sources along the two adjacent walls. As shown in Figure 10–3A, the detection pattern actually consists of a number of sensitive, angular beams, shown shaded, which are separated by inactive areas. An intruder is detected when crossing a boundary between an active area and an inactive area, moving in either direction. Best detection occurs when an intruder crosses the beam pattern. Poorest detection occurs along the beam. Some detectors use multilevel beam patterns, with different patterns on different levels. With the detector aimed slightly downward, an intruder walking along a beam would cross from an upper to a lower pattern or vice versa. Thus not all detection capability would be lost in that direction of travel.

Another detection pattern is a long-range one consisting of a long, narrow beam. Some units use two beams that are balanced to provide better immunity to false alarms, as shown in Figure 10–3B. These are used typically in halls or aisles and are sometimes used in place of photo beams. Ranges vary from 100 to 1000 feet (30 to 300 meters). The longer range units are used by governmental agencies and may not be generally available. A similar unit has twin beam patterns at right angles to each other. This pattern can be used to cover right angle walls, hallways or aisles.

Passive IR detectors are available as both stand-alone units and as master-slave systems. The latter can accommodate up to eight detectors and are generally more economical than several stand-alone units where large area or multiple area coverage is required. Most master-slave systems can accommodate a mixture of wide-angle and long-range detectors. Both stand-alone and master-slave units are available for both surface mounting and for flush (recessed) mounting. Unlike stand-alone ultrasonic units, IR units will not false alarm each other even if two or more cover the same area. This is because IR units are passive detectors.

10.2.1   Failure to Alarm

The most important thing to remember when applying passive IR detectors is that the detection pattern is unsupervised. Any obstruction will block out the detection since the IR energy does not penetrate any building materials, and there will be no alarm or other indication of this loss of coverage. Detection units occasionally get knocked out of alignment too. Again, loss of coverage may go unnoticed. As with ultrasonic and microwave detectors, the only solution is for the subscriber to walk test the area regularly.

When the long-range, narrow-beam passive IR detectors that use a double beam are used, it is essential that the unit be mounted so that the two beams are side by side. If it is mounted incorrectly (with one beam on top of the other), an intruder would intercept both beams at once. This could result in a failure to detect an intrusion.

10.2.2   False Alarms

Passive IR detectors respond to heat or, more properly, changes in temperature. Anything that changes temperature rapidly is a potential false alarm cause. Typical examples

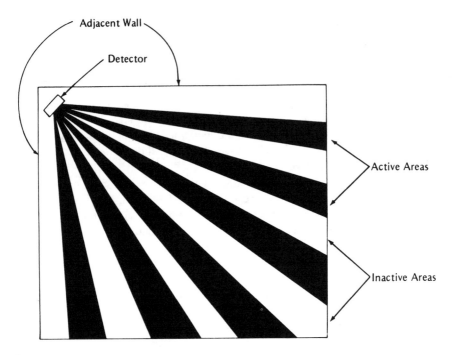

A. Wide angle pattern of coverage, seen from above

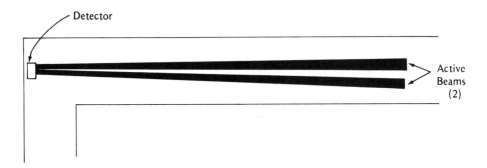

B. Long range pattern

Figure 10–3   Passive infrared coverage patterns (as seen from above). (A) Wide-angle pattern. (B) Long-range pattern.

are lights and certain types of heaters, such as open element electric heaters. Most radiators and other heaters warm up slowly enough so that they will not be detected. Lights installed after the alarm system has been put in can also cause problems. Suspect this problem if troubles occur after the alarm system has been working satisfactorily for some time.

The wide-angle type IR detectors can often be realigned so that a light or other offending source falls within a blind segment. If this is not practical or if there are two or more offending sources that can not be accommodated, then an alternative is to either relocate the offending source or sources or to shield them from the detector's view. Nearly any material will do as a shield. Examples are wood, cardboard, paper, foil, any masonry, sheet metal, and dry wall. If shielding is used, keep the following in mind: Don't create blind areas any larger than necessary where an intruder could move about undetected. Don't place combustible materials so near a heat source as to cause a fire hazard. Do not place any material in such a way as to interfere with normal operation of heaters or other devices. Do not use expanded metal or other material with holes in it as a shield. Whatever corrective action is taken, it is wise to make sure the subscriber understands the need for and the method of the correction and so won't undo your efforts later.

Another method is to mask a part of the detector's coverage. This is done by covering one or a few segments of the detector's segmented lens or mirror with opaque or nonreflecting tape. Some manufacturers furnish precut self-adhesive segments to fit the various lens or mirror segments. Determination of where to place the segments is done by placing a visible LED at the detector location. By looking at the detector from the location of the offending source, you can see in which segment the LED is visible, then mask it. Obviously, you wouldn't cover too many segments or much of the detector's coverage would be lost.

Another potential source of false alarms is animals. Dogs and cats can cause problems depending on their relative size and distance from the detector. Mice and birds are unlikely to cause problems unless they pass within a few feet of the detector. The best bet is to keep birds and larger animals out of the protected area. The long-range, narrow-beam type IR detector can often be mounted and aimed to avoid animals at floor level. The wide-angle type detectors usually have protection beams that point downward to provide detection close in front of the detector to prevent approach and tampering. With these types of IR detectors it may be difficult or impossible to aim the unit high enough to avoid animals at floor level while still maintaining good intruder detection capability.

Normally passive IR detectors are relatively easy to apply and are well behaved. They will not usually be affected by wind, rain, two-way radios, air turbulence, moving signs, and other causes that may trigger ultrasonics or microwaves. Also, bear in mind that passive IR units have the best sensitivity when the intruder moves across the detection beam pattern and the lowest sensitivity for motion toward or away from the detector. This is just the opposite for ultrasonic and microwave units.

10.3   ULTRASONIC MOTION DETECTORS

An ultrasonic motion detector is an active, volumetric type device. It sends out an ultrasonic sound, from one or more transmitters, which fills the volume (room or portion of a room) to be protected. The sound frequency is too high for most people to hear, but dogs and other animals may be disturbed. When an intruder moves through this space, the motion creates a shift in frequency of the transmitted sound energy, known as a Doppler shift. These shifted frequencies are picked up by one or more receivers and are detected as an intrusion.

When the ultrasonic Doppler idea was first used as an intrusion detection device, there were tremendously high incidences of false alarms due to a wide variety of then unknown causes. In addition, there was a race to advertise greater coverage than the competition. This led to overdriving the transmitters. This, in turn, led to transmitter failures and opened the door to undetected attacks by burglars.

These problems nearly spelled the end of ultrasonics as an intrusion detecting device. The problem areas, however, were gradually identified. As word spread, the alarm companies could spot and avoid some of these problems. Improvements were also made in the equipment. One of the earlier attempts was a circuit that automatically reduced sensitivity in response to small disturbances to reduce false alarms. This often resulted in systems putting themselves to sleep and thus being unable to detect an intrusion. Reputable manufacturers no longer use this technique for obvious reasons. Many more recent improvements have greatly reduced the ultrasonic's tendency to false alarm while still maintaining a reasonable detection capability. There are still problem areas that have to be understood and either avoided or corrected for reliable operation. These will be examined later after looking at ultrasonic equipment.

Ultrasonic equipment can be divided into three categories: (1) self-contained single units, often referred to as minisonics; (2) master-slave; and (3) multiple head.

The self-contained unit is the smallest and least expensive. It provides an elliptical coverage pattern typically about 25 feet (7.6 meters) long and about half as wide at the widest point. Aiming the pattern of coverage usually requires mounting the entire unit on a swivel bracket. With their limited coverage, these units are typically used to protect one small room or a high-value area in a larger room.

If necessary, two or more units can be used, but the master-slave type system is usually more economical, at least by the time three or more miniunits are required. If two or more self-contained units are to be used in the same area, they must be crystal controlled so that they all operate at exactly the same frequency. If not, they will most likely false alarm each other because of slight differences in frequencies. Even ultrasound going through an open doorway to a unit in a room or two away can cause this problem.

The master-slave system consists of a master unit that contains a pair of transducers (a transmitter and a receiver), the necessary electronics, and an optional standby battery. Although it costs more than a self-contained unit, it provides a somewhat greater range (40 by 20 feet; 12 by 6 meters), and some units also have a provision for changing the shape of the pattern of coverage.

The big advantage of a master-slave type system is that inexpensive slave transducers can be wired to the master, thus providing greatly increased coverage for a small additional cost. Various systems can accommodate a maximum of one to eight slaves to provide additional coverage. Slaves are often available in look-alike (to the master) enclosures. Some systems can also accommodate separate transmitters and separate receivers or directional transducers to provide greater flexibility in coverage.

Multiple head systems were once used for large area coverage. Unlike the master-slave system, the ultrasonic control box that contained the electronics and standby battery did not include transducers. Separate transmitting and receiving transducers were wired to the ultrasonic control. These systems, to the best of my knowledge, are no longer available.

Some systems use receivers with built-in electronics. This provides preamplification of the weak receiver signal so that twisted pair wire, rather than shielded wire, can be run to the ultrasonic control box. This reduces installation cost.

10.3.1   False Alarms

Ultrasonic system false alarms stem from two causes: ultrasonic noise and motion. Ultrasonic noise of the correct frequency will be detected as a Doppler shift, hence, as an alarm. In addition to audible noise, devices such as bells, whistles, steam or compressed gas leaks, and squealing (dry) machinery bearings also produce ultrasonic energy that can cause false alarms. The audible portion of such noises is often helpful in identifying the source of such problems.

Telephone bells that ring at random times may be hard to identify as a source of a problem. If suspected, dial the number, let the phone ring and observe its effect on the system. If troublesome, place some tape on the gongs inside the phone or place a sound-absorbing mat under the phone. With improved ultrasonic systems telephone bells are not the problem they once were. Other kinds of bells controlled by time clock or machinery may start automatically, thus making such causes of false alarms hard to identify. The best method is to ask your subscriber if such things exist. If so, ring the bells, start the machinery manually, etc., and note the effect on the system.

An indirect cause of false alarms is changes in temperature and relative humidity. At a temperature of about 70°F (21°C) and a relative humidity of about 38 percent, the range of the ultrasonic detector is at its minimum. Above or below these points, the effective range can be as much as double. If a system were set up at the minimum conditions, then when the temperature and relative humidity changed significantly (say to 90°F (31°C) and 90 percent relative humidity), the range could extend into areas where no coverage was intended, thus detecting possible false alarm causes in these areas.

Compressed air and gas or steam leaks should be repaired by the subscriber. In an emergency, sound-absorbing material such as rags, foam rubber, or building insulation can be placed over the leak to absorb trouble-causing ultrasonic noise.

Any object in motion within the area of coverage is a candidate for causing false alarms in ultrasonic systems. Typical examples are large doors shaken by the wind, swinging signs or other displays, fans, and machinery. Even air turbulence, caused by fans, heaters, and air conditioners, can produce false alarms. Again, today's systems that have improved filtering techniques are not troubled nearly as much by these factors as were earlier ultrasonics. This is particularly true of back-and-forth type movements such as swinging signs and rattling doors. This is not to deny such conditions will cause false alarms. Particular attention must still be given to strong turbulence, such as that produced by unit heaters suspended from ceilings and large moving objects or objects that move more than 1 foot (30 centimeters).

10.3.2   Failure to Alarm

In addition to false alarms, there are a number of things that can prevent proper operation. Blockage of the transducers is a common example. This might happen if the subscriber installs new walls to construct a new office or storeroom, or if a drop ceiling is added and the transducers are mounted above it on the original ceiling. Another example is the stacking of cartons or other stock in front of transducers during busy times of year, such as the Christmas sales season. System wiring can also get damaged and transducers can get bumped out of alignment so that they no longer cover the intended area. Changes in temperature and relative humidity can also reduce range, as previously explained under ultrasonic noise problems. The only sure solution to any of these causes is to have the subscriber walk test the system daily and report inadequate or excessive coverage.

10.3.3   Troubleshooting Ultrasonic Alarms

When troubleshooting an ultrasonic system there are a lot of points to consider. Many of these were already mentioned. As in any other troubleshooting situation the correct procedure is to know what you are doing and have a good plan of attack.

When looking for sources of false alarms, divide the potential problem into the two areas discussed, that is, noise and motion. Disconnect all transmitting transducers at the ultrasonic control box. If this is not easily done, such as in a self-contained or master unit, cover the transmitter with several layers of cloth. Do not disconnect or cover receiving transducers.

Now connect a test meter to the ultrasonic control per the manufacturer's instructions. Observe the amount of noise as indicated by the meter. It may be necessary to cause telephones, other bells, or whistles to sound; to start machinery or fans; or to do whatever else is necessary to cause the suspected problem to appear. Once it is identified, take the necessary steps to eliminate it. If the problem cannot be eliminated, try reducing the problem by swapping the transmitter and receiver locations so that the transmitter is closer to the noise source. This puts the receiver further from the problem source and may solve the problem.

In master-slave or multiple head systems, it is first necessary to isolate the noise source. This can be done by disconnecting groups of receivers, then individual receivers within the group, until the offending receiver or receivers are isolated, thus pinpointing the area of the source of the problem.

If the problem does not appear to be ultrasonic noise, then object motion or air turbulence must be investigated. This can be done by reconnecting the transmitters or removing coverings over them. If the meter, previously mentioned, indicates the problem is present, your suspicions are confirmed. Remember, it may be necessary to start fans, blowers, or other suspected machinery to get accurate test results.

Again, a procedure of divide and conquer is applicable on systems with more than one set of transducers. Disconnect transmitters in zones or groups, then individually within the offending zone or group until the problem is isolated. When testing is completed, don't forget to reconnect all devices and remove all covering cloths to restore full coverage.

10.4 MICROWAVE MOTION DETECTORS

Microwave motion detectors are somewhat similar to ultrasonic motion detectors in that they transmit energy and look for a frequency shift due to intruder motion. Instead of operating at a frequency just above that of human hearing, they operate at a high radio frequency. The earlier detectors operated at a frequency of 915 MHz. These devices were omnidirectional. That is, they had a 360° detection pattern around the antenna. This system was sometimes referred to as a radar system instead of microwave.

Today's microwave detectors operate at 10.525 Gigahertz (GHz), which is over eleven times the frequency of the old systems. The new system is highly directional. The coverage is determined by a horn antenna in front of the transducer. Different horns can provide different ranges and angles of coverage as shown in Figure 10–4. Most microwave units are single ended. That is, they transmit microwave energy and detect the energy reflected back to the same unit. Of course, the unit is looking for a Doppler shift in frequency as a means of detecting an intrusion.

Typical coverage is 75 by 35 feet (23 by 11 meters). There is another type of unit that is double ended. It has a long but relatively narrow detection pattern. Typical coverage is 300 by 15 feet (95 by 5 meters) with the same height. These units are typically used for perimeter detection either indoors or outdoors within a fenced area. In this respect they are used similar to the way a standard double-ended photo beam would be used. The advantage of a microwave over a photo beam is that the microwave beam pattern had height and width. This makes it highly unlikely that an intruder could go over or under the protection, as might be done with a photo beam, which has an essentially pencil-sized beam.

Although a single microwave unit is more expensive than a single ultrasonic unit, it provides greater coverage and may, therefore, be more economical. In fact, one microwave unit may be able to cover an area that would require several ultrasonics or several ultrasonic heads. The reduced amount of installation labor should also be considered. On the other hand, don't try to use a microwave if conditions indicate the probability of high false alarms, even if it is more economical.

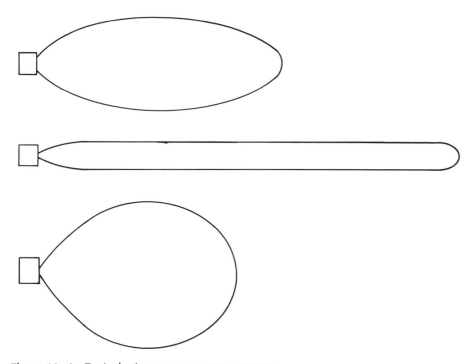

Figure 10–4   Typical microwave coverage patterns.

10.4.1   False Alarms

The biggest incidence of false alarms probably stems from the fact that microwave energy penetrates building materials. The older 915-MHz units would easily penetrate nearly any building materials except metal. The newer 10.525-GHz units have less penetrating power but will still go through wood, glass, drywall, and plaster very easily. Masonry walls (brick, concrete, stone) will not be penetrated so easily.

Wall penetration is sometimes advertised as an advantage, as several rooms can be protected by one unit. Unless great care is exercised, the detection pattern will penetrate exterior or party walls where innocent people can cause false alarms. Even if the sensitivity is adjusted to avoid this problem, difficulties may still arise. For example, a truck passing on the street outside can cause false alarms. Even though farther from the premises, it is so much bigger than a pedestrian on the sidewalk that false alarms are possible.

Since large trucks are not always handy to test for potential penetration problems, try this test. Walk close along the outside of exterior walls carrying a screen door held flat to the wall, with the system turned on. Screen doors are light and easy to carry. Use one with metal screen mesh. Plastic or fiberglass screen mesh will not work. Even though a screen door is not as large as a truck, it will be much closer to the outside wall and so should serve as a fairly reliable test. An exception might be an alley where a truck could pass very close to the building.

If false alarms are generated in the above tests, the tendency is to first reduce the sensitivity. This may be acceptable but, eventually, a point will be reached where detection inside becomes unreliable in the desired areas of coverage. A better approach is to attempt to relocate the detector so that it will be pointed at a different wall where penetration will be less of a problem. Sometimes it will be possible to mount the detector high, looking more down toward the floor. This can often reduce or eliminate penetration problems. As a more extreme corrective measure, penetration can be controlled by shielding with metal. Solid sheet metal, metal screen wire, or metal foil can be used. For a pleasing decorative effect, foil wallpaper can be used. In one application, microwaves penetrated drywall and plastic soil pipe (sewer pipe). A false alarm resulted when the toilet in the upstairs bathroom was flushed at night. After great difficulty in identifying the source of the problem, foil wallpaper was used to correct it by shielding.

Fans and other moving machinery will also cause false alarms. Metal screen wire can sometimes be used to shield the moving items so that the microwave will not "see" it. The subscriber will have to be told of the need to keep these screens clean so that accumulations of dust and dirt will not interfere with the proper operation of fans or other equipment. The subscriber will also have to be told of the need to keep the screens in place. Rather than using shielding techniques, it is generally easier and better to turn off fans or machinery when the alarm system is on. This may not be possible in the case of automatically controlled fans or machinery.

Shielding can be a help, but metal surfaces, in general, can be a mixed blessing. Although microwaves will not penetrate metal or fine mesh metal screen wire, it will be reflected by them. This can result in the microwaves being reflected into unexpected areas where false alarms can be generated. An example of this was a store with a microwave detector correctly mounted above the front show windows and aimed back into the store. All worked fine until the store located some new, metal display shelves across the front of the store. The microwaves bounced off the metal shelves and out the front windows. Every time a truck went by at night, the system falsely alarmed. Since the store manager refused to remove the shelves, the microwave had to be relocated.

Other potential causes of false alarms are metal roofs; walls and doors shaking in the wind; two-way radios such as police, fire, ambulance, aircraft, armature, and CB; and fluorescent lights. With improved system designs, these causes are not as troublesome as with earlier systems. In particular, back-and-forth type motion and fluorescent lights present little problem today. Two-way radios, depending on their power output, distance, and frequency, can sometimes cause false alarms. Animals can also cause false alarms depending on their relative size and distance from the microwave unit. By way of comparison, microwave detectors are not set off by air currents, noises, or bright lights.

10.4.2   Failure to Alarm

As explained in the preceding section, metals can be used to shield problem areas. Installation of metals can just as well cause loss of coverage. Examples are redecorating with metal foil wallpaper or addition of metal storage shelves. The only way to detect such loss of coverage is to have the subscriber periodically walk test all areas of coverage and report any loss of coverage. Tampering with the system can also cause loss of detection capability. Walk testing is, again, the proper way to check coverage.

An exception to the foregoing is the double-ended microwave perimeter type system. Here, obstruction of the signal path would create an alarm condition. As with the double-ended photo beam, the signal path is supervised.

10.5   PROXIMITY ALARMS

Proximity alarms are often known as safe alarms because they are most often used to protect a safe, money chest, file cabinet, or similar metal object. They are also known as capacitance alarms because they sense the capacitance of an intruder's body approaching within a few inches of the protected object.

A variation of the proximity alarm is used to protect a fence. In this case the sensing element is a wire strung a few feet inside a chain link fence and insulated from the ground. Two sensing wires are used in a balanced arrangement or guard wires are used to reduce the probability of false alarms. A chain link or other suitable metal fencing is required to shield the sensing wire(s) from anybody outside the fence.

10.5.1   False Alarms—Object Applications

When protecting a safe or other object, that object must be well insulated from the ground. Failure to insulate the object will usually result in false alarms. Manufacturers of capacitance alarms usually offer suitable insulating blocks. Also when a proximity system is installed, it is essential that the proximity control be connected to a solid ground (earth). Failure to do so will result in unreliable operation.

A common problem is the tendency to set the sensitivity too high. A detection range of a few inches is usually adequate. Setting the range at a foot or more will usually result in excessive false alarms. Another common problem is a telephone, lamp, or other electrical appliance placed on the safe or protected object. Even though the appliance may be electrically insulated, its capacitance will often trigger the alarm.

If a safe or protected object is located against or close to an outside or party wall, it is possible that a person outside the protected premises could trigger the alarm. To avoid this problem, move the protected object further from the wall or reduce the sensitivity. Do not reduce the sensitivity to the point where reliable detection is lost. If the above methods do not work, relocate the safe or protected object. If this is not possible, the last resort is to place a piece of metal behind the safe. Most any metal sheet can be used. Expanded metal (the kind with small holes, i.e., less than ½ inch or 1 centimeter) will work as well and is more attractive. It should extend 6 to 12 inches (15 to 30 centimeters) beyond the sides and top of the safe and should be secured to the wall so that it can't fall against the safe or protected object. After installing a shield, it will be necessary to readjust the detection system. It may be necessary to move the safe further from the wall (shield) to reduce its capacitance.

In normal operation a safe or money chest is connected to an alarm line to the central station that is separate from the premises' alarm. This allows securing valuables at the close of business, before the premises are secured. Sometimes cleaning personnel or late workers are in the area. If they approach the secured object too closely, they will create a false alarm. Such people must be instructed to keep a sufficient distance.

10.5.2   Failure to Alarm—Object Applications

A common cause of failure to respond is turning the sensitivity too low in an attempt to avoid false alarms. Corrective actions outlined under false alarms plus readjustment should eliminate this problem.

Another problem arises when attempting to protect too many objects. Although you are unlikely to find more than one or two safes or money chests at one location, metal desks and file cabinets are very common. Don't exceed the manufacturer's instructions on the maximum number and types of items that can be protected by one detection system. A very similar problem occurs when trying to locate the proximity detector system control box too far from the protected objects. A practical limit is 10 to 20 feet (3 to 6 meters), but this will depend on the type of cable used and the number and size of protected objects. Follow the manufacturer's recommendations.

10.5.3   False Alarms—Fence Applications

Grass, bushes, or weeds that are not kept trimmed back from the sensing lines can cause false alarms, as can tree limbs blowing in the wind. Larger animals, like dogs, can cause problems, but smaller ones like mice won't. Damaged, broken, or sagging sensing wires and damaged fencing can cause problems. Fencing should be kept in good repair and sensing wires can be provided with springs to keep them taut while providing give to allow for thermal expansion and contraction. Keep grass cut low and shrubbery and tree limbs well away. Tree limbs blowing in the wind can easily cause false alarms.

10.5.4   Failure to Alarm—Fence Applications

Setting the sensitivity too low or attempting to protect too great a length of fence can cause failure of the system to detect an intruder. Insufficient spacing of the sensing wire(s) from the fence can cause the same problem.

10.6   SOUND DETECTION SYSTEMS

There are six types of sound detection systems. One is the Doppler shift sonic system, mentioned separately under ultrasonic motion detectors. A second type consists simply of a microphone, amplifier, and relay. It is intended for vault protection where it is used to pick up the sounds of physical attack on the vault. Since it usually has no discrimination, it responds to all sounds. It is therefore limited to vault applications where outside noises are not likely to penetrate the vault walls to cause false alarms.

A third type of sound alarm is called a sound discriminator. It is similar to a vault alarm but has discriminators (filters) in the amplifier that are intended to ignore normal background noises but detect sounds of breaking and entering. This appears good on paper but actual operation is not always so clear-cut. Audio discriminators are available as either stand-alone units or as modules that can be used in local bell or central reporting systems. Care must be used in applying these devices, and careful testing should be done during installation to avoid false alarms from background noises.

A fourth type, the audio central station system, uses microphones and an amplifier at the protected premises. The audio signal is then sent over a voice-grade telephone circuit to a special receiver at the central station. The receiver sounds an audible alarm and lights an indicator when an adjustable noise threshold is exceeded. An operator then listens to the sound over a small speaker in the receiver. A trained operator can usually distinguish between normal background noises and sounds of intrusion and can then ignore the signal or summon an appropriate response. The sound signal can also be recorded for later use, if desired. This type of system relies primarily on sound. Some systems can also accommodate a protective loop containing magnetic contacts or other types of intrusion detection devices. In schools and other institutions, it is sometimes possible to use existing public address or intercom systems instead of installing new microphones. This will depend on the nature of the existing public address or intercom system. If possible, it could represent a sizeable savings on an installation.

A fifth type of system is not really a detection device but a feature that is available with some tape and digital dialers that allows a central operator to listen in via a microphone at the protected premises. Obviously, this cannot happen until after an intrusion has been detected by some other device and the dialer activated. A trained operator may be able to distinguish between normal background noises and an actual intrusion. Unlike the previous system, a dialer may be equipped with only one microphone, which might not provide adequate coverage. Also, the listen-in time is usually limited to only a few minutes.

A sixth type is also a sound discriminator. It is similar to the type mentioned above. The main difference is the use of filtering to detect only the sounds of breaking glass. This device is discussed further in Section 10.7.3 on glass break detectors.

10.6.1 False Alarms

False alarms are caused by noises that do not represent an intrusion. Continuous noises are easily avoided. Intermittent noises may not occur during installation and so they may be overlooked. Examples are telephone bells, cars, trucks, airplanes, factory whistles, automatic machinery, furnaces, air conditioners, time clocks, hail, rain, children playing outside, thunder, and dogs barking.

Depending on the source, it may or may not be possible to disable internal false alarm sources. For example, it may be possible to disable a time clock bell during secured hours but not possible to turn off a furnace for a weekend in winter because of the danger of pipes freezing. External noise sources can sometimes be controlled by replacing broken windows, repairing sloppily fitting doors, and blocking other openings where sounds can enter.

Some general techniques that may help reduce false alarms are to relocate microphones farther from suspected interfering noise sources and to adjust microphone or system sensitivity. In doing so, care must be used to avoid loss of detection capability. Unlike motion detectors, which can be walk tested with known size and speed of steps, there is unfortunately no standard for testing sound detectors. You could invent your own method. Examples are breaking sticks, shaking a jar of marbles, hitting a board with a hammer, or whatever you find gives a reliable indication with the make and model of system you use.

10.6.2 Failure to Alarm

Failure to alarm can result from too few microphones, poor placement of microphones, or low sensitivity. Failure can also result from cut or shorted microphone wires. Not all systems supervise the wiring. Cartons or other objects in front of a microphone could considerably reduce its sound pickup effectiveness. This is particularly true of cloth or other absorbent material. In general, the addition of sound-absorbing materials to a room, such as carpet, draperies, or acoustic ceilings, can reduce effective pickup.

Some systems used to employ a sound cancellation channel. The idea was to place a microphone close to a known false alarm-causing noise source. This signal was fed into a cancellation circuit to eliminate false alarms. Improper positioning of microphones or too high a sensitivity on the cancellation channel sometimes resulted in the bypass of legitimate intrusion sounds.

10.6.3 Review

Of the six types of sound systems, only the audible Doppler system has not gained any great popularity. Bank vault type systems are generally false alarm-free due to the heavy vault construction. Audio discriminators must be applied, installed, and tested with care if satisfactory results are to be obtained. An audio central station system has the added advantage that a properly trained operator can distinguish between normal background and intrusion sounds. Dialers with a listen-in feature may be of limited benefit because the listen-in time is limited and because the operators may have limited training since sound is an extra, not a standard method of operation as it is in the audio central station system.

10.7 MISCELLANEOUS DETECTORS

There are a wide variety of other types of detectors available. Some of these serve special applications. Most have not gained wide usage, due to either their special nature, cost, difficulty of installation, or reliability. You should be aware of these devices so that you can use them when a special application arises or when you feel one of the following may do a better job than the more common type detectors.

10.7.1 Seismic Detectors

There are a number of seismic or pressure detectors. These are normally buried in the ground for exterior perimeter protection. One of the earlier efforts used a simple hose or tube, usually filled with a freeze-proof liquid. A better method was to use two hoses or tubes, placed several feet apart. The hose was connected to a sensitive switch (when two, to a differential switch) to sense the pressure created when an intruder stepped on or near a hose or tube. The double hose system is less susceptible to false alarms as earth tremors will affect both hoses equally.

Another type of seismic detector uses a string of geophone detectors, similar to those used by geologists for oil exploration. Detectors are spaced per manufacturer's recommendations based on the type of terrain. Detectors and cables are usually buried for concealment.

10.7.2 Stress Detectors

Stress detectors are small devices, about the size of a magnetic contact, that are cemented to the underside of floor joists, fire escapes, etc. The weight of an intruder walking above creates a slight deflection in the floor joist. This is sensed by the stress detector and analyzed by a companion electronic unit. The output of the electronic unit is connected to the alarm protective loop. I doubt these devices are manufactured any more.

10.7.3 Glass Break Detectors

Glass break detectors are gaining in popularity because they are easy and quick to install and not nearly as easily damaged as foil. These are small devices that are attached to glass, usually near the top, using either glue or double face tape. A thin layer of clear room-temperature-vulcanizing glue (RTV) is excellent because it sticks well, is waterproof, and does not unduly deaden the shock waves on their way to the sensor from the glass.

Some models are specialized mechanical switches in unsealed plastic cases and are subject to corrosion, although the manufacturers use plating on contact surfaces to minimize this problem. About the only other problem with the mechanical switches is that they can become detached from the glass. They should not come loose from the glass when gently but firmly pried with the fingers during periodic inspection.

Other models use special mercury switches that are tuned to the frequency characteristic of breaking glass. Sensitivity is adjusted by loosening a screw and rotating the device. These can be connected directly into the protective loop, but their response time is fairly short so they must be tested carefully to see that they will, in fact, trigger the system. Testing is done by hitting the glass with a special hammer or with a plastic screwdriver handle. If adjusted too tight, they will fail to detect. If set too sensitive, they are likely to false alarm. The best bet is to connect the devices in their own loop connected to a pulse stretcher (available from the manufacturer), which is then wired into the regular loop. Sensitivity can then be set fairly low to avoid false alarms, yet the pulse stretcher will insure reliable detection. Loop response time must be less than 5 milliseconds to ensure adequate sensitivity (unless a pulse stretcher is used). When a mercury type unit is used on a loop with a speed of 25 to 100 milliseconds, it may respond to the test hammer but not respond to a glass break that lasts only a few milliseconds.

10.8   GENERAL APPLICATION INFORMATION

Throughout this book, you may have noticed the use of generalities such as usually, often, sometimes, relatively, most, and some. This conveys the fact that the selection, application, and servicing of intrusion detection devices is seldom an exact matter. This point was rather emphatically impressed upon me when I attended a panel discussion some years ago.

This particular session consisted of a panel of noted experts in the industry, representing a variety of different intrusion detection manufacturers. Several weeks prior to the meeting, each of these representatives was furnished with diagrams of a jewelry store, an office, a warehouse, a factory, a department store, and a small store. Notations were included pointing out potential problem areas. At the meeting, each person presented recommendations for protecting each type of premise. Needless to say, there were as many recommendations as there were participants. Although there was little agreement on what would work, there was much closer agreement as to what would not work.

During the course of the discussion, panel member and audience stories related a wide variety of usual, and often amusing, experiences with false alarm causes and with failure to alarm. Although many incidences were amusing, they all caused a lot of hard work in locating and correcting the problems. One example is the cockroach that took a shortcut through a hole in a wall. In doing so, it tripped a photo beam aimed through that hole so that one beam could be used to protect two rooms for the price of one. Another is the garbage truck air brakes that falsely alarmed an ultrasonic system due to the sound of compressed air escaping from the brakes. Replacing a broken window kept out this source of ultrasound noise. Another example is that of a loiterer who was picked up by police when a jewelry store alarm went off for the umpteenth time. While waiting for his girlfriend to get off work at a movie theatre across the street, he leaned against a wall opposite the jewelry store safe, tripping the proximity alarm.

Such stories can go on forever. Each installer and serviceperson has one to tell, yet others may never encounter that particular problem. The objective of this book is to explain principles. If you understand how each type of detector works and some of the typical causes of false alarms and of failure to alarm, then you are well on the road to being a professional in the industry. As you gain experience of your own, often in the school of hard knocks, you will be building a career.

In addition to the technical knowledge presented earlier, there are a number of general concepts that are important to the selection, application, and servicing of any type of intrusion detection device. In fact, most of these points apply just as well to an entire alarm system. The point here is that a system, when properly chosen and properly applied, will minimize the amount of service required later.

In the selection of any system, the premises must be carefully surveyed and the necessary questions asked to find out such things as what is to be protected; how valuable it is; who is likely to be interested in illegally getting their hands on it; how they might gain access to it; what is the best way to detect such attempts; and what kind of response is needed to prevent the loss. Table 10–1 lists a number of things that have to be considered.

Table 10–1   Alarm equipment selection factors

1. What is to be protected?
2. How valuable is it?
3. Who might want to steal it?
4. How might someone go about stealing it?
5. Where are the valuables located?
6. What physical protection is provided?
7. What are the weaknesses in the physical protection?
8. What type of alarm system can best protect the valuables?
9. What interference problems might cause false alarms?
10. How can these problems be overcome?
11. What problems might cause failure to alarm?
12. How can these problems be overcome?
13. How much will the alarm equipment cost?
14. How much will it cost to install it?
15. What is the system's value to the customer?
16. How much is the customer willing to invest?
17. What amount of alarm detection coverage is required?
18. What combination of volumetric, area, beam, and spot coverage will best do the job?

Table 10–1   (continued)

19. What is your company's reliability experience with the intended equipment?
20. How familiar are you and your company with the application and servicing of the proposed equipment?
21. What kind of training and service support is provided by the manufacturer and distributor for the proposed equipment?
22. How easy is the equipment to install?
23. How easy is the equipment to service?
24. Is the system expandable if greater coverage is needed in the future?
25. How easy is the system for the subscriber to use?
26. What is the dependability of the subscriber personnel who will be responsible for controlling the system?
27. What is the rate of turnover of these people?
28. Must the system meet UL requirements?
29. What are the requirements of the subscriber's insurance carrier?
30. What changes have taken place in all of the above since the system was installed? Last modified? Last serviced?
31. What alarm ordinances must be complied with?

A review of Table 10–1 points out not only that there are a lot of items, but also that some of these are mutually exclusive. For example, a system adequate for a high-risk application will be expensive, which contradicts economy. All too often though, an inadequate system proves to be poor economy in the long run. It's too late to lock the barn door after the horse is stolen. I wish I could give you easy answers in this book. The best I can hope for is to provide a good basics of alarm systems.

PART FIVE

The chapters in Part Five attempt to outline working practices in the alarm business. Each company has its own practices and procedures that it has developed over the years. No company will agree on every point presented here. Employees are advised to comply with all legal and proper practices and procedures established by their employer. The intent here is to outline some generally good practices, to provide the newcomer with some idea of what the work will be like, and to provide ideas for possible improvement.

11 A Day in the Life of an Alarm Serviceperson

Chapter 5 presented the seven basic steps of troubleshooting. Now let's expand on this a little and look at a typical daily routine of an alarm troubleshooter.

The following twenty steps provide a rough outline of an alarm serviceperson's day-to-day activity.

1. Receive an assignment from the service dispatcher (in a large company) or supervisor (in a smaller company). This includes the address where service is required and the name of the person to contact there.

2. Get information on the kind of system to be serviced, such as local bell, silent or monitored, McCulloh, polarity reversal, direct wire, multiplex, monitored by central station, monitored by police department, proprietary, etc. If possible, also find out the types, makes, models, and quantities of equipment used in the system; areas of coverage; and other such helpful information. Obtain diagrams if available. This information should be available from job files, if they are maintained.

3. Next, obtain manufacturer's service instructions for the equipment involved. The best setup is to have a service manual in the truck at all times that covers the equipment you will normally have to work on. If you suspect from the trouble report that you may have to work on new or unusual types of equipment, take the necessary instruction manuals with you if available. Instructions should include a picture or sketch of the equipment, make, model, a list of options and variations, if any, a description of how it operates, wiring diagrams, instructions on how to make adjustments, troubles to be avoided, and a troubleshooting guide. All too often the manufacturer's instruction sheets are not detailed enough to be of as much help as they could. Sometimes none will be available to you. In that case, you're on your own. If you anticipate needing special replacement parts that are not normally carried on the service truck, now is the time to get them from your stockroom. An extra trip to pick them up later is wasted time. Delays seldom make subscribers or customers happy, especially if they are waiting to close and go home.

4. When you arrive, check with the subscriber or owner to verify the nature of the problem. Often you can get helpful hints from them, and this is your chance to

find out if the problem is due to subscriber error. Chapter 13 offers suggestions on how to handle this delicate matter.

5. If you are working on a silent alarm, notify the central station, police department, or whoever is monitoring it, so that they will not respond to any alarms you may create while working on the system.

6. Look for obvious problems such as doors or windows left open, broken wires, damaged foil, motion detectors in constant alarm (observe walk test light), and blocked photo beams. A quick look around often reveals such problems in seconds, whereas a great deal of time would be spent using test instruments to eventually find them. Experience will soon tell you how much time you should spend looking and when to haul out the test instruments. One old hand says he solved 90 percent of his cases without using any test equipment.

7. If you haven't already received the information from your dispatcher, supervisor, or files, find out what kind of equipment is in the system so that you know what you are working on. If you are familiar with the kind of equipment, you can work from experience. If not, at least you will know which instruction manuals to refer to. Now is also the time to verify the file information, if files are kept on each job, and to correct and update them as necessary.

8. Know how the equipment is supposed to operate. You may have worked on it before. This is certainly to your advantage. If you are working on new equipment or on equipment with which you are not too familiar or if you encounter unusual problems on otherwise familiar equipment, it is wise, and usually essential, to carefully review the equipment manufacturer's instructions. Now you can understand the need for step three. Without the necessary instructions, you will most likely end up having to call your supervisor or fellow worker who is familiar with the equipment. Better this, though, than to proceed blindly, make a wrong assumption, and go down the wrong path.

9. Determine possible causes of the problem. This involves making a list, at least mentally, of possible causes. This gives you an idea of what to look for and, more importantly, what can be eliminated. This can save you a lot of time.

10. Once located, the necessary repairs are usually obvious: tighten a loose screw, realign a photo beam, splice a broken wire, close a window or door that has been left open, clean and solder loose or corroded wire splices, tape bare wires, etc. Take time to make the repair properly. The small amount of extra time spent will pay dividends in the long run. Coming back in six months or a year to redo the work just isn't good business.

11. Notify the phone company if the problem is in the phone line. Follow your company procedures, if any, when doing this. Give them all the information you can to help locate the problem. For instance, does the problem appear to be an open, a short, a ground, or a cross with somebody else's phone line? If it is a short or a ground, what resistance do you measure from the subscriber's end and from the central station's end of the line? Is the problem continuous or intermittent? When did the trouble first appear? What voltage do you apply to the line and at which end? A little cooperation with phone company people will often help in speeding

repairs. Before notifying the phone company, though, be certain the problem is, in fact, in the phone line. Some telephone companies charge the alarm company for their service time if they find no problem in their phone circuits.

12. Once the repair has been made, check for additional problems. What you have just fixed may have been close to causing a problem but may not have been the cause of the present problem.

13. Repeat steps 9 through 12 if more trouble is found.

14. When all repairs have been made, check the system for normal operation. As a professional troubleshooter, you can do without the embarrassment of being called back to fix what you previously told your boss had already been fixed.

15. Advise the subscriber that repairs have been made. It is also wise to keep the subscriber informed in case you have to leave for some reason before repairs have been completed. Give an honest reason for leaving, when you expect to return, and what the condition of the alarm system is. This can be a sensitive matter, so be sure to follow your supervisor's instructions. Your supervisor may not want you, the troubleshooter, to tell the subscriber anything if repairs are incomplete; some prefer to take that responsibility on themselves. Once repairs are completed, the system is working properly, and subscriber has been advised, you can go to the next step.

16. Fill out the service ticket, service record, service invoice, or whatever paperwork is required. Have the subscriber sign it if necessary.

17. Notify the central station or police department or other monitoring agents that the system is now back to normal operation. Conduct the necessary tests to verify normal signal transmission. Note on the paperwork the time and the name of the person notified if required. This can avoid arguments later.

18. Notify the service dispatcher or your supervisor that the job has been completed. If it is not completed, explain why and what the system status is.

19. Get your next assignment.

20. At the end of the day, turn in your paperwork, restock your truck to replace the items used, and head home, proud that you've licked another bunch of troubles.

12 Work Hazards

Many alarm people give little or no thought to safety, but stop and reflect for a moment on what safety, or rather the lack of it, can mean to you. An unsafe act can lead to loss of income, loss of job, loss of limbs, a life in a wheelchair, or a one-way trip to the cemetery. When your unsafe acts are considered, not just as possible injuries but as end results such as these, you will begin to place the proper emphasis on safety. The same consideration should be given to the safety of those around you as well as to yourself. Our lives are surrounded by hazards, not just at work but all around us. By being aware of the hazards and by knowing and taking the correct precautions, we can greatly swing the odds in our own favor. If you don't believe the effort to learn and improve your odds is worthwhile, then put this book down for long enough to visit someone recovering from a serious accident at home or in the hospital.

If safety is so important, what is it? First, safety is a state of mind. It is a state of mind in which you are constantly asking yourself, "What will be the consequence of each thing I do?" before you do it. This may sound like an onerous task, and at first it will take conscious effort. Learning the alarm trade takes a conscious effort. Safety is part of the trade. Learn it too. As with other parts of the job, safety will become second nature with adequate practice. And "second nature" must be your goal!

The nature of our work takes us to all kinds of premises where a wide variety of hazards are present. The following is not intended as a complete listing of all of them. No single book could list all possible hazards and how to deal with them. With the safety awareness that you will develop, and the common sense you should already have, you will be a much safer, healthier, and happier worker.

12.1 FALLS

Falls are a constant hazard. You will often have to work in poorly illuminated areas, often in storerooms or little-used areas where junk of all kinds tends to collect. Such items pose hazards. Crawling over obstacles can be dangerous. Often things are stacked unevenly or precariously, and can fall on you or out from under you if used as a makeshift ladder. Where possible, work from a well-placed ladder. If this is not possible, remove obstacles or rearrange things so they will safely support you. This will often be a matter of judgment. Be conservative about safety and do not take shortcuts to rush the job. Even when you are working in open, well-lighted areas, the hazard still exists. Often you will be looking upward at wiring or system components. Always watch your footing when you get ready to move.

12.1.1 Ladders

A great deal of alarm work involves ladders, another safety risk. Falls from ladders tend to be more hazardous because of the added height. To reduce accidents, ladders should be in good shape. Avoid those that are unstable, have loose or missing parts, or wooden ladders that are split or broken. All ladders should have antiskid feet. Extension ladders should be placed with a firm, even footing. The bottom end should be placed out from the wall one-fourth of the length to which the ladder is extended. Placing ladders too nearly vertical increases the tendency to topple backwards. Placing them with too much of a lean increases the tendency to kick out at the bottom. If necessary, use short pieces of planks to level the ladder and provide a firm footing. Place them securely and at a tilt so the ladder feet won't slide off. If the ladder feet are resting on a backward slope, particularly outdoors, or if you feel there is a chance the bottom end might kick out, tie the bottom end. A tree, pipe, large rock, or even a stake driven into the ground can be used as an anchor. A short piece of rope is preferred but wire or cable can be used. Generally it won't take much to hold the bottom from kicking out. Also note that the higher you climb, the greater the tendency is to have the ladder kick out at the bottom. When working from the top of any ladder, be careful about pushing on the wall or on tools, such as while drilling holes in a concrete, tilt-up wall to mount a bell box.

When climbing a ladder, avoid a balancing act. Put tools in your tool belt and small parts in a tool pouch or a pocket. Tie a rope onto large objects such as bell boxes and haul the box up after climbing into position. Don't stretch or lean from any ladder. If you cannot reach your objective, climb down and reposition the ladder.

12.1.2 Ceilings

Another falling hazard is through ceilings. Stringing alarm wiring often takes you into attics and crawl spaces that have no floorboards. Ceilings below can be plaster or various types of acoustic tile. None will safely support a person's weight. Missing a rafter up above can quickly put you through the ceiling. An acquaintance fell all the way through and was off work for many months. Since he worked on a contract basis, he had no income during this time. I was luckier. I only put one foot through an acoustic tile ceiling.

12.2 CUTS, PUNCTURES, AND ABRASIONS

An alarm serviceperson is no stranger to cuts, punctures, and abrasions. Working in unfinished areas such as attics and under floor crawl spaces exposes you to protruding nails and splinters. Some types of roofs bristle with protruding nails in the attic.

Standing up under them can be a painful experience. Working any area where junk collects presents a variety of hazards, from loose board with protruding nails to broken glass and pointed objects. The best safety precautions are to look before you move and to take your own light in dim areas.

While cuts often bleed freely, thus cleansing the wound, this is not true of many puncture wounds. Even seemingly minor puncture wounds should receive medical attention. If you have not already done so, it would be wise to get a tetanus shot. Booster shots are needed every two years.

12.3   ELECTRIC SHOCK

Electric shock is an ever present hazard. It's not uncommon to find live junction or fuse boxes without covers. Reaching into one or poking a wire or fish tape (electrician's tape) into one could result in a dangerous shock. Drilling holes in walls to fish out alarm wires can result in drilling into power wires hidden in the walls. A double insulated drill with exposed metal parts provides no protection against this hazard. A drill with a three-wire grounding cord and plug will provide protection, but not if the grounding pin is cut off of the drill or extension cord or if a nongrounding outlet or extension cord is used.

12.4   FALLING OBJECTS

Falling objects are another type of hazard. New construction sites and industrial areas or plants almost always require the wearing of hard hats. Large falling objects are not the only hazard. Much alarm work is done above head level. This requires looking up. Wear glasses or safety goggles to keep dirt and drill chips out of your eyes. If assisting a helper working above you, look out for falling tools, drill chips, wire clippings, etc. If you are above, take care to avoid dropping things on your helper or a bystander. If something is dropped, "headache" is the standard warning.

12.5   ANIMALS AND INSECTS

Critters can pose hazards too! Some dogs bite and trained guard dogs can do serious injury to alarm personnel responding to alarms. Records should be kept and personnel advised if guard dogs are kept on the premises.

Smaller animals such as black widow spiders, brown recluse spiders, wasps, bees, and hornets can pose dangers, too. Poisonous snakes can be encountered outdoors and even occasionally indoors. Scorpions are common in western desert regions. Fortunately, none of these is usually deadly. Snake bites and scorpion stings should receive immediate medical attention. Insect bites are painful but not dangerous unless received in large numbers or unless you are hypersensitive to them. Pay particular attention to an animal that you might accidentally corner while proceeding through areas, especially in dark areas or in confined quarters. Even a normally nonharmful animal can cause a fall or other injury if it startles you. I nearly fell off a ladder when startled by a bird that suddenly flew from a nest near a bell box.

12.6   WEATHER

Although most alarm work is inside, you will sometimes find it necessary to work outside, such as when hanging bell boxes. Sunburn can be a hazard if you have not acquired a tan. A few people are extremely sensitive to the sun and should be particularly careful when working outdoors. Adequate clothing cover and suntan lotion are required. Sun protection factor (SPF) ratings of suntan products sold in the United States range from two to twenty-five or higher. The higher the number, the better the protection from the sun.

In the winter, frostbite of fingers and toes is a potential hazard. Since working with gloves is often cumbersome, the inclination is to remove them, which only increases the danger. Handling tools, metal bells, boxes, and the like has a further chilling effect. Even if temperatures are not too low, a strong wind greatly increases the chill factor and the danger.

Rain, while not directly dangerous, will make ladders and other outdoor work surfaces slippery. Wet feet from tracked-in rain will cause similar hazards indoors. Wet clothing can lead to excessive body heat loss, chills, and illness. Do not work on ladders or on rooftops during electrical storms. If the storm is in your immediate vicinity, it is best to cease installation work entirely. System wiring can act like a big antenna to attract static buildup when lightning strikes nearby. On completed systems, one side of the loop and other wiring is usually grounded. This will normally drain off static. If you receive a shock, discontinue work until the storm has passed.

12.7   FIBERGLASS AND DUST

Working in attics and other areas with fiberglass or other insulating materials poses special hazards. Dust accumulations make matters worse. In addition, it is usually hot and perspiration only adds to your discomfort. I have found the following steps of great help:

1. Wear a dust mask. Disposable masks come five to a package and are available at hardware, paint, and discount stores and cost about two dollars per pack. These are essential to prevent nose and throat irritation and excessive coughing. Smokers will probably find them of even more importance.
2. Protect your eyes. Working in hot attics produces sweat, which can wash dirt and fiberglass particles into the eyes. To prevent this, fold a large handkerchief into

a narrow band and tie around your forehead. Elastic bands from sporting shops serve the same purpose.

3. Cover your arms and hands. Even in heat I prefer long-sleeve shirts to keep out dirt and fiberglass. Button the cuffs and, if necessary, the collar too. If you are really bothered, wear thin rubber gloves and tape shirt cuffs to the gloves.

4. Take a cool shower after working in fiberglass. This washes away the particles. A hot shower or bath opens the pores of the skin, allowing fiberglass particles a chance to enter the pores where they tend to cause itching.

5. If you will be working in a hot attic for any length of time, put a fan on a small board placed across the rafters and aim it into your work area. An oscillating fan works nicely for this purpose.

12.8   TOOLS

Alarm people use and misuse a wide variety of hard and power tools. Without going into extensive detail on each tool, there are a few general points to consider. Keep tools sharp. Although a sharp tool would, at first, appear the more dangerous, it is more likely to do its intended job. By comparison, a dull tool is more likely to require excessive force and to slip, which is often what causes an accident. The result can be a stab wound or a fall from a ladder. Keep all of your tools sharp. This includes screwdrivers, chisels, pocketknives, wire strippers, saws, and drill bits. Most tools can be sharpened. If not, replace them.

Use the correct tool for the job. There's an old adage, "To the person whose only tool is a hammer, the whole world looks like a nail." Misused tools are dangerous, take longer, and don't do quality work. I once tried to do some prying with a drill. Of necessity, drill bits must be hard in order to keep a sharp cutting edge, but they are also quite brittle. I'm just glad the broken piece hit me on the cheek, not in the eye.

12.9   BURNS

If you must smoke, do it in a safe place. Do not smoke in attics or where dust or trash collects. A carelessly discarded match or a glowing ash that gets knocked off a cigarette can easily lead to a fire or to an explosion. In an enclosed space, such as an attic, you could get burned. Worse yet, fire could cut off your escape route. For the same reasons, don't "solder" with a match. Use a cordless soldering iron or use a crimp type connector and the correct crimping tool. Never smoke or use an open fire or flame where there is evidence of leaking gas or flammable vapors such as gasoline, paint solvents, or cleaning solvents.

12.10   FIRST AID PROCEDURES AND EQUIPMENT

Despite even the best efforts accidents will happen. These are usually the result of lapses in safety consciousness or of encountering a new and unexpected hazard. The following topics will help handle accidents.

12.10.1   First Aid Kit

In your service vehicle, you should carry a first aid kit stocked to handle minor problems. It should also contain the necessary supplies to provide immediate emergency treatment of more serious injuries until competent medical help can be provided. Table 12–1 lists suggested items. Various sizes of kits are available from industrial suppliers and drugstores. Some alarm distributors now stock them too. For their reasonable price, they are a good investment. Keep them where they are readily available and restock them as the items are used. An empty box does you no good.

Table 12–1   Typical contents of 24-unit size first aid kit

1-inch adhesive compress	2 units
2-inch bandage compress	2 units
3-inch bandage compress	2 units
4-inch bandage compress	2 units
3-inch × 3-inch gauze pad	1 unit
Eye dressing pack	1 unit
Plain absorbent gauze (24 inch × 72 inch)	3 units
Plain absorbent gauze (½ square yard)	4 units
Gauze roller bandage	2 units
Triangular bandage (40 inches)	4 units
Tourniquet	1 unit
Scissors	1 unit
Tweezers	1 unit

12.10.2   Training

A first aid kit, no matter how elaborate, is of no use if you don't know what to do. Worse yet, you can cause additional injury if you do the wrong thing. The only answer is to get proper first aid training. The topic is much too lengthy to cover here. Excellent training is available through the Red Cross in most cities and towns. It is useful at home and on vacations as well as on the job. The training will teach you the correct way to handle minor injuries. More important, it will teach you techniques for the immediate, temporary handling of major emergencies; the techniques are designed to sustain life and minimize further injury until competent medical help is available.

12.10.3   Sources of Help

Quite often you may be working alone. What would you do if you had an accident? Would anybody miss you and come looking if you were disabled or trapped? Do you know your options?

When working alone make sure your supervisor or dispatcher knows where you are and when to expect you to call in or to return. If you do not show up, you know help will be on its way. By the same token, be faithful in calling in. Too many ''false alarms'' will cause you to lose your credibility.

When arriving at a job, find out where the nearest help will be available. Are there other workers or people around who could help or summon help in case of need? If not, where is the nearest telephone? Is it in working order? If it is a pay phone, do you have change in your pocket? Do you have a two-way radio in your truck? Searching for a means of summoning help after sustaining injury, a broken leg for instance, may become impossible. Do you know your location so you can direct help to you if necessary? A little foresight can help you in the event an emergency arises.

12.11   PREVENTION

What is safety? It is a state of mind! It is caring. It is caring about yourself and about others. It means stopping a moment to plan your actions, to look for and consider possible hazards, and to plan how you will avoid those hazards. It is constant attention to what you are doing and how you are doing it. I speak from experience. Recently, I was too intent on what I was doing and ignored what was going on around me. Now I have only 9½ fingers. They don't grow back. It's too late for prevention. Don't you be too late for prevention.

13 Dealing Effectively with Customers

In addition to a thorough technical knowledge, any serviceperson who expects to be successful in the trade must also have a knowledge of proper conduct when dealing with a customer. This is more easily said than done, but it is certainly possible, as anyone who has this knack can tell you. Someone new to dealing with customers, may say, "Yes, the old timers know how, but I don't, and I don't know how to learn." Before going into some of the detail, let's set up a little background.

In your job as troubleshooter, you are probably more accustomed to dealing with objects. Things, such as alarm controls, wire, bells, and detection devices, behave according to well-known laws of physics. Even when defective, they follow these laws, although in a different manner. It is your understanding of the equipment that enables you to find and fix the problems. Equipment is not moody. It doesn't swear at you or talk back, nor does it have feelings or emotions. Customers do have feelings. They do get mad and they do talk back. You can, if you want, lump all these human characteristics under the term "psychology." Yet you don't have to study formal psychology to be able to get along with people and to get your job done in a professional way.

The position of the serviceperson on a trouble call is not the easiest one but, even at its worst, is never impossible. Part of the reason is that the customer may be unhappy because the alarm system is not working. In addition, the customer may have got out on the wrong side of bed that morning or may have just had something else happen to make him or her unhappy. These are things over which you have no control. Yet you will sometimes have to live with the consequences, such as grouchy customers. With a little understanding, you can still do a good job.

The key words in dealing with a customer are "courtesy" and "consideration." Remember, your mission is to get the system fixed and to make the customer happy again. Some of the snags you may run into occur when the customer is angry or very angry; is abusive; is actually wrong; doesn't understand the system; is the cause of the problem; hasn't done or refuses to do what is required in regard to system operation; or any combination of these.

The following points, if you keep them in mind, will do more to smooth your job than any other. When you encounter an angry, abusive customer, remember that he or she may be mad at your company or at something totally unrelated and not at you individually. Therefore, there is no reason for you to take any insults personally and no reason for you to become angry and abusive in return. If you were to do so, you would only make matters all the worse.

The second point is not to be apologetic and not to admit that either you or the company are at fault. To do so only gives the customer reinforcement for being mad. To admit fault could also have serious legal consequences for your company or even for yourself, should the customer later decide to sue.

Do not tell the customer that it isn't your fault. The problem may very well not be your fault but to say so only antagonizes the customer. Again, don't take any accusations personally. Even more so, do not tell the customer, "It's your fault," even if it is the truth. Never blame the customer.

Well, if you are not supposed to take insults personally and you are not supposed to admit fault or wrongdoing and you are not supposed to blame the customer, what are you supposed to do? Be positive, courteous, and businesslike. By being so, you instill confidence in the customer or subscriber. You want to convey the idea that you are somebody that is here to help, that is *able* to help, and that *will* help.

A good approach is to let the customer or subscriber know of your empathy. Say something along the line of, "I understand how you feel," pause briefly, then continue, "What seems to be the problem?" Don't be disturbed if you get a reply something like, "The damned thing don't work." Just remain calm and ask questions that will get you specific answers about what is not working. Don't expect an irate customer to calm down instantly. The general technique is to use phrases like, "I understand," or "I can appreciate how you feel," or "I understand your position," or "If you can be a little more specific, I may be able to go directly to the trouble and get it fixed more quickly for you." Then, you want to ask questions that get the answers you need. Asking the questions transfers the ball to the owner or subscriber. It is then up to him or her to do something. The more specific the information they give, the more customers help themselves.

Be as honest as you can with your subscribers and customers. A lie may get you off the hook for the moment, but lies always seem to come back to haunt you or the next serviceperson to show up. Remember, you are that other person for all the rest. If you don't know the answer, and you often won't, say you'll look it up in the manual or call your supervisor or do some testing first to find answers. You are there to get answers, especially those needed to get the system back in service.

By the same token, don't make promises you know you can't keep. For instance, don't promise you'll have the system fixed in ten minutes unless you're sure you know just what the problem is and can fix it in that amount of time. A qualified statement, such as, "If the problem is such-and-such then I should be able to fix it in ten minutes," is slightly better. But if four hours have gone by without results, I'll guarantee that the waiting customer will have forgotten that "if." If you use this approach then report back to the customer after ten minutes and explain how things stand.

When servicing a system, keep your eyes open for little things that you can fix or adjust. Let your subscriber or customer know about these little extras in a polite way. This is not only good public relations but good business too. These extras can help avoid future service calls, which keeps down expenses and helps keep subscribers happy down the road too.

Glossary

abort A feature available in some tape dialers and digital communicators that discontinues the transmission of an alarm signal if the alarm system is turned off. This allows the alarm user to reduce false alarms caused by accidental tripping.

absorption The property of materials such as carpeting, drapes, and acoustic ceilings that causes them to soak up or deaden sound. These materials deaden ultrasonics too, so a higher than normal range setting may be required. See also *acoustics; reflection*.

AC See *alternating current*.

AC induction The tendency for alarm system wiring to pick up alternating current when located close to power wiring, motors, generators, transformers, etc. If strong enough, these unwanted AC signals will cause failures of the alarm system. Such problems can be intermittent, making them more difficult to find. See also *RF pickup*.

access control (1) Any means of limiting entry into a building or area to those who are authorized. (2) A system that does this by use of coded cards, push-button sequence, fingerprint comparison (by holography and computer), hand geometry, or other means.

account A subscriber to an alarm company's services.

accumulating circuit A counting circuit that must receive a certain number of input pulses (often adjustable) before signaling an alarm. Used on motion, shock, audio, stress, vibration, and other detectors to prevent false alarms due to random events.

acoustic alarm See *audio alarm*.

acoustics The aliveness or deadness of sound in a room, an important consideration in adjusting for correct ultrasonic coverage. See also *absorption; reflection*.

active detector A detector that sends out or transmits energy in order to perform its detection function. Examples are ultrasonics, microwaves, photoelectric beams, E-field fences, and capacitance alarms. Compare *passive detector*.

activity report A record of alarm signals received by a central station. May also include opening and closing signals if the system is designed to send these. A copy of this record may be forwarded to the subscriber for review.

AF See *audio frequency*.

aiming light A visible light used to mechanically aim photoelectric beams.

air turbulence Air disturbance or churning caused by a breeze or draft from a fan, furnace, air conditioner, or other source. Air turbulence in the vicinity of an ultrasonic transducer can produce false alarms.

alarm condition The presence of a dangerous or undesired situation, such as fire, intrusion, or holdup, that is sensed and signaled by an alarm system.

alarm line A wire or telephone line used to report an alarm condition to a remote location such as a guard station or an alarm central office.

alarm screen (1) A window screen (insect screen) with fine, insulated wires woven into or sewn onto the screen fabric and connected to the protective loop in such a way that cutting the screen or removing it frame and all will trip the alarm. (2) An arrangement of wooden dowels and framing members made to cover a window opening. The wooden pieces have grooves in which are embedded fine wires held in place with varnish. When the screen is broken or torn off, the wires are broken, triggering an alarm. Seldom used anymore due to cost and poor appearance. Now largely superseded by motion detectors.

alarm signal   An indication that some dangerous or unwanted condition is occurring, such as an intrusion, fire, or holdup.

alarm system   A collection of detection devices, control unit, annunciation or reporting equipment, control station(s), wiring, phone lines, radio channels, power supply, and other associated equipment connected together to detect and report the existence of an undesirable condition such as an intrusion, a fire, or an unsafe condition in an industrial manufacturing process.

alignment   (1) The physical aiming of a photoelectric beam and its mirrors (if any). (2) The physical aiming of a motion detector. (3) The electronic tuning of RF circuits. This requires proper training and equipment and is best left to the manufacturer or repair shop.

alignment shutter   A device, used to test some types of photoelectric beams, that reduces the intensity of the transmitted beam by a fixed or adjustable amount. If the system still works with reduced beam intensity, it is considered to have enough of a safety margin to avoid common false alarm causes in normal operation. This is particularly important on any installation that is near the published maximum usable range.

alternating current (AC)   An electric current that continuously reverses direction. House current in the United States is 60 Hz AC. Compare *direct current*.

ammeter   A meter that indicates the amount of electric current flowing in a circuit.

ampere (amp)   The rate of electrical flow. Represented by ''I'' (intensity) in Ohm's law.

ampere-hour   The capacity of a battery to deliver electrical energy.

annunciator   A device, typically a small horn or light, used to attract the attention of someone close by.

answering machine   See *telephone answering machine*.

answering service   See *telephone answering service*.

anticlash   A feature of some McCulloh transmitters that causes all other activated transmitters to wait if one is already using the line to transmit a signal. This prevents garbling of signals due to two or more transmitters operating at the same time. Also called hold-out or noninterfering.

area protection   (1) A detector that is sensitive over a two-dimensional space, such as a strain gauge sensor or a seismic detector. (2) A misnomer for volumetric protection (which is three-dimensional).

armed   The condition of an alarm system when it is on and ready to be tripped.

armed light   A light or light-emitting diode, usually red, that indicates the alarm system is armed or set.

attack   (1) An attempt to burglarize or vandalize, successful or not. (2) An attempt to defeat an alarm system, successful or not.

audible alarm   An alarm that makes noise, as opposed to a silent alarm. Also called a local bell alarm.

audio alarm   A detection device that is triggered upon detecting noises, such as the sounds of breaking and entering. See also *audio discriminator; sonic detector; vault alarm*.

audio discriminator   A type of detector that triggers an alarm when it detects noises. In an effort to minimize false alarms, some models have built-in circuitry to trigger only on certain frequencies of sound, only on sounds above a certain level, only on sounds lasting a certain length of time, or a combination of these and other techniques. See also *audio alarm*.

audio frequency (AF)   A frequency within the range of human hearing, generally about 20 to 15,000 Hz.

audit trail   See *event log*.

automatic reset   A feature of certain alarm systems that silences the alarm automatically after a certain time delay (see *bell cutoff*) or that returns the system to the non-alarm condition automatically, usually after a time delay.

azimuth coverage   The floor plan coverage pattern of a microwave or other detector. See also *elevation coverage*.

BA   Burglar alarm. See *intrusion alarm*.

balanced magnetic contact   See *high-security magnetic contact*.

battery   An assembly of two or more cells used to obtain higher voltages than that available from a single cell.

beam   See *photoelectric beam*.

bell   An electromechanical noise-making device in which a hammer hits a gong. Used in alarm systems to scare off intruders and to alert people of an attempted intrusion.

bell cutoff   A timing circuit that automatically turns off an alarm bell after a given time interval. Also called a bell time-out.

blind areas   Loss of detection (often unexpected) of a motion detector system, particularly due to objects blocking the view of an ultrasonic or passive IR system or a metallic object blocking the view of a microwave system. Such blind areas are often created when the subscriber rearranges office furniture or warehouse stock or adds new partitions without advising the alarm company. Also called shadowing.

bounce-back   A short-range (up to about 75 feet) photoelectric beam that has both the transmitter and receiver in one physical unit (thus simplifying installation). The far end of the beam is bounced back by a simple retro-reflector.

break alarm   An alarm caused by an opening (breaking) of one wire in a direct wire system.

break-and-cross loop   Another name for the milliamp signaling method described under direct wire.

bug   (1) A detector. (2) A magnetic contact.

(3) To install a contact on; as in, "to bug the front door."

burglar alarm (BA)   See *intrusion alarm*.

burglary   The illegal taking of property from a premises. Compare *robbery*.

buzzer   An electromechanical noise-making device similar to a bell but without a gong. Generally not as loud as a bell. Sometimes used as an annunciator or as an indoor warning device.

bypassed   See *defeat; zoned-out*.

cable   A bundle of wires covered by a common jacket or sheath.

call back   A security measure used for downloading and uploading that works as follows: The programmer at the central station calls the alarm control via dial-up telephone line. The control answers and acknowledges the call, then hangs up. The control then calls back to the central station programmer using a preset telephone number to permit uploading or downloading. Thus an unauthorized person who called the control panel would not be able to obtain any information or to change anything.

call forwarding   A feature offered by some phone companies that allows the telephone subscriber to have incoming calls automatically forwarded to another number. Incoming calls from the central station to a digital communicator will also be forwarded when this feature is in effect, making it impossible to reach the communicator.

call waiting   A feature offered by some phone companies that sounds a tone to let the telephone user know of a second caller waiting on the line. Such a tone will generally garble uploading and downloading communications.

cancellation   See *noise cancellation*.

capacitance detector   A device that detects an intruder's close approach to or touching of a protected metal object. Often used to protect safes and file cabinets. Protected objects must be metal, well insulated from ground, and not too large. Also called safe alarm or proximity alarm. See also *E-field detector*.

carrier current system   A type of wireless alarm system where the receiver and several transmitters are connected to the 120-volt house wiring, usually by plugging in. The transmitted alarm signal is a high frequency (much higher than the 60-Hz line frequency) that travels over the power wiring within one house or building and sometimes from one building to another.

casement window   A type of window that hinges outward and is usually opened with a crank. It is often difficult to mount contacts on casement windows. Tamper switches are sometimes used successfully.

CCTV   See *closed circuit television*.

cell   The basic unit of a battery, consisting of a positive electrode, a negative electrode, an electrolyte, and a container. See also *battery; primary cell; secondary cell*.

cellular radio   (1) For alarm systems: providing multiple long-range receiving stations with widely overlapping coverage so that each transmitter is provided with redundant receiver coverage. (2) For mobile telephone service: providing many short-range receivers with slightly overlapping coverage to increase the number of simultaneously available conversations. See also *long-range radio*.

central office   Another name for *central station*. Since the telephone company also has central offices, many persons in the alarm industry prefer to use the term ''central station.''

central office relay   See *reversing relay*.

central station   A central location where an alarm company monitors a large number of its accounts. (Alarm systems with a local bell only are not monitored.)

certificated alarm system   An alarm system that is installed by a UL certified alarm company and that meets certain requirements for installation, service, and extent of coverage.

charge   To put electrical energy into a battery for later use. See also *float charge; overcharge; undercharge*.

circuit breaker   An electrical safety valve; a device designed to interrupt dangerously high

currents. Unlike a fuse, a circuit breaker can be reset to be used again; thus, no replacements are needed. Some circuit breakers can also be used as switches. Compare *fuse*.

circumvention of alarm   See *defeat*.

Class 2   Low-voltage, limited energy electrical systems, per article 725 of the National Electrical Code. Most alarm systems meet Class 2 requirements.

Class 2 transformer   A transformer that limits energy per the National Electrical Code. Class 2 transformers are almost universally used for alarm work and are usually of the plug-in type. See also *Class 2*.

closed circuit loop   See *double closed loop; single closed loop*.

closed circuit television (CCTV)   An on-premises TV system used to enable a guard to watch one or more critical areas, such as entrances and high-value areas. The TV signal is usually transmitted by coaxial cable or fiber-optic cable and is usually limited to distances of a few hundred to a few thousand feet.

closed window bridge   A method of connecting subscribers' phone lines, in a telephone exchange, to a common channel to an alarm central station in such a manner that a failure or attempt to jam on one subscriber's line will not disable the transmission of alarm signals from another subscriber. Used in multiplex systems. Compare *open window bridge*.

closing signal   A signal transmitted by an alarm system to the central station when the proprietor secures and leaves the premises at the close of business. Usually done on a prearranged time schedule. See also *opening signal*.

coaxial cable   A special kind of shielded cable that has one center conductor surrounded by relatively thick insulation, which in turn has a shield (usually braided wires, spirally laid wires, or foil) over it. An outer plastic jacket is usually included. Used primarily for radio frequency work, such as antenna lead-in and for closed circuit television cameras.

code wheel A wheel with teeth that rotates by either a windup or an electric motor to generate a code as it rotates. Teeth are removed as required to generate unique pulse codes that will identify a particular subscriber or location when an alarm is transmitted. Used in McCulloh loops.

coded transmitter A transmitter whose output is a string of pulses that identify the origin and type of alarm. McCulloh transmitters and digital dialers are examples.

coincident (1) Occurring at the same time. (2) Two detectors, usually of different kinds, wired so that both have to be in alarm at the same time in order to trip the alarm system. This technique is based on the idea that conditions that would trip a microwave system, for example, would probably not trip a PIR system, and vice versa; only an intruder would trip both types of detector at the same time. Their higher cost limits their popularity. Compare *redundant*.

color code, resistor A color code developed by the Radio, Electronic, Television Manufacturers Association (RETMA) to identify the value of resistors. For valves, see Table 1–5 in the text.

color code, telephone cable Telephone cable is sometimes used for alarm systems when many conductors are required. Since most telephone cable is paired (i.e., two wires twisted together), it is not easy to assign an orderly color code such as that used for resistors. The easiest method is to use the telephone industry's color code:

Column 1	Column 2
Blue	White
Orange	Red
Green	Black
Brown	Yellow
Slate (gray)	Plum (purple)

The first five wires consist of the five colors (in order) in column 1 paired with white, the first color in column 2. The next five repeat column 1, this time paired with the next color in column 2, namely red, and so on. This will accommodate 25 pair, which will be bundled together with blue thread, the next 25 pair with orange thread, then green, etc.

commercial alarm An alarm installed in a commercial or business location, as opposed to a residential alarm.

compromise To defeat or bypass an alarm system or part of it, to render it inoperative.

conductor Any material that is a good carrier of electricity. Metals such as copper, aluminum, and silver are good conductors.

conduit A pipe specially made to run wires through. Sometimes used in alarm systems to provide tamper protection, mechanical protection, or physical support of alarm wires.

connection diagram See *wiring diagram*.

constant current charging A charging method usually used for nickel-cadmium batteries. A constant (or nearly so) current is fed into the battery regardless of its level of charge.

constant voltage charging A charging method usually used for lead-acid batteries. A constant (or nearly so) voltage is fed into the battery regardless of its level of charge.

contact A switch, either magnetic or mechanical.

continuity The quality of an electrical circuit that is not interrupted, broken, or open.

control The nerve center of the alarm system located at the protected premises. It monitors the loop for a trip condition and rings a bell or transmits a signal, or both, but only when the system is armed. Also called a panel or control panel.

control key switch A key switch mounted on the control box or transmitter box, used to turn the entire alarm system on and off. Some control switches are also equipped with a loop (or circuit) test and bell test positions. The key is removable in the on and off positions but not in any test positions. See also *shunt switch*.

control panel See *control*.

control station See *remote control station*.

coverage (1) The extent of protection of any

alarm system. (2) The space protected by a motion detector.

CPS Cycles per second. The preferred term is now hertz (Hz).

crimp wire splice A device that makes a reliable electrical splice or connection by mashing a metal sleeve over the wires to be joined. Can be insulated or uninsulated. The reliability of the splice can be very poor if the proper tool is not used to make the crimp. The proper tool depends on the type of crimp device used. Diagonal cutters or pliers give poor results on most types of devices. Crimp devices are popular because they do not require soldering and save time.

cross alarm An alarm caused by shorting (crossing) the two wires of a direct wire protective loop.

crossover foil (1) Insulated or uninsulated, tinned brass shim stock (thin brass) about ¼ inch wide. (2) Self-adhesive, clear plastic tape (for insulation), ½ inch wide, over which is placed extra heavy, ⅜ inch wide, self-adhesive foil. Either kind is intended to carry the protective circuit from one window to another nearby window without the use of foil connectors. A short (1½ inch) piece of either type also makes excellent reinforcement for the foil at foil connectors.

cut wire options Some control units have short loops of various colors of wires protruding from the module. By cutting or not cutting the various colored wires in accordance with the manufacturer's instructions, the installer or serviceperson can select various operating features, such as continuous ringing bell or automatic bell time-out.

cutoff See *bell cutoff*.

cycles per second See *frequency; hertz*.

data base A table or listing stored in a computer that shows related data. For example, a subscriber data base could include address, telephone number of the control, zone assignment information, and so on. Such databases are used for uploading and downloading, alarm response, maintenance history, billing, etc.

day-night switch A switch located at the subscriber's premises, used by the subscriber to signal the opening and closing of the premises to the central station. Used only on direct wire, supervised accounts (the milliamp signal method), and multiplex systems.

DC See *direct current*.

dead (1) Describing a circuit without voltage. (2) Describing an ultrasonic transducer or any other motion detector, that does not work. (3) See *absorption*.

decibel (db) (1) Technically, a measure of relative power levels. (2) A measure of the loudness of a bell, siren, horn, or other noisemaker. (3) The strength of an audio signal.

decode The reverse process of *encoding*.

dedicated line or circuit A phone line or circuit that is dedicated solely to transmission of alarm signals. Examples are derived channel; direct wire; McCulloh; multiplex. Compare *dial-up*. See also *long-range radio*.

defeat Circumvention or bypassing of an alarm system, rendering it or a portion of it inoperative.

delay See *time delay*.

derived channel The use of a subcarrier signal on a normal, usually existing, dial telephone line to convey alarm signals without interfering with phone service. This type of service does provide line supervision.

detector Any device that senses the presence of an intruder, an intrusion attempt, fire, smoke, or any other dangerous or undesirable condition.

detector cell A small, pressure-sensitive switch, about 1½ inch in diameter and ⅛ inch thick. It can be thought of as a microsize mat switch. A valuable object can be placed on a detector cell so that removal of the object will signal an alarm.

deterrent Anything that discourages. The presence of an alarm system should, in the first place, discourage a potential intruder from attempting to break in.

diagnostics A program provided by manufacturers of microprocessor-based controls that performs a sequence of tests to determine current status and possible problems in the panel itself, in the loop wiring, and in *system keypads* and their wiring. Can be a tremendous troubleshooting aid.

dialer See *digital communicator; tape dialer.*

dialer programmer See *programmer.*

dial-up A telephone line that uses the dial telephone network as opposed to a telephone circuit that is dedicated only to alarm use. Since most businesses and residences already have dial telephone lines that can be used with digital communicators, there is no additional line charge. The disadvantage is that there is no line security. Compare *derived channel.*

digital communicator A device used to report alarm signals over the conventional dial telephone network. It operates digitally rather than by using a recorded tape with voice message as does a tape dialer. It requires a matching receiver at the monitoring location to receive, decode, and display the alarm message. Since it uses a regular telephone line, it saves the cost of leased telephone lines. Although more sophisticated than a tape dialer, it shares the same limitation: the line is unsupervised. It is generally acceptable for low-risk applications or where low cost is important. Compare *derived channel; tape dialer.*

digital dialer See *digital communicator.*

digital display See *liquid crystal display.*

digital multimeter (DMM) A very sensitive electronic replacement for a volt-ohm-milliamp meter (V-O-M). Readings are displayed digitally rather than by a moving pointer.

digital receiver A device that receives, decodes, and displays alarm signals transmitted by digital communicators. One receiver can typically service several hundred communicators.

diode A solid-state device that allows current to flow in one direction only. Sometimes called a rectifier.

direct connect An alarm system connected directly to a police station. Usually, but not always, employs the polarity reversal method of sending an alarm signal. Some police stations will accept direct connects, others will not.

direct current (DC) An electric current that flows in one direction only. Batteries provide direct current and most alarm equipment operates on DC. Compare *alternating current.*

direct line (DL) See *direct wire.*

direct wire (DW) A private line method of sending an alarm signal directly from the protected premises to the alarm central station, as opposed to the party line McCulloh method. There are several ways of doing this. One is the polarity reversal method (see *reversing relay*). Another is a break-and-cross circuit that uses specific milliamp signals over the wire, with different milliamp signals representing day secure, night secure, and various types of alarm conditions (usually referred to as a direct line). Another method is multiplexing and another is a derived channel. The term direct wire was most often used to refer to the break-and-cross circuit just described. This method is seldom used in new service anymore.

disarm To turn off an alarm system when opening the protected premises for entry.

discharge To use electrical energy out of a battery.

discharged Describing a battery with little or no energy left in it.

disconnecting door cord A special door cord with a plug and socket (or jack) in the middle of the cord. Typically used on overhead truck doors where opening the door disconnects the cord, triggering an alarm. Used when it is necessary to protect a pilot (personnel) door or windows on an overhead door. See also *door cord.*

distributed resistance loop In this type of loop, instead of one end-of-line resistor, small value resistors are manufactured inside each switch, and similar resistors are added to foil and to the outputs of motion detectors.

The distributed resistance loop requires a very special type of control and special switches. It needs great care in installation and is somewhat expensive and hard to find, but it does offer excellent security. Any attempt to cut, short, or ground wires, or any attempt to jumper or bypass even one switch, will trigger an alarm.

DL   Direct line. See *direct wire*.

DMM   See *digital multimeter*.

door cord   A very flexible, sturdy, jacketed wire used to carry an alarm circuit onto a door, window, or other movable object to connect to foil or other protective devices. Door cords are available in 12-inch to 24-inch lengths and in coiled cord versions, some of which can extend to 12 feet or more. The coiled types are used on sliding doors or truck doors. Available in two- or four-conductor form.

door shunt   See *shunt switch*.

door switch   See *magnetic contact*.

doppler shift   The apparent frequency shift due to motion of an intruder in ultrasonic and microwave detection.

double circuit lacing   A method of protecting openings, such as ducts and skylights, by stringing bare wire over the opening at about four-inch centers. Two such layers are placed at right angles about one inch apart, then connected to opposite sides ($+$ and $-$) of the loop. The wires are supported on insulators. Breaking or shorting the wires causes an alarm. One of the few detection devices to be intentionally connected in the grounded side of a loop (one layer). Double circuit lacing is seldom used any more.

double closed loop   Often called simply a double loop. A type of loop that can accommodate switches in series, preferably all in the hot (ungrounded) wire, and can also accommodate open circuit devices, such as mat switches, connected in parallel across the loop. Cutting either wire or shorting them together will trip the alarm.

double drop   A system of running two separate wires (each two-conductor) from a telephone terminal to a protected building,

preferably from two separate terminals and preferably to opposite ends of the building. Both lines are then connected to the Mc-Culloh transmitter inside. Should an intruder cut a wire prior to breaking in, the McCulloh transmitter can still send the alarm signal over the uncut drop. It is unlikely that an intruder will be aware that the second drop exists. A similar arrangement can also be used with dialers or digital communicators if line cut monitors are used.

double hung window   A type of window popular in older construction. The lower sash (window) can be raised and the upper sash can be lowered. Two contacts are usually used to protect both sashes.

download   The procedure whereby information is sent from a programmer, which is usually a personal computer, to a microprocessor-based control. This is usually done via dial-up telephone lines, although it could be done locally by temporarily plugging a programmer into the control. Using this method, it is possible to change the status or option settings of the control. See also *upload*.

drill mount   Generally refers to a contact that can simply be mounted in a drilled hole. See also *recessed contact*.

driver   See *siren driver; warbler driver*.

drop   The wire running from a telephone pole to a building.

drop relay   A more heavy-duty relay that operates to ring a bell and to perform the latching function when the sensitive relay drops out (releases) when an alarm condition is detected by the protective loop.

dry cell   A type of battery that is not rechargeable. Dry cells are occasionally used in alarm work, but because of the required periodic replacement, rechargeable batteries are usually favored. (Rechargeable batteries also have to be replaced periodically, but not as often as dry cells.) See also *lead-acid battery; nickel-cadmium battery*.

dual alarm service   Protection of premises by two separate alarm systems, usually serviced by different alarm companies. Thus protected, there is less likelihood that both systems could be successfully compromised and less chance of collusion among dishonest employees of the two alarm companies. Use is limited to high-risk applications because of the cost.

duress code Same function as duress switch except initiated by a special code entered on a keypad.

duress switch A special type of key switch that can be turned in either of two directions or can be operated with two different keys. One direction or key operates the alarm system in a normal manner. The other direction or key signals the central station that the owner of the protected premises is under duress (is held at gunpoint, for instance). A holdup switch is activated secretly, whereas a duress switch is activated openly, the bandit being unaware of its duress signaling function.

DW See *direct wire*.

dynamic battery test Part of a *diagnostics* test that places a heavy load (about 10 amps) on the battery briefly, during which time the voltage is checked. This is a relatively good method by which to predict imminent failure before total failure occurs. This test should be done with the charger disabled.

E-field detector Electomagnetic field detector. Detects an intrusion by the close approach of an intruder to a sensing wire. The sensing wire is supported on insulators a few feet inside a chain link fence or other physical barrier. Usually used for outdoor applications.

electronic key switch An electronic switch actuated by the pushing of the correct sequence of push buttons. Sometimes used in place of a key switch.

electronic siren An electronic device with a speaker, used to simulate the sound of a motor-driven siren.

electronic warbler An electronic device with a speaker, designed to produce a loud, penetrating, attention-getting noise that is unlike that of a siren. Many different sounds

are available, some of which have their own characteristic names or trade names. Sometimes used to circumvent antisiren ordinances.

elevation coverage The floor-to-ceiling (vertical) coverage pattern of a microwave or other detector. This is not necessarily the same as the azimuth (horizontal) coverage. Some microwave detectors intentionally have a small detection pattern pointing nearly straight down (in addition to the main, outward pattern) to prevent an intruder from sneaking directly under the unit to attempt to defeat it.

emergency button A push-button switch (usually NO) connected to a local bell alarm system so that momentarily pushing the button will immediately sound the bell, even if the protective loop part of the system is turned off at the time.

encoding (1) A method of converting alarm signals and uploading and downloading information into signals suitable for transmission over phone lines or radio. (2) The process of scrambling text or command signals used in uploading and downloading so that they would be meaningless even if intercepted. Also called encryption.

encryption See *encoding*. Encryption can also be applied to a data base stored in a computer in such a way that theft of the data base would be meaningless without the correct key, needed to decrypt the data.

endless loop The tape in a tape dialer cartridge is arranged in an endless loop so that it can be tripped repeatedly without having to be manually rewound after each operation. A sensing device stops the tape after one complete playing to avoid its running forever once tripped.

end-of-line battery loop A double closed loop in which the loop power is provided by a battery or power supply separate from that which supplies the control or transmitter. This battery or power supply is often, but not always, remote from the control.

end-of-line resistor loop A type of double closed loop that has a resistor of usually a few thousand ohms connected across the end of the loop that is distant from the control. It provides loop supervision against opens and shorts if the loop is properly wired and does not require an end-of-line battery or the need to return both ends of the loop to the control panel. Provides easy installation, no maintenance.

end-of-line terminator loop A type of double loop that has a terminator at the far end. The terminator is usually a resistor, but some fire alarms use a diode instead.

energized (1) The condition of equipment to which electrical power has been applied. (2) The condition of a relay coil to which electrical power has been applied, holding its contacts in the opposite normal condition.

entry-exit delay A feature of some alarm systems, particularly in residential applications, that permits locating the on-off station inside the protected premises. When exiting, the user turns the system on, which starts the exit time delay cycle (typically 30 to 120 seconds). The user can then exit through a designated protected door without tripping the alarm during this delay. Later, when the user returns, the system is tripped when the door is opened. This action starts an entry delay cycle but does not cause an immediate alarm (although a small prealert alarm may sound as a reminder). The user then has, typically, 15 to 60 seconds to turn the system off. An intruder would not have a key to turn the system off, therefore the alarm would ring or a silent signal would be transmitted after the entry delay expired.

environmental considerations Factors that must be considered in the proper application of alarm detectors to reduce false alarms, particularly with motion sensors. Such factors include rain, fog, snow, wind, hail, humidity, temperature, corrosion, moving or swaying objects, vegetation growth, and animals and depend on the type(s) of detectors being considered and where they are to be located.

E-O-L End-of-line. See *end-of-line battery loop; end-of-line resistor loop*.

event log A list of events maintained by a computer or microprocessor-based control. Such a list can be invaluable in determining what happened and what needs to be fixed, if anything.

E volts The electrical pressure in a circuit that causes electricity to flow. Derives from the term electromotive force.

Exor-system® The trade name of a troubleshooting test instrument that is particularly useful in locating swingers. No longer available. See also *Loop-Sticks®*.

failure to alarm A fault or problem existing in an alarm system that prevents detection of a dangerous condition such as an intrusion. Compare *false alarm*.

false alarm An alarm signal that does not represent a dangerous or unwanted condition. This condition is caused by some fault or problem in the system, by subscriber error, or by phone line problems. Compare *failure to alarm*.

fault A problem or trouble condition in an alarm system. A fault can prevent the system from working when it should or can cause false alarms.

fence alarm Any of a variety of devices mounted on or near a fence to detect someone climbing over, cutting through, or lifting fence fabric when going under the fence.

fiber-optic cable A hair-fine glass strand that is covered with a "cladding" (coating) of a different kind of glass and usually covered with a plastic jacket. Used primarily for closed circuit TV in place of coaxial cable, with use of proper adapters.

field disturbance detector See *capacitance detector*.

first-in alarm The ability of some controls to store and to later indicate the first zone to go into alarm. Helpful in determining point of entry or in resolving false alarm causes.

float charge To put just enough electrical energy into a lead-acid battery from a constant voltage charger to keep it fully charged without overcharging.

floor trap See *trap*.

foil   See *wall foil; window foil.*

foil connector   The terminal or connector between foil and wire. Also called a foil take-off or foil takeoff block.

foot rail   A switch that is actuated by the foot to signal a holdup. It is usually operated by inserting the toe under the rail and lifting, rather than pushing down on the rail, as it is less likely to be accidentally triggered that way.

forced arming   A feature, of dubious value, that automatically bypasses unsecured zones to permit the user the convenience of immediately arming the alarm system. This may leave much of the protective service out of operation and the user unaware of this fact.

form A contact   Single-pole, single-throw, normally open relay or momentary switch contact. Abbreviated SPST-NO.

form B contact   Single-pole, single-throw, normally closed relay or momentary switch contact. Abbreviated SPST-NC.

form C contact   Single-pole, double-throw (SPDT) switch or relay contact. Also called a transfer contact or a break-and-cross contact. SPDT toggle switches can be two-position or three-position, the third or center position being "off." Two-position SPDT switches can be spring-loaded (momentary). Three-position SPDT switches can be spring-loaded in one or both directions, the center position being "off."

freq.   See *frequency.*

frequency (freq.)   The rate at which AC electricity completes a cycle (two polarity reversals). Frequency is expressed in hertz (Hz), formerly called cycles per second (CPS). Typical house power in the United States is 60 Hz.

frequency shift keying   A method of transmitting digital information over a line by using two different frequencies to represent binary ones and zeroes.

FSK   Frequency shift keying.

fuse   Electrical safety valve; a device designed to blow or open the circuit to interrupt dangerously high currents that could damage equipment or cause a fire. A fuse can be blown only once. Fuses are available in ratings of 1/100 amp to several thousand amps. Typical alarm work involves fuses from about 1/4 to 5 amps. Fuse ratings must be matched to the service (both current and maximum voltage), and replacements should always match equipment manufacturer's recommendations. Compare *circuit breaker.* See also *slow-blow fuse.*

gauge, wire   (1) A measure of the size of electrical wires (excluding the insulation). Around the world there are various wire gauge systems in use, but in the United States the standard reference is to American wire gauge, which is also known as Brown and Sharp or B & S wire gauge. The higher the gauge number, the smaller the wire. Typical sizes used in alarm work vary from 16 gauge through 18, 20, 22, and 24 gauge. (2) A device used to measure wire size.

gel/cell®   (1) Trade name of Globe Union Inc.'s lead-acid battery. (2) Sometimes used colloquially to indicate a similar battery. The term derives from the use of a gelled electrolyte rather than a liquid electrolyte.

geophones   Another name for a seismic detector. These devices are sometimes used in outdoor intrusion detection systems. Sensors are usually buried and detect intruder footfalls or vehicle vibrations.

giga-   A prefix meaning one billion, as in gigahertz (GHz).

glass break detector   A device mounted on or near windows that detects the breakage of glass by the sound frequencies generated when the glass breaks. Some detectors are self-contained and are connected directly into the protective loop. Others include an electronic discriminator. See also *vibration contact.*

glazing   The clear material set in windows, usually glass, sometimes plastic.

grade of service   Usually, the AA, A, B, or C grade of alarm service outlined in UL Standard 681.

ground   (1) A conductor that is in direct electrical contact with the earth, or any wire that is in turn connected to such a conductor. Cold-water pipes or long (6 to 8 feet) rods driven into the earth usually make good ground connections. (2) A common point in an alarm system or other electrical circuit or any wire connected to such a point. In this instance, "ground" is just a convenient reference point and does not have to be connected to the earth.

ground start A type of telephone system in which you have to first short one side of the telephone line to ground momentarily in order to get a dial tone before you can dial an outgoing number. Requires a special feature on a digital communicator or connection into the phone line ahead of a private branch exchange; otherwise the communicator will be unable to report an alarm.

guard See *runner*.

guardrail A device mounted around photoelectric beams and mirrors to protect them mechanically from bumps and misalignment.

handshake signal A series of query and acknowledgment signals exchanged by two computers or between a computer (programmer) and a microprocessor-based control in order to correctly establish communications, usually over a phone line, preparatory to exchanging data or for uploading and downloading.

hang-up signal The signal, usually a tone, programmed onto a tape dialer to cause it to hang up (disconnect from the phone line) at the end of the voice message. The same tone, in short pulses, is used to generate the dial pulses of the phone number(s) to be called. This tone is generated by the dialer programmer.

hard-wire system A system in which the detectors are connected with wire, as opposed to a wireless (radio) transmitter. (2) The connecting of any parts of an alarm system with wire.

head (1) Usually, an ultrasonic transducer. (2) A transducer of a photoelectric beam or other motion detector. (3) The part of a tape dialer that picks up the recorded signal from the tape.

headset An audio listening device clamped over one or both ears by a headband. Useful for testing alarm circuits by listening for the click when connected to a live circuit.

hertz (Hz) Unit of measurement of frequency. Formerly called cycles per second (CPS).

hide-in burglar One who hides inside a protected premises before closing time with the intent to commit thefts undetected after closing time. The burglar would then trip the alarm upon breaking out and make a fast getaway before police had a chance to respond. Interior photoelectric beams, traps, or motion detectors can often detect a hide-in burglar early on to permit response and apprehension.

high-risk account An account that stands to suffer a high dollar loss in case of a successful burglary, such as jewelry stores, banks, precious metals handlers, and some museums.

high-security alarm The term is usually used to refer to a kind of system that offers better security than others, but the user must be well aware of the alarm dealer, distributor, or manufacturer's reputation and of the particular application, because what might offer excellent security in one application could represent poor security in another.

high-security magnetic contact A special magnetic contact that uses a balanced magnetic circuit that will alarm upon attempted defeat with an external magnet of either polarity. It is enclosed in a housing with a cover protected by a tamper arrangement (preferably on a 24-hour circuit) and with provision for protecting the wiring, preferably by running it in conduit. Few magnetic contacts meet these requirements, even those called "high security" by their manufacturers. High-security magnetic contacts are expensive, costing typically twenty to thirty times more than standard magnetic contacts, but they do offer improved security.

hit and run attack   See *smash and grab attack*.

hold-out   See *anticlash*.

hold up   If sunlight or other bright light falls on the receivers of some kinds of photoelectric beams, this extra light source will hold up the beam so that an intruder walking through the regular beam will not trip the alarm. Pulsed type photoelectric beams will go into an alarm condition rather than being held up.

holdup   A robbery.

holdup alarm   A means of notifying a remote location, such as an alarm central station or police station, that a holdup is in progress. Holdup alarms are always silent and are actuated secretly, otherwise the noise of a local alarm or the obvious pushing of an alarm button could prompt the burglar to violence. A holdup alarm should not be confused with a panic alarm or a duress alarm.

Holmes, Edwin   Inventor of the electric burglar alarm, 1853.

horn   (1) An electromechanical noise-making device that uses a vibrating diaphragm to generate sound. Used as an annunciator or as an indoor warning device. Commonly found on single-station fire alarms. (2) An electronic horn, such as Mallory's Sonalert®, used as in definition one and also as a test device. See also *Sonalert®*.

hot   (1) Electrically live; having a voltage present. Often used to refer to voltages high enough to cause a shock, such as 120 volts, but can be used to refer to the presence of any voltage. (2) See *hot wire*.

hot key   A special key used in place of the regular key in a control or shunt lock to signal a duress condition. See also *duress switch*.

hot wire   (1) The ungrounded wire in a protective loop. This is usually the positive wire, but not always. (2) The ungrounded wire in 120-volt power wiring, usually black, sometimes red.

hydraulic detector   An outdoor perimeter detector that is buried a few inches in the ground. It senses an intruder by the pressure on the ground and transmits this pressure signal through a hydraulic (fluid-filled) tube to a very sensitive pressure switch. See also *seismic detector*.

hydrostatic sensor   See *hydraulic detector*.

Hz   See *hertz*.

I   The abbreviation for current (amperes). Derives from "intensity."

impedance   The resistance of an AC circuit. It is composed of line resistance, capacitive reactance, inductive reactance, and leakage resistance and is a vector (complex number). Very rarely needed by alarm servicepeople.

indicator light   Any light, either incandescent or **LED**, that indicates the status of an alarm system, such as the "ready" light.

infrared detector   (1) Passive type—one that detects an intruder by body heat (IR energy). This type does not emit any IR energy but only detects it. (2) Active type—a photoelectric beam that uses IR instead of visible light. This kind does emit IR energy. See also *photoelectric beam*.

instructions   Every alarm troubleshooter should have written instructions readily available to explain each piece of equipment on which he or she has to work. Unfortunately, this is seldom the case. A few minutes spent reading instructions can often save hours of wasted effort.

insulating block   Safes and other metal objects protected by capacitance detectors must be insulated from ground for proper operation. Insulating blocks for this purpose are available from several alarm suppliers.

insulator   Any material that is a very poor conductor of electricity, such as plastic, glass, Bakelite, dry wood, and dry paper. See also *insulating block*.

intrusion alarm   An arrangement of electrical and electronic devices designed to detect the presence of an intruder or an attempted intrusion and to provide notification either by making a loud noise locally or by transmitting an alarm signal to some remote monitoring location or both. See also *silent alarm*.

invisible beam   See *photoelectric beam*.

IR   Infrared.

jalousie window   See *louver window*.

keypad   A collection of push buttons mounted on a plate, used to enter a secret code that arms and disarms alarm systems. Often resembles a touch-tone phone pad. Used to replace key operated switches. Decoding of the correct combination is done by electronics mounted behind the pad. Also called a stand-alone keypad. Compare *system pad*.

kilo-   A prefix meaning one thousand as in kiloohms.

kiss off   A signal used to terminate communications between a digital communicator and its receiver or programmer.

L A battery   Lead-acid battery.

lacing   Fine wire stretched across openings such as skylights and ducts to detect entry; breaking a wire triggers the alarm. Lacing is also sometimes used over door panels that might get kicked in or cut through. The wires are covered with masonite to conceal and protect them during everyday use. Sometimes two sets of lacing are installed at right angles to each other so that breaking or shorting the wires (bare wires are used and are supported on insulators) will trigger an alarm. With the advent of motion detectors, lacing is now seldom used. See also *trap* (4).

lamp cord   Two-conductor, parallel construction, 18 gauge wire typically used on 120-volt floor and table lamps and in light-duty extension cords. This kind of wire is sometimes used in alarm systems for bell runs or power runs. See also *zip cord*.

LCD   See *liquid crystal display*.

lead-acid battery   One type of rechargeable battery used for standby service in alarm work. Produces 2 volts per cell and requires a constant voltage charging source. See also *nickel-cadmium battery; sealed battery*.

leased alarm   Usually, a type of alarm service where the customer does not buy the alarm system. Technically, a lease refers to equipment. An alarm company generally does not lease equipment; it provides a protective service. This service does involve the use of alarm equipment, but that is not the same as a lease. There is an important tax angle in this terminology. See also *subscriber*, and your tax advisor.

leased line   A line, pair of wires, or circuit that is leased from the local telephone company and used for alarm-reporting service.

LED   See *light-emitting diode*.

levels of authorization   In a computer system, particularly one used for uploading and downloading, various levels of access are established. For example, an alarm monitoring person may be granted access to determining whether a subscriber's system is armed or not. The supervisor may have a higher level of authority that would enable him or her to arm or disarm a system from the central station. A manager could have even higher authority, to change other operating functions of the subscriber's control.

light beam transmission   A technique of sending an alarm signal a short distance (up to about 1,000 feet) via a photoelectric beam. An alarm signal is used to turn off the photoelectric beam transmitter. This puts the receiver into alarm, which in turn trips an alarm control wired to it. Light beam transmission is a handy method where it is impossible to run wires, such as from one building to another. See also *wireless*.

light-emitting diode (LED)   A transistorized light bulb; a small, solid-state device that gives off light when current is passed through it. LEDs are used extensively as indicators in alarm systems. They are preferred over bulbs because of longer life and low current drain (typically 10 to 50 mA). Available in red, yellow, and green. They are polarity sensitive and must have a current-limiting resistor, otherwise the excessive current flow will destroy them in a fraction of a second.

line cut monitor   A device attached to a dial-up type telephone line that will detect a cut or short in the phone line. Can be used to enable a local bell or to transfer a dialer or digital communicator to a back-up telephone line.

lined box   An alarm system control, bell, or equipment box that has an interior metal lining that is insulated from the box. Box and lining are both connected to the protective loop. Drilling or chiseling through the box will signal an alarm. Used on grade A systems.

line security   See *line supervision*.

line seizure   (1) The act of a tape dialer or digital communicator seizing the phone line, as when a person picks up the receiver of a telephone. (2) An arrangement whereby a tape dialer or digital communicator disconnects all telephone instruments from the line when tripped. This prevents the burglar from defeating the system by simply picking up a phone receiver.

line supervision   An arrangement where a known current, either AC, DC, pulses, or a combination, is present on the line to the central station. Cutting or shorting the line will change this current, signaling an alarm. In high-security systems, complex line supervision systems are used, the better to detect attempts to defeat the system.

line voltage   (1) 120-volt AC house power. (2) The voltage on a telephone line used for alarm service.

liquid crystal display (LCD)   A display method that can show letters, numbers, and special characters to form instructions in English (or other language). Typically used on system keypads and consisting of from one to four rows of twenty to thirty-six characters each. The same technology is used on wrist watches and on portable computers. Requires very low current drain.

listen-in feature   A feature available on some tape dialers and digital communicators that enables monitoring personnel to listen for sounds of intrusion via a microphone at the protected premises. The listen-in period takes place after the necessary identifying message has been transmitted. By having the monitoring personnel classify the sounds, false alarms can be reduced.

live   (1) Describing a circuit with a voltage present on it. See also *hot*. (2) Describing a motion detector that is working. (3) See *reflection*.

live trap   See *trap* (3).

load   The general name given to any electrical power-consuming device. Examples of loads in alarm work are bells, buzzers, horns, sirens, lights, strobes, beacons, and resistors.

local bell alarm   An alarm system designed only to sound a bell at the protected premises when the system is tripped. Compare *silent alarm*; see also *monitored alarm*.

lock cover   A device mounted over an outdoor key switch to keep rain, snow, and dirt out of the keyhole.

lockout   The disabling of a control or the alarm reporting portion of a control via downloading. Used primarily on those subscribers who don't pay their bill. Be sure to comply with all contractual and legal re quirements, such as notification of subscriber via certified letter, prior to taking such a step.

log-on   (1) Procedure required to gain entry to a computer or to a specific computer program as an authorized user. Usually involves the use of a user identification number and one or more passwords. (2) Similar procedure to establish authorized access to a control for uploading and downloading. See also *levels of authorization*.

long-range radio   A method of transmitting alarm signals via radio. Typical ranges are five to twenty-five miles. Two-way systems are available, as are a number of different frequency bands.

loop   See *protective loop*.

loop diagram   A diagram or drawing that can greatly simplify troubleshooting by showing the physical arrangement of the protected premises and the layout of the alarm system. Unfortunately, such diagrams are seldom made.

loop status indicator   A light bulb, LED meter, or digital display that tells the user whether the protective loop is in the secure condition.

Loop-Sticks®: A highly sensitive device for testing protective loops. The transmitter, connected to the loop, senses loop condition and transmits a low radio frequency of the test results, using the loop as an antenna. The receiver is carried by the troubleshooter as the loop is mechanically disturbed, e.g., by tapping on loop wires with a small stick or rapping lightly on a foiled window with a screwdriver handle. Poor connections are indicated by a beep on the receiver.

louver window A window consisting of many slats of glass about three or four inches wide that all open simultaneously by pivoting on their long axis as a crank is turned. Difficult to protect. Alarm screens may be used, or several sets of magnetic contacts can be used with switches and magnets glued to alternate pieces of glass. Also called jalousie window. More popular in warmer climates.

McCulloh circuit A party line arrangement for transmitting alarm signals from many subscribers over one pair of telephone wires. Each subscriber and each type of alarm condition (burglary, fire, holdup, etc.) has a unique code signal, enabling the central station operator to identify the source and nature of the alarm signal. See also *multiplex*. A McCulloh circuit, often called a McCulloh loop, is not part of the protective loop. Also note that McCulloh transmitters at the various subscribers' premises are connected in series. Seldom used in new installations.

McCulloh loop A means of transmitting alarm signals from many subscribers over telephone wires to the alarm central station. The loop refers to the telephone lines. The receiver and all transmitters are wired in series. Signals are sent as a string of pulses that identifies the location and nature of the alarm. The McCulloh loop is seldom used anymore because it requires metallic telephone lines (i.e., DC continuity). Do not confuse it with the protective loop. See *code wheel; coded transmitter; metallic; register, McCulloh; round.*

mA Milliampere ($\frac{1}{1000}$th of an ampere).

magnetic contact A magnetically operated switch, typically used on doors and windows to detect opening. The switch is mounted on the frame or fixed part while the magnet is mounted on the movable door or window. Generally much easier to use than earlier, mechanically actuated switches. Available in NO, NC, or SPST contact forms.

magnetic contact cover See *terminal cover.*

magnetic tape The material on which the telephone number and voice message of a tape dialer is recorded.

magnetometer A device that is sensitive to small changes in the earth's magnetic field. Used mainly for vehicle detection when buried under or alongside a driveway.

maintained contact switch A conventional switch, one that stays in its last set position. Compare *momentary contact switch.*

make contact The normally open contacts of a relay or push button; the ones that close when the coil is energized and open when de-energized. The opposite of break contacts.

manual reset A type of alarm that must be silenced or restored to the nonalarm condition by someone going to the protected premises to reset it.

master A unit, usually a type of detector, that can stand alone but can also accept the inputs from one or more slave units for expanded coverage. Occasionally used in ultrasonic systems.

master code A secret code used to access that part of the program in the PC (or programmer) that permits the downloading of program changes to a microprocessor-based control.

mat coupler A small electronic device used to connect a mat switch, which is an open circuit device, into a single closed loop type alarm system. May not work with solid-state controls as loop current is too low.

mat switch A very thin, pressure-sensing switch placed under carpets (and carpet padding) to trip an alarm when an intruder steps on it. Typical size is 30 × 36 inches. Sizes vary from 7 × 24 inches (stair tread size) to 30 × 45 inches. Typical thickness is ³⁄₃₂ inch to ⅛ inch. Runner mat is 2½ × 25 feet and is cut to the desired length with scissors. With one exception, all mat switches are normally open. Supervised mats have two sets of leads. For damp or wet locations, sealed type mats should be used.

maximum loop resistance All alarm controls or transmitters have maximum loop resistance limits. If a protective loop is used that has a higher resistance, the system may not work or will not work reliably. This problem will usually be worsened if the alarm supply voltage happens to be low. The loop resistance limit depends on the make and model of equipment. It can vary from about 100 ohms for some of the older, relay-operated systems to over 100,000 ohms on some new solid-state systems. Most of the newer equipment will accommodate loops of any practical length. Loops that are too long should be zoned for convenience in any case. Controls with extremely high limits have the disadvantage that moisture, dirt, or corrosion can more easily shunt the system. A few thousand ohms would seem a good compromise, which is the limit of most E-O-L resistor loops.

medical alert An alarm system by which an invalid or elderly person can push a button near the bedside to alert someone that a doctor, ambulance, or other medical assistance is required.

mega- A prefix meaning one million, as in megahertz.

mercury tilt switch A switch that is sensitive to position. The switch contains a small globule of mercury, which is a liquid metal and therefore a conductor. The globule rolls around inside the switch as it is tilted and either makes or breaks the circuit, depending on how it is mounted and the position it is in. Mercury tilt switches can usually be adjusted so that they can be used on closed or open circuit alarms. They are commonly used on transoms and on overhead and tilt-up doors. Their sensitivity should not be set too high, or false alarms will result from vibration.

metallic A term from the telephone industry meaning a circuit of solid copper, one having DC continuity from one end to the other, as opposed to a typical voice-grade telephone circuit that has AC continuity through the various repeater, carrier, and multiplex systems used by the telephone company, but without DC continuity. DC continuity is required for reversing relay, direct wire, and McCulloh loops. In some areas, particularly in some large cities, it is becoming increasingly difficult, if not impossible, to get the necessary interoffice metallic pairs for new alarm circuits. This fact is making new alarm multiplex systems, long-range radio, and derived channel circuits more popular because they do not require metallic pairs.

metallic foil See *window foil*.

micro- A prefix meaning one-millionth, as in microampere.

microphone A transducer that converts sound energy to electrical energy. Used in audio alarms and sometimes as a listen-in device on tape or digital dialers. Also used in some vault alarms.

microprocessor A computer on a microchip, the heart of all personal computers. Now used as the heart of alarm control panels. With a microprocessor designed into a control, it is possible to obtain features that would be prohibitively expensive otherwise. Some examples are dozens of zones, information displays in English (or another language), and zone parameters (speed of response, perimeter-interior, entry-exit, instant response, etc.) assignable for each zone. Most important, these things can be changed, often without requiring a service call to the premises. First introduced by Ron Gottsegen of Radionics in 1977.

microwave detector A device that senses the motion of an intruder in a protected area by a Doppler shift in the transmitted radio frequency energy. Microwave detectors generally operate at 10.525 GHz. Older units operated at 915 MHz.

milli- A prefix meaning one-thousandth, as in milliampere.

milliammeter method   A method of troubleshooting a protective loop, utilizing a milliammeter instead of a voltmeter. Used primarily on the milliamp signal method of alarm.

milliamp signal method   A method of sending secure and alarm signals over telephone lines in which different current levels (measured in milliamps) represent such conditions as day secure, night secure, foil or wire break, door or window open, and motion sensor alarm. A milliammeter at the alarm central station indicates the line current and thus the alarm condition. Most often referred to as a direct wire system. Do not confuse with reversing relay.

minimum loop leakage resistance   Any open loop or double closed loop alarm control or transmitter has a minimum leakage resistance. Any resistance lower than this value will produce an alarm or will be unreliable in operation. For example, a mat switch, when stepped on, will present a resistance that is essentially zero to produce an alarm. Possible sources of leakage resistance are moisture, dirt, and corrosion, which can cause false alarms. On a double closed loop system the leakage resistance value that will cause an alarm condition will depend on where in the loop the problem occurs.

minisonic   An ultrasonic detector with the transmitting and receiving transducers and all the electronics in one box, as opposed to multiple-head or master-slave systems.

mirror   An item used to change the direction of a photoelectric beam to obtain greater coverage. Each mirror worsens the alignment problem, reduces maximum beam length by 25 to 30 percent, and can get dirty and knocked out of alignment. It is not a good idea to use more than one mirror. The recommended practice today is not to use any mirrors.

modulated beam   A photoelectric beam that uses a pulsed rather than steady beam of light. The advantage is that a modulated beam cannot be held up (defeated) by an intruder holding a flashlight in front of the receiver or by sunlight. Either will create an alarm. Another advantage in IR-emitting diode transmitter designs is greater range.

momentary contact switch   A push-button or similar type of switch that returns to normal when released. Opposite of maintained contact switch. See also *push-button*.

money clip   See *money trap*.

money trap   A special switch placed in the bottom of a cash drawer. It is activated during a holdup by pulling out the bottom bill of the stack, which has been previously inserted into the trap. To prevent a false alarm, care must be taken not to remove that bottom bill at any other time.

monitored alarm   A local bell alarm that is also monitored at a remote location, usually via telephone lines; a combination local bell alarm and silent alarm.

motion detector   Any of several devices that detects an intruder by motion within a protected area or protected volume. See *area protection; infrared; microwave; ultrasonic; volumetric protection*.

mounting bracket   A mechanical device for mounting a detection device in the necessary position. Simple ones are used for magnetic contacts on two-way swinging doors. More complex ones are used for motion sensors and usually allow for correct aiming. They are also used to mount CCTV cameras.

multicircuit key switch   A key-operated switch that has two or three form C contacts. Generally used on an alarm control or transmitter for on-off-test operation. By comparison, a shunt switch has only one pole (SPST or SPDT contacts). See also *form C contact*.

multimeter   The basic piece of alarm test equipment. An electrical device used to measure AC and DC volts, ohms, DC current (amps and milliamps), and sometimes AC current. See also *digital multimeter; V-O-M meter*.

multiple head   (1) A motion detector that is not self-contained; one that operates as a master with one or more slaves connected to it. (2) In particular, an ultrasonic system that has separate transducers connected to the master unit, as opposed to a self-contained minisonic.

multiplex (1) In general, any method of sending many signals over one communications channel. (2) Specifically, any method of sending alarm signals from many subscribers over one pair of wires to a monitoring location. (Technically, a McCulloh circuit does this, but the term multiplex is generally used to refer to the newer, electronic techniques using polling computers and similar methods.)

nano- A prefix meaning one-billionth, as in nanosecond.

National Electrical Code (NEC) A code detailing safe wiring methods and the safe use of electricity. Article 725 of this code outlines requirements for the safe installation of alarms (and other low-voltage, limited-energy equipment). These requirements are few and simple compared to power wiring. Most cities and counties adopt the NEC (or a very similar code) as law. These requirements deal only with electrical safety and not with security.

NC See *normally closed*.

NEC See *National Electrical Code*.

Ni-Cad See *nickel-cadmium battery*.

nickel-cadmium battery (Ni-Cad) One type of rechargeable battery occasionally used for standby service in alarm work. Produces nominally 1.25 volts per cell and usually requires a constant current charging source for sealed types. The large, vented cell nickel-cadmium battery (generally found only in some large fire alarm systems) can use constant voltage charge. Nickel-cadmium batteries are seldom used in burglar alarm systems due to loss of storage capacity, known as the "memory effect." See also *lead-acid battery; sealed battery*.

NO See *normally open*.

noise cancellation A technique used in audio alarms and, in particular, in audio discriminators to help reduce false alarms. Cancellation microphones are placed near known background noise sources (such as furnaces or machinery) or outside. These signals are then subtracted from or cancelled out of the sounds picked up by the regular detection microphones. Thus, noises from known sources or those originating outside are less likely to cause false alarms. Must be used with caution to prevent loss of protection.

normally closed (NC) A switch whose contacts are closed when the button is not pushed (or the magnet is away from the switch), or a relay whose contacts are closed when the relay coil is not energized. Used in open loop alarm systems, as the switches are in the opposite-normal condition when the premises are secured.

normally open (NO) A switch whose contacts are open when the button is not pushed (or when the magnet is away from the switch), or a relay whose contacts are open when the relay coil is not energized. Same as make contact. Used in a closed loop alarm system, as the switches are in the opposite-normal condition when the premises are secured.

normally open loop A type of protective loop in which all switches are wired in parallel and are open in the secure mode.

object protection See *spot protection*.

ohm (Ω) The unit of electrical resistance or friction. A measurement of what slows down or limits the amount of current flow in a circuit. It is represented by R (resistance) in Ohm's law.

omnidirectional In all directions. Early microwaves that operated at 915 MHz (often called radar alarms) were omnidirectional. Some ultrasonic transducers are also omnidirectional; that is, they have a 360-degree pattern.

on-off switch (1) A switch used to turn an entire system on or off, as opposed to a shunt switch, which bypasses only one door or a portion of the system. (2) A switch on any device that is used to turn its power on or off.

open and closed loop A combination of an open loop and a closed loop, used on some controls. Note that, unlike the double closed loop, the open loop conductor in this system is not supervised. That is, cutting this wire will disable part of the system without causing an alarm condition.

open circuit loop See *normally open loop.*

opening (1) Any possible point of entry for an intruder, such as a window, door, ventilator, or roof hatch. (2) Any such point that is protected by an alarm detection device. (3) See *opening signal.* (4) See *scheduled opening; unscheduled opening.*

opening signal An alarm signal transmitted by the alarm system to the central station, representing the normal opening of the protected premises for business. The difference between an intrusion signal and a normal opening signal is based mainly upon an opening time agreed on in advance by the subscriber and the alarm company. The alternative is to use a shunt switch or entry delay to permit the subscriber to enter without transmitting an alarm signal. See also *closing signal.*

open window bridge A method of connecting subscribers' phone lines, in a telephone exchange, to a common channel to an alarm central station in such a manner that a failure or attempt to jam on one subscriber's line may disable the transmission of alarm signals from another subscriber. Used in multiplex systems. Compare *closed window bridge.*

operating procedures See *procedures.*

optics (1) The lenses, reflectors, and mirrors used to control the direction of photoelectric beams. These surfaces must be kept clean to help reduce false alarms. (2) Lenses or reflectors that determine the coverage pattern of a PIR. Many PIRs now have interchangeable units to permit the installer or system designer to choose the best coverage pattern without having to stock a large variety.

ordinance A local law. The alarm industry is now concerned with those ordinances regulating the installation and use of alarm systems. Many ordinances specifically address the false alarm problem.

overcharge To put too much electrical energy into a rechargeable battery. The excess energy destroys the battery or shortens its service life and might cause it to explode (although the batteries usually have safety vents). For these reasons, it is important always to use the correct charger for the type of battery being used and never to substitute types of batteries. See also *charge; lead-acid; nickel-cadmium.*

overhead door A truck, loading dock, or garage door. It comes in many varieties. They usually need wide-gap magnetic contacts and are best protected by overhead door contacts, which are made specially for them. See also *pilot door.*

P Power (watts).

pad See *mat switch.*

pair Two. Usually, two wires, such as a pair of telephone wires.

panel See *control.*

panic alarm A local bell alarm, triggered manually, usually by pushing a button. Usually found only in residential systems. The panic button permits the subscriber to trigger the alarm manually in case of intrusion, even though the alarm system happens to be turned off at the time. A panic alarm (which is audible) should not be confused with a holdup alarm, which is always silent.

parallel pair wire Two wires that run side by side and are held together by a web of plastic (part of the insulation) between them. Lamp cord and speaker wire are examples. Compare *twisted pair wire.*

party wall A common wall between two stores or premises. Typically, in a shopping center, party walls are only plaster or drywall. This makes an easy entry for a burglar from an adjacent store that has no alarm system. In such cases, interior detectors such as photoelectric beams or motion detectors are essential.

pass code A secret code used to allow a properly authorized programmer access to a digital communicator.

passive detector One that does not emit or

send out any kind of energy in order to perform its detection function. Most often refers to passive infrared, ambient light, stress, and seismic sensors, but also includes simple devices such as contacts, mat switches, pull traps, and foil. See also *active detector*.

passive IR See *infrared detector* (1).

pattern The shape of the area or volume of coverage of motion detectors. For instance, various horns on a microwave detector produce different patterns of coverage, some being long and narrow, others being more nearly round. PIRs usually have a wide variety of lenses or reflectors to permit a wide variety of detection patterns. Note that vertical coverage may well be quite different from horizontal coverage for any given pattern.

PC Personal computer. Used to upload and download information to a microprocessor-based alarm control. Can also be used to track and report alarm signals at a central station and for billing and other business uses.

PCM See *pulse code modulation*.

penetration (1) Breaking into a protected premises without tripping the alarm. (2) The ability of microwave energy to pass through certain building materials such as wood, plaster, glass, and drywall. The microwave system may thus detect movement in unwanted areas, causing false alarms. (3) A hole made through a wall, floor, or ceiling for the purpose of running wires, conduit, pipes, or ducts.

perimeter protection A scheme of protection that uses devices to detect intrusion at points of entry into a protected area such as doors, windows, skylights, and trap doors. Devices typically used in perimeter protection include magnetic or mechanical contacts, foil, lacing, and screens. Compare *motion detectors*.

pet mat A special mat switch that is less sensitive than the regular mat so that small pets will not trip the alarm if they walk on it. Running or jumping on the mat could still cause false alarms.

photo beam See *photoelectric beam*.

photoelectric beam A device that detects an intruder who interrupts a light beam. Most units now use invisible infrared beams instead of visible light so that an intruder cannot see and thus avoid them. Various units have range limits from 20 to 1,000 feet. Beam paths can be reflected with mirrors, but this is no longer advisable.

pico- A prefix meaning one-trillionth, as in picosecond.

pilot door An overhead door that has a smaller door built into it to permit entry of people without having to open the overhead door. See also *disconnecting door cord*.

pinch roller In a tape dialer, the rubber roller found opposite the capstan that holds the tape against the capstan when the dialer is in operation. It should be kept clean to prevent the tape's becoming stuck to it and jamming the machine.

PIR Passive infrared. See *infrared detector* (1).

plug-in transformer A transformer that has prongs to plug directly into a 120-volt AC wall outlet for simple, quick installation. Output (low voltage) usually has screw terminals for easy connection of alarm wiring. Usually has mounting tab to prevent accidental unplugging. These are usually rated Class 2. See also *Class 2*.

point protection See *spot protection*.

polarity Positive or negative in DC circuits. Usually it is important to connect alarm wires to the correct terminals, that is, those with the correct polarity. If the two wires are reversed, that is, connected with the wrong polarity, the system may not operate properly or may be damaged.

polarity-reversing relay See *reversing relay*.

police connect See *direct connect*.

police control An alarm control unit with a built-in reversing relay. Often used for silent alarms to police stations or other remote monitoring locations equipped with polarity-reversing monitors. See also *reversing relay*.

police response   Arrival of the local police at a location from which an alarm signal has been received, in the hopes of apprehending an intruder. Often refers to the length of time it takes the police to get there.

polling computer   A method of multiplexing in which a computer at an alarm central station interrogates, in turn, each subscriber on the circuit (often a telephone line). The response to the interrogation indicates the alarm condition or secure condition of each premises.

portable detector system   A complete alarm system in a self-contained package that is easy to transport and quick to set up. Portable systems usually employ a motion type detector to eliminate wiring. Most are local bell or siren units, although some include a dialer. Intended mainly for temporary service where immediate protection is a must.

power   The rate at which electrical energy is converted to another type of energy. Expressed in watts (W). Abbreviated with the letter P. In DC circuits power = volts × amps.

power consumption   The amount of electricity used by any given piece of equipment or system. It is expressed in watts. Most alarm equipment uses very little power in order to provide long standby battery operating time.

power supply   Any source of electrical energy. More specifically, power supply usually refers to an electronic device that converts AC to DC for use by alarm equipment. It may also reduce the voltage from 120 volts to the voltage needed by the alarm equipment. Some power supplies have provision for connecting a standby battery. Others will accommodate a rechargeable battery and will provide the necessary charging current for that battery.

premises   See *protected premises*.

pressure detector   See *hydraulic detector; mat switch*.

pressure-sensing tape   See *strip switch*.

preventive maintenance   Testing and checking out alarm systems on a regular schedule to locate and repair potential problems before false alarms or system failures result. Unfortunately, preventive maintenance is usually forgotten until trouble occurs.

primary cell   Any of several kinds of electrochemical devices that deliver DC electrical energy on demand. They are not rechargeable. The most common kind is the carbon-zinc cell used in flashlights. Sometimes called a battery.

procedures   The steps necessary to correctly operate an alarm system. Procedures are important for three reasons: (1) improper procedures will cause false alarms; (2) improper procedures can leave the premises unprotected; and (3) improper procedures can create vulnerabilities in the system. For instance, loosely controlled procedures used to authorize unscheduled openings could permit even a burglar to authorize such an opening.

programmer   (1) A device used to enter information into a microprocessor-based alarm control to obtain the desired operation. Examples are assigning zones to entry-exit delay and entering a phone number to which to report an alarm. A programmer can be a dedicated portable device, a portable computer, or a computer at another location. See also *downloading; uploading*. (2) A unit used to enter the desired telephone number(s) and recorded message(s) onto a tape for a tape dialer.

proprietary alarm   A silent alarm system that is monitored by subscriber personnel, such as guards at the subscriber's premises, rather than by an alarm company central station or other remote location. This could be a leased or a purchased system. Usually limited to large office buildings or large business or industrial complexes.

protected area   That portion of a premises (store, factory, house, etc.) that is covered by an alarm system. Due to cost considerations, the entire premises are often not covered. See also *protected premises*.

protected opening   See *opening* (2).

protected premises   The store, factory, warehouse, office, home, or other place where an alarm system is installed and operating properly.

protective loop The wiring connecting all of the detecting devices to the alarm system control or transmitter. The term comes from the days when the wiring was routed from the control, proceeded around the premises past each detector, then back to the control. With today's wide use of E-O-L resistance loops, there is no longer any need to loop the wiring back to the control box. Today's standard practice is also to use multiple zones, with each zone covering only one or a few detection devices. There are many kinds of protective loops. See *break-and-cross loop; distributed resistance loop; double closed loop; end-of-line battery loop; end-of-line resistor loop; normally open loop; single closed loop.*

proximity alarm See *capacitance detector.*

pull-apart door cord See *disconnecting door cord.*

pull trap See *trap.*

pulse code modulation (PCM) A method of transmitting signals in which the data to be sent is digitally encoded as a string of pulses.

pulsed beam See *modulated beam.*

pulse stretcher An electronic device that will sense a very brief input pulse, such as from a glass break detector. The output pulse is then stretched to ½ to 5 seconds (depending on manufacturer) to trip a control or transmitter. Thus a pulse too brief to trip a control or transmitter directly will give reliable operation. A pulse stretcher can be built into a control or can be a separate module which can be connected to any control or transmitter, provided the proper power is available to operate it.

push button (1) A momentary switch which is actuated manually. Used for panic buttons and sometimes used to arm or disarm a residential system from indoors. (2) A momentary switch used in the protective loop. See *tamper switch.*

R See *resistance.*

radar alarm A term sometimes used to refer to the now obsolete, omnidirectional, L-band microwave systems operating at 915 MHz. Now replaced by microwave.

radio frequency Frequencies above about 100 kHz.

radio transmission The sending of an alarm signal from the protected premises to an alarm central station via radio. Usually called long-range radio. Not to be confused with the term wireless, which is usually limited to on-premises signaling.

range control An adjustment on some ultrasonic or microwave detectors that determines the maximum range at which an intruder can be detected. This should not be confused with the sensitivity control.

ready light A light or LED, usually green or white, used to indicate whether the protective loop is in the secured condition, with all doors and windows closed, for example. In most systems the light goes on to indicate "secure" and off to indicate "not secure," but in some systems the opposite is true.

receiver (1) A unit that accepts or receives an alarm signal, such as a McCulloh receiver or digital receiver. (2) The unit at the end of a photoelectric beam that receives the light or infrared energy. (3) The ultrasonic transducer that receives the ultrasonic energy sent out by the transmitter.

recessed contact Any contact (switch), either magnetic or mechanical, that is designed to be mounted in a hidden manner, usually in a drilled hole. Most recessed magnetic contacts mount in a ¼-inch diameter hole, while most recessed flanged contacts mount in ⅜-inch diameter holes. Some designs require larger holes, typically ½ inch, ¾ inch, or 1 inch. Sometimes it is helpful to drill slightly oversized holes, as some brands of contacts run slightly oversize.

recessed flange contact A magnetic contact designed for recessed mounting that includes a flange larger in diameter than the body of the switch or magnet. The flange prevents the switch or magnet from falling into the mounting hole or from being pulled in by the wires. Many brands mount in a ⅜-

inch hole with a ¾-inch diameter flange, while some are larger. Sometimes only the switch is equipped with a flange, while the magnet is bare and mounts in a ¼-inch diameter hole. If necessary, on a tight-fitting door, the flange can be recessed by first drilling a hole the diameter of the flange with a flat wood bit (depth equals thickness of flange), then drilling the hole for the body. This assures proper centering.

rechargeable battery   A battery, such as a lead-acid or nickel-cadmium, that can be recharged. Compare *dry cell*.

rectifier   A device that converts alternating current to direct current. Also called a diode.

redundant   Overlapping. In a redundant alarm system, any of two or more detectors covering the same area could detect an intruder and could, by itself, trigger the alarm. If one detector failed, the other(s) would be there as a backup to detect an intruder. In a redundant system, if any detector falsely detects an intrusion a false alarm will result. Compare *coincident*.

reed switch   A type of magnetically operated switch made by sealing two small steel leaves or reeds inside a glass tube. When the magnet is brought near, the reeds flex slightly, touching each other to complete the circuit. When the magnet is removed, the reeds spring apart, breaking the circuit. See also *magnetic contact*.

reflection   The property of materials such as concrete, glass, wood, and tile to bounce back sound. These materials also bounce back ultrasonics, so that a lower than normal range setting may be required. See also *absorption; acoustics*.

reflector   See *bounce-back*.

register, McCulloh   A recording device that either punches holes in a paper tape or marks a paper tape with pens in response to a McCulloh receiver so as to permanently record the alarm signal codes sent by the transmitters on the McCulloh loop.

relay   An electrically operated switch.

release signal   See *hang-up signal*.

remote control station   A device that ena-

bles the user to turn the alarm system on or off at a location remote from the control unit. It is equipped with a key switch, toggle switch, or push button (depending on the type of alarm control unit) to do the switching and is usually equipped with a light or digital display to indicate loop status. When mounted outside the protected premises, it should have a tamper switch behind the cover. See also *key pad; system pad*.

remote zone annunciator   A device, located away from the control, to indicate which zone is in alarm or unsecured.

reporting line   See *alarm line*.

reset   (1) To silence a ringing local bell alarm. (2) To restore a transmitter to the nonalarm condition.

reset time   Some detection devices, once tripped, cannot be tripped again until a fixed reset time (usually several seconds) has elapsed. This makes no difference when detecting an intruder but must be remembered when walk testing such devices.

residential alarm   An alarm installed in a private home, as opposed to one installed in a business. Compare *commercial alarm*.

resistance   The property of an electrically conductive material that limits or restricts the amount of current flow. Measured in ohms.

response, police   See *police response*.

RETMA   Radio, Electronic, Television Manufacturers Association. See also *color code; resistor*.

retractable door cord   A special door cord made in a coil that permits stretching to 12 feet or more, depending on the model. Used on sliding doors with glass and on overhead garage or truck doors with pilot doors or with windows in them. They can have two or four conductors and resemble the coil cords often seen on telephones. See also *door cord; pilot door*.

retro-reflector   See *bounce-back*.

reversal   Generally refers to polarity reversal. See *reversing relay*.

reversing relay   (1) A method of transmitting an alarm signal over a telephone wire by reversing the DC polarity. In the secure mode, a voltage is sent over the phone line from the protected premises to the monitoring location to provide line supervision. An alarm signal is transmitted by reversing the polarity, usually by operating a double-pole, double-throw relay in the subscriber's control. (2) The relay used to reverse the polarity.

RF See *radio frequency*.

RFI Radio frequency interference. See *RF pickup*.

RF pickup Interference occurring when the loop wiring (occasionally other wiring) of an alarm system acts as an antenna, picking up a radio, TV, or shortwave broadcast, which can cause improper system operation. See also *AC induction*.

ridged conductor A ridge or stripe molded into the plastic insulation of one conductor on some twisted pair or parallel conductor wire. Permits polarity identification without cutting or stripping the wire. See also *tinned conductor*.

rigid mounting Required for all photoelectric beams and mirrors and for all motion detectors. Loose or sloppy mounting is sure to cause false alarms, and the cause of these will usually be hard to identify.

ring back circuit See *vault alarm*.

ringer (1) Another name for a local bell alarm system. (2) An alarm bell that is ringing. For instance, a policeperson might report, "I have a ringer at First and Main Streets."

ripple The result of imperfect filtering of a DC power supply that operates from an AC source. It is the amount of AC that comes out of a DC power supply on top of the DC. It can be measured by setting a multimeter to the "db" or "output" setting and reading the AC volts scale. On a normally operating power supply, it is usually a small fraction of one volt, too low to cause any alarm system problems.

RJ-31, RJ-38 Eight-conductor, modular telephone jacks used to connect alarm equipment to a dial-up phone line. Preferably installed by the phone company, ahead of any telephone subscriber equipment. Unplug-

ging maintains normal telephone service while disconnecting the alarm equipment. Excellent for troubleshooting phone line problems. RJ-38 provides supervision against unplugging via pins two and seven.

robbery The forcible and illegal taking of property from a person. A holdup. Compare *burglary*.

rotating beacon A bright light with a motor-driven, rotating reflector or lens. Sometimes used on local alarms as an additional means of attracting attention and to confuse and frighten away intruders. See also *strobe light*.

round (1) One revolution of the code wheel in a McCulloh transmitter. (2) The code signal transmitted by such a revolution. Typically, three rounds are transmitted for an alarm or for an opening signal and one or two rounds for restore signal. Some transmitters also send closing rounds.

round key A key often used for alarm work that is round and has notches cut in the end, rather than a conventional flat key that has notches along one or both edges.

RTV glue Room temperature vulcanizing glue, dries to a rubberlike consistency. Sticks very well on wood, glass, metal, hard plastics, and many other surfaces if applied to a clean, dry surface. Available in clear, white, black, and aluminum colors, with clear being the most useful. Available at most hardware, drug, and building supply stores. RTV glue has many uses in alarm work, both for mounting and sealing.

runner An alarm company employee who is sent to investigate the premises from which an alarm signal has been received. Also called a guard.

safe alarm See *capacitance detector*.

scheduled opening The regular time a protected premises is opened for business, as prearranged with the alarm company. Applies only to supervised, silent alarm accounts.

schematic diagram A drawing that shows, by use of appropriate electronic symbols, the design of an electronic circuit. Should not be confused with a wiring diagram.

screen See *alarm screen*.

screen hanger A metal device or set of devices used to physically support an alarm screen and to make electrical connections to it.

sealed battery Most rechargeable batteries used today in alarm service are of the sealed construction type, which means they can be used in any position and can be used in close proximity to electronic components with little likelihood of corrosion. Although called sealed, they all have safety vents that will open to release excess pressure if overcharged. Overcharging shortens battery life and can cause corrosion. See also *lead-acid battery; nickle-cadmium battery*.

secondary cell Any of several kinds of rechargeable cells. The most common type is the lead-acid cell. Often called batteries because they are usually used as such.

secure condition The method of operation of an alarm system when it is set, armed, or on and is ready to detect an intrusion.

seismic detector An outdoor perimeter or fence detector that is usually buried in the ground. It senses the seismic (shock) waves of an intruder walking or a vehicle driving over or near it. See also *hydraulic detector*.

self-adhesive foil See *self-stick foil*.

self-restoring alarm system A system that restores itself to the nonalarm condition after transmitting an alarm signal when tripped, provided all detection devices have returned to the secure condition.

self-stick foil Window foil that has an adhesive layer on one side. It is generally easier to apply than conventional foil because no varnish is needed as an adhesive. A protective coat or two of varnish should still be applied after the foil is installed.

self-supervising circuitry A circuit that is designed to go into alarm should any of the key electronic components fail.

sensitive relay A relay used to sense the current in the protective loop. It is designed with a very high sensitivity so that it needs very little current to keep it operated. This keeps battery drain low.

sensitivity control An adjustment on some ultrasonic and microwave detectors that determines the number of footsteps an intruder must take before an alarm is triggered. This should not be confused with the range control.

sensor See *detector*.

set To arm or turn on an alarm system when closing the premises.

set light See *armed light*.

shadowing See *blind areas*.

shaker alarm A vibration detector used on some vehicle alarms.

shelf life The length of time a piece of equipment will remain in good condition while sitting on the stockroom shelf. About the only item of concern in alarm work are dry cell batteries and lead-acid batteries, which should be placed in service within a few months.

shielded wire Any wire or cable that is covered by metal, which can be in the form of braided fine wires, spirally wrapped fine wires, or foil or aluminized plastic (usually with a drain wire). Metal conduit also acts as a shield. When the shield is grounded (usually earth grounded) it can greatly reduce electrical interference from static, adjoining power wires, electrical machinery, etc. Use of shielded wire is not a cure-all but it usually helps. Shielding is important on lowlevel signals, such as for some ultrasonic receiver wiring.

shock detector See *seismic detector*.

shunt (1) Any short. (2) See *shunt switch*.

shunt switch A key-operated switch located outside the protected premises that allows the subscriber to bypass usually just one door to permit entry without tripping the alarm system. The subscriber will normally proceed to the control or transmitter to turn off the entire system with the on-off switch, usually using the same key. Upon closing, the procedure is reversed.

signal processing A generalized term used to refer to electronic manipulation of intrusion-sensing detectors in an effort to reduce false alarms.

silent alarm   An alarm system that does not ring a bell or give any other indication of an alarm condition at the protected premises, but instead transmits an alarm signal to an alarm central station or other monitoring location.

single closed loop   A type of protective loop where all switches are wired in series and all switches are closed in the secure mode.

single-pole, double-throw switch (SPDT)   A switch or relay contact composed of a combination of an NO and an NC contact with one terminal shared (a total of three terminals).

single-pole, single-throw switch (SPST)   A switch having only two contacts. The contacts can be touching each other (switch closed) or not (switch open) depending on the position of the switch handle. In a momentary switch or relay, the contacts, in the normal or unoperated condition, can be open (NO) or closed (NC).

single-stroke bell   A bell that operates like a single-note chime. It rings only once each time the correct power is applied. Used primarily in coded fire alarm systems where the number of rings identifies the fire zone.

siren   (1) Traditionally, a motor-driven noisemaker used on police cars, fire trucks, ambulances, etc. (2) An electronic replacement for a motor-driven noisemaker producing a very similar sound.

siren driver   An electronics module or circuit that generates the electronic siren signal. A high-power (5 to 30 watts) speaker converts this signal to sound.

slave   A remote or extension unit that is incomplete in itself but works in conjunction with a master unit to which it is connected. An example is a detection slave unit that cannot be used by itself because it does not have complete electronic circuitry. Instead, it works with a master unit that is designed to work with one or more slave units. Slaves cost less than master units, so they are used to increase coverage at a cost less than that of providing many master units. Used in some ultrasonics. See also *master*.

slow-blow fuse   A fuse that is designed not to blow or open as rapidly as a regular fuse. This type of fuse can better withstand momentary surges such as the starting of a motor-driven siren.

smash and grab attack   A burglary in which, typically, a display window is smashed, valuable items are grabbed, and the burglar flees within seconds, too quickly for the police to respond to an alarm signal. Only physical protection can stop such attacks.

soft key   A feature used on some *system keypads* whereby the functions available to the user at any given time are shown on an English language display. Buttons located next to the display are used to select these functions. This is less confusing than labeled buttons that often have multiple functions shown on or next to each button. Multiple labels are necessary because each button serves a variety of purposes depending on where in the sequence the user is. Soft keys display only those functions currently available at any given point in the sequence.

solderless wire splice   See *crimp wire splice*.

solid-state   Describing an alarm system (or other electronic device) that uses transistors instead of vacuum tubes or relays.

Sonalert®   Trade name of a small horn by Mallory Company often used in testing alarms, as a prealert warning on residential alarm systems having an entry delay, and as an annunciator on alarm receivers and monitors. One model is advertised to work from 6 to 28 volts but will work down to about 2 volts (softly).

sonic detector   (1) A Doppler principle detection device much like ultrasonic except that it uses an audible frequency. Not very common. (2) A misnomer for ultrasonic.

sound cancellation   See *noise cancellation*.

sound discriminator   See *audio discriminator*.

space alarms   See *volumetric protection*.

spacer   (1) A nonmagnetic material, usually plastic, used to space magnetic contacts and their magnets away from iron or steel surfaces to prevent loss of operating distance. One quarter inch to ⅜ inch is usually adequate. (2) A device used to obtain correct mechanical alignment between a magnetic contact and its magnet when mounting on unequal surfaces.

SPDT   See *single-pole, double-throw switch*.

splice   (1) The connection of two or more wires. For long-term reliable results, all splices should be soldered and taped or should be made with a good quality crimp connector that has been correctly crimped with the proper tool. (2) A foil splice or patch made by overlapping foil ends several inches, pricking with a pointed tool, then varnishing over.

spot protection   (1) Protecting a specific small area or object such as a safe or a valuable piece of art work. Can be done with a magnetic or mechanical contact, a small pressure sensor or mat, or a capacitance alarm. (2) A detector that is sensitive only at one spot or small area, such as a mat switch, strip switch, or spot switch.

spot switch   A tiny mat switch about 1½ inches in diameter, designed to be placed under an object to detect its removal.

SPST   See *single-pole, single-throw switch*.

stand-alone keypad   See *keypad*.

standby battery   A battery used to supply electricity to an alarm system only in case of AC line power failure.

stay-behind burglar   See *hide-in burglar*.

step mat   See *mat switch*.

storage battery   See *rechargeable battery*.

strain gauge sensor   A device that is glued to the underside of a floor beam, fire escape, stair, passageway, etc., to detect the flexure (quite small, to be sure) of the floor as an intruder walks over or near it.

stress detector   See *strain gauge sensor*.

strip switch   A detector that is sensitive to physical pressure. It is similar to a mat switch but is long and narrow, typically about 1 inch wide or less and up to 25 feet long. Some models can be cut to any desired length. Typically used on window sills and on stair treads.

strobe light   A light that flashes with very short, very bright flashes. Used to confuse and scare away intruders and to alert nearby personnel.

subscriber   The company, agency, or person that buys the protective services (but not the physical equipment) of an alarm company. See also *leased alarm*.

subscriber error   A false alarm or loss of alarm protection caused by the subscriber not following the correct procedures in the use of the alarm system.

supervised account   A silent alarm system in which opening signals and closing signals are sent to the central station, where they are verified for correct procedure and time. If incorrect, an intrusion is assumed.

supervised loop   Any type of closed loop; any loop where cutting the wire will trip the alarm. Properly, an alarm should also be signaled if the wires are shorted.

surveillance system   Usually, a closed circuit television system or a film camera system. Used extensively in banks or high-risk locations. See also *closed circuit television*.

swinger   A term used in the alarm industry to indicate an intermittent problem. It is often very hard to locate these problems because they vanish by the time the alarm serviceperson arrives to troubleshoot the system. Swingers are often the cause of repeated false alarms on the system.

switch   A mechanically or magnetically operated device used to open and close electrical circuits.

system pad, system keypad   A group of push buttons mounted on a plate, usually with an LCD display (in English), used to arm and disarm an alarm system, to control other functions, and to display system status. All signals are multiplexed over usually a 4-wire circuit, and all decoding and other functions are performed by the microprocessor-based control. Compare *keypad*.

takeoff block   See *foil connector*.

tamper-proof box   This term is somewhat of a misnomer because few things are proof against attack. The term is usually used to indicate that a control, bell, or equipment box is equipped with a tamper switch to signal an alarm when the door is opened. Tamper switches are preferably connected to a 24-hour protective circuit. Bell boxes or other boxes outside the protective area should also be equipped with a double door. Opening the outer door triggers the tamper switch, while the inner door denies the attacker immediate access to the bell or its wiring.

tamper switch   A switch, usually mechanically operated, used to detect opening of alarm equipment boxes.

tape   (1) An electrical insulating material. (2) See *wall foil; window foil.*

tape dialer   A device that uses magnetic recording tape to report an alarm condition to a remote location over the regular dial telephone network. When tripped by an alarm system, the dialer starts the tape, which dials a preprogrammed telephone number and then plays a prerecorded voice announcement, identifying the nature and location of the alarm. Seldom used now.

tape programmer   See *programmer.*

tape switch   See *strip switch.* Also a trade name.

telco   The telephone company, whose wires are used to transmit alarm signals.

telephone answering machine   A device attached to a telephone line to answer calls and record messages when nobody is home or when a business is closed. These devices can interfere with attempts to call a subscriber's control for purposes of uploading and downloading. There are a number of ways around this problem. Contact the manufacturer of your control unit.

telephone answering service   A business designed to answer the telephones of its customers and to give and take messages. Since they are often operated on a 24-hour basis, they are sometimes used by small alarm companies to monitor alarms. Such monitoring service is highly variable and depends on how intelligent and well trained the answering service personnel are, the rate of personnel turnover, how complex the alarms are,

how well the alarm company instructs the answering service personnel, and, in general, how cooperative they are. A better option today is to choose an alarm monitoring service. Several provide nationwide service and they are trained in handling alarm signals.

telephone test set   A device used by telephone company personnel to test telephone lines. It is a telephone handset with a built-in dial and a talk-listen switch. Often called a "butt-in." Useful when checking dialers or digital communicators.

terminal cover   (1) A plastic cover designed to fit over the terminals of a magnetic contact to reduce the likelihood of tampering. (2) Any insulating cover that fits over a terminal strip. Used to prevent accidental shorts and to prevent shock hazards on high voltage. Often used by telephone companies on alarm circuit terminals.

terminal strip   A convenient place for connecting wires. Usually of the screw type but can also be solder type.

terminating resistor   A resistor, typically a few thousand ohms, connected at the end of an end-of-line resistor loop to complete the circuit.

tester   A generalized name given to a wide variety of devices, often homemade, used to test alarm systems.

tilt switch   See *mercury tilt switch.*

timed alarm   See *bell cutoff.*

time delay   A time interval, measured by an electronic circuit, used to provide a desired feature such as an entry delay, exit delay, or bell time-out.

time-out   See *bell cutoff.*

tinned conductor   A silver color sometimes plated over one conductor of two-conductor wire (the other conductor being copper-colored). Permits polarity identification, but only after cutting or stripping. See also *ridged conductor.*

tolerance   The amount by which a component or device may vary from the advertised nominal value, as specified by manufacturer or by the buyer. It is usually specified as a percentage but can also be stated in measuring units, such as inches.

tone coding   A method of multiplexing in which the signal to be sent turns a tone of a particular frequency on or off. Many signals of different frequencies can be sent over one line. At the receiving point, detectors sense the presence or absence of the various frequencies. See also *frequency shift keying*.

touch detector   See *capacitance detector*.

transducer   Any device that changes one form of energy to another. Examples are bells, horns, buzzers, ultrasonic heads, microphones, speakers, motors, and generators. In alarm work the term most often refers to ultrasonic heads.

transfer contact   See *form C contact; single-pole, double-throw switch*.

transformer   A device that converts high-voltage AC to low-voltage AC (or vice versa). Will not work on DC.

transients   Basically, electrical noise. Such noise can be caused by nearby lightning strikes, motors and other electrical equipment starting and stopping, radio interference, light dimmers, and many other causes. The protective loop and other wiring in an alarm system acts as a giant antenna to pick up this noise. Other noise gets into the alarm via the AC power. If not well designed by the manufacturer, alarm equipment can be damaged and false alarms or false operation can result from such noise. Usually transients do not present a problem in alarm work, but when they do, it can be very hard to track down the cause.

transmitter   (1) A device that sends an alarm signal to a remote point, such as a McCulloh transmitter. (2) The unit at the end of a photoelectric beam that sends out the light or invisible infrared energy. (3) The ultrasonic transducer that sends out the ultrasonic energy.

trap   (1) A device that detects an intruder who trips over a taut, fine, black string or wire, usually located about knee level, and pulls a clip out of the device, thus breaking or making the circuit to trigger an alarm. (2) A dead trap, one that uses a string and triggers an alarm only when the clip is pulled

out. (3) A live trap, one that uses a wire (instead of a string) that is made part of the protective loop. Triggers an alarm if the clip is pulled out or if the wire is broken. See also *two-way trap*. (4) To protect an opening, as to trap a door using a magnetic contact.

trigger   See *trip*.

trip   To actuate or set off the alarm system; to ring a bell or cause an alarm signal to be transmitted.

trip wire   See *trap* (2) and (3).

trouble alarm   (1) An indication that there is a problem in the system, as opposed to an alarm signal.

troubleshooting table   A troubleshooting aid, prepared by better equipment manufacturers, that lists symptoms, possible causes, and corrective action in a table or list form.

tubular key   See *round key*.

tuning   The adjustment that must be made to a capacitance detector to make it work properly.

turbulence   See *air turbulence*.

twisted pair wire   Two wires that are held together by spiraling around each other. Compare *parallel pair wire*.

two-way trap   A trap that uses a spring-loaded, balanced switch, held in its midposition by proper string tension. It triggers an alarm if pulled or if the string is cut. Thus, it provides the protection of a live trap, but with the simple, one-point wiring of a dead trap. See trap (2) and (3).

UL key and switch   A key-operated switch listed by Underwriters' Laboratories for alarm service. It offers higher security than most unlisted key switches.

UL listed alarm company   An alarm company that meets the requirements of Underwriters' Laboratories and is so designated by appearing on a UL published list.

UL standard for alarms   Underwriters' Laboratories publishes many standards outlining the requirements that must be met by alarm equipment and alarm companies in order to obtain UL listing. The most important of these is UL 681, which outlines alarm system installation requirements. Many others cover various kinds of equipment. It is important to bear in mind that there are many UL listings for many UL standards, many of which are unrelated to security (such as electrical safety). Therefore the term "UL listed" is meaningless unless the exact nature of the list is detailed. UL 639 outlines transient protection requirements. UL 611 outlines central station units and systems.

ultrasonic detector   A device that senses motion in a protected area by a Doppler shift in the transmitted ultrasonic energy. The sound is of too high a frequency to be heard by humans.

unauthorized opening   Any alarm signal for which the monitoring alarm company does not have advance authorization. The alarm company assumes an unauthorized opening to be an intrusion. Applies only to silent alarm, supervised accounts.

under-carpet mat, pad, or switch   See *mat switch*.

undercharge   To put too little electrical energy into a rechargeable battery to keep it fully charged. The battery will not be able to deliver its required capacity when needed; it will run down too quickly.

under-dome bell   An alarm bell on which the gong completely covers the ringing mechanism. See also *single-stroke bell; vibrating bell*.

unscheduled opening   Opening of a protected premises at an unscheduled time. Silent alarm, supervised account subscribers notify the monitoring alarm company in advance of their standard opening and closing times. If the owner or authorized person wishes to enter at any other time, he or she has to make special arrangements with the alarm company, either by phone and prearranged secret code word or, preferably, by letter.

upload   The procedure whereby information is sent from a microprocessor-based control to a programming device, which is usually a personal computer. The usual procedure is performed via dial-up telephone lines, although a local programming device can be temporarily connected locally. See also *download*.

varnish   Used to coat window foil after installation, to provide mechanical and electrical protection to the foil. Also used to adhere non-self-stick foil to glass. Any varnish used on foil should be obtained from a reputable alarm supplier. Some hardware store brands tend to yellow or to crack and peel after a while.

vault alarm   An alarm system used to protect a vault, such as a bank vault or storage vault. It is a special type of audio alarm and usually has a test feature via the ring back circuit that can be actuated from the alarm central station.

vibrating bell   A bell that rings continuously as long as the correct power is applied. Compare *single-stroke bell*.

vibration analyzer   An electronic circuit used to evaluate a vibration signal as to intensity, duration, repetition rate, count, interval, etc., in an effort to reduce false alarms caused by occurrences other than human intrusion, such as an earthquake. Can be used with seismic, fence, glass break, and strain gauge detectors.

vibration contact   A normally closed switch that bounces open in response to vibration, generated by a break-in attempt, of the surfaces on which it is mounted. It has a screw type adjustment to set sensitivity. It is sometimes used on windows as a glass break detector, but provides questionable protection in such service unless connected in a separate loop to an analyzer made specifically for that purpose. See also *glass break detector; shaker alarm; vibration analyzer*.

video motion detector   (1) A light sensor that mounts on the face of a CCTV monitor screen, usually by suction cup, to detect changes in brightness level that might represent the presence of an intruder (or of fire). (2) A device that electronically looks at a portion of the CCTV picture to serve the same function.

volt   The unit of electrical pressure. It is what forces the current to flow through the circuit. Represented as E (electromotive force) in Ohm's law.

volt-ohm-milliamp meter (VOM meter)   The alarm troubleshooter's basic testing instrument. See also *digital multimeter; multimeter*.

volumetric protection   Any type of detector that will detect an intruder in a three-dimensional space. Specifically, ultrasonic, microwave, sonic, and some passive infrared systems (not photoelectric beam systems).

V-O-M meter   See volt-ohm-milliamp meter.

W   See *watt*

wait-in burglar   See *hide-in burglar*.

walk test   A procedure of actually walking through the area protected by a motion detector to determine the limits of its coverage. Indication is usually provided by an LED mounted on the detection unit. This indicator should be disabled or covered when not used for walk testing to prevent a would-be burglar from walk testing during open-for-business hours to determine holes in the coverage.

wall foil   Lead foil usually 1 inch wide and .003 inch thick used to cover walls and ceilings at 8-inch intervals to detect entry. It is time-consuming and expensive to install, easily damaged, hard to maintain, and, with the advent of motion detectors, now practically never used.

warbler   See *electronic warbler*.

warbler driver   An electronic module or circuit that generates the electronic noise signal. A high-power speaker (5 to 30 watts) converts this signal to sound.

warm-up time   Some detection devices require a definite warm-up time when first turned on, even if solid-state design. Manufacturer's instructions should be followed when turning equipment on before testing.

watt   The rate at which electrical energy is converted to other kinds of energy. It is equal to volts times amps in DC circuits.

weather   See *environmental considerations*.

wide-gap magnetic contact   A unit that uses an extrasensitive switch, an extrastrong magnet, or both, in order to obtain a wider than usual operating range. Although there is no definite separating point, wide-gaps usually operate over ¾ inch or more.

window foil   A strip of lead foil usually ⅜ inch wide and .001 to .003 inches thick that is glued to glass, usually with a special varnish that does not yellow or peel. When the glass is broken the foil usually breaks, interrupting the loop current to signal an alarm. Sometimes called tape.

window screen   See *alarm screen*.

wire color code   See *color code, resistor; color code, telephone cable*.

wire gauge   See *gauge, wire*.

wireless   (1) A method of sending alarm signals from a detection device to a control using small radio transmitters at the detectors and a receiver at the control. This eliminates the need for hard wiring the protective loop. (2) See *light beam transmission*. (3) See *radio transmission*.

wire markers   Tags or devices (numbered, lettered, or written upon) attached to ends of wires or cables to permit easy identification. Unfortunately, these are seldom used by alarm companies, yet they could save troubleshooting time.

wiring diagram   A drawing showing the external wiring connections to an alarm control, motion sensor, etc. See also *loop diagram; schematic diagram*.

wood screen   See *alarm screen*.

zapping   A technique of troubleshooting foil by discharging high-voltage (about 300-volt) capacitors through the foil to burn open hairline cracks or bad patches.

zip cord   Any parallel construction wire, usually two- or three-conductor and 16-gauge or smaller. See also *lamp cord*.

zone   Large protected premises are divided into areas or zones, each having its own indicator or annunciator. This helps pinpoint the specific area of intrusion and is a great aid in narrowing down a problem when troubleshooting. Today's control units may have 16, 30, 48, or more zones.

zoned-out Describing a zone that has been bypassed, disabled, or switched out of service. An area can be zoned-out to allow access to that zone while the other zones are in service or to temporarily bypass a zone in trouble until repairs can be made, thus allowing the rest of the system to remain operational.

zone light A light or LED used to indicate the status of each zone in a multiple zone system. One or more indicators can be provided per zone to indicate any of the following: ready, armed, alarm, zoned-out.

Index